Costs and Challenges of
Local Urban Services

Costs and Challenges of Local Urban Services

Evidence from India's Cities

KALA SEETHARAM SRIDHAR
OM PRAKASH MATHUR

OXFORD
UNIVERSITY PRESS

OXFORD

UNIVERSITY PRESS

YMCA Library Building, Jai Singh Road, New Delhi 110001

Oxford University Press is a department of the University of Oxford. It furthers the
University's objective of excellence in research, scholarship, and education
by publishing worldwide in

Oxford New York
Auckland Cape Town Dar es Salaam Hong Kong Karachi Kuala Lumpur
Madrid Melbourne Mexico City Nairobi New Delhi Shanghai Taipei Toronto

With offices in
Argentina Austria Brazil Chile Czech Republic France Greece Guatemala
Hungary Italy Japan Poland Portugal Singapore South Korea Switzerland
Thailand Turkey Ukraine Vietnam

Oxford is a registered trademark of Oxford University Press
in the UK and in certain other countries

Published in India by Oxford University Press, New Delhi

ISBN-13: 978-019-806084-0
ISBN-10: 019-806084-X

Typeset in 11/13.2 in Adobe Garamond Pro
by Excellent Laser Typesetters, Pitampura, Delhi 110 034
Printed in India by Pauls Press, New Delhi 110 020
Published by Oxford University Press
YMCA Library Building, Jai Singh Road, New Delhi 110 001

To the urban local bodies
with a wish that they understand
the implications of the several critical messages in the book

Contents

Tables and Figures

Figures

Preface

The origin of the book owes itself to a grant the authors received from the South Asia Network of Economic Research Institutes (SANEI)-Global Development Network (GDN) to undertake a field-level study of the costs of key urban services such as water supply, sewerage systems, municipal roads, solid waste collection and management, and street lighting, and the price at which these were sold for domestic and non-domestic purposes. The original study was undertaken in six cities—Bangalore, Lucknow, Surat, Chandigarh, Jaipur, and Pune, using primarily the accounts and budgets of the corporations of these cities and the respective parastatal entities and utilities who held responsibility for providing these services. For evaluating the adequacy of the pricing structures, we examined the extent to which the pricing structures conformed to the marginal cost pricing principles. Preliminary results of this study were presented at a meeting held in Islamabad in December 2005.

As the study drew to a close, the authors who were simultaneously engaged in several other urban studies saw a lot of synergy in looking at service pricing issues in conjunction with urban growth strategies. As a result, fresh perspectives emerged, which form the core of the book.

Many individuals who have been acknowledged separately have contributed to making of this book. In particular, we appreciate the contributions made by Anindita Nandy, Subhro Dutta, Sandeep Thakur, A.K. Halen, Astha Singh, Simanti Bandyopadhyay, Akshat Vipin, and Poulomee Basu. We would like to also acknowledge Navroz Dubash for his contribution to the chapter on Rajkot. All errors, however, remain ours.

Acknowledgements

This book is a result of the work of several individuals. First of all, we would like to thank the South Asia Network of Economic Research Institutes (SANEI) and the Global Development Network (GDN) for funding the work presented in Chapters 1–4, 6, and 7. We would like to thank SANEI's Research Advisory Panel members, specifically T.N. Srinivasan and S.R. Osmani, Arvind Virmani, Chairperson of the session, and Dhilliraj Khanal, the discussant of the paper, for their comments during SANEI's annual conference held in Islamabad in December 2005. We are grateful to A.R. Kemal and Saba Anwar of the Pakistan Institute of Development Economics for their support of the work and for patiently answering all our questions pertaining to the project.

We also thank M. Govinda Rao, Director, National Institute of Public Finance and Policy (NIPFP), for his encouragement and support of the proposal and the work from the initial stages. We would like to thank Simanti Bandyopadhyay of NIPFP for her work on the project, including the questionnaire and field visits to Chandigarh and Bangalore for this project, prior to submission of the draft report. We acknowledge with thanks the excellent research assistance offered by Anindita Nandy, who made all the field visits, collected the data, and analysed it, following our guidance meticulously. She also actively contributed to the methodological discussions, which we acknowledge and thank. We are also grateful to Astha Singh and A.K. Halen for their field visits to Bangalore and Lucknow, respectively. We thank Sweta Singh at NIPFP for assisting us with tables during the last stage of preparing the manuscript. We are also grateful to Subhro Dutta who worked on this project in its early stages, and was helpful in gathering data during the field visits and formatting the data obtained.

Next, we would like to thank the Commissioners and staff members of the Municipal Corporations of Chandigarh, Bangalore, Surat (specially R.P. Patel), Pune, Jaipur (specially R.L. Krishnani), and Lucknow (specially Santosh Kumar Rai, Additional Municipal Commissioner, and the Municipal Commissioner, Lucknow Municipal Corporation) for the cooperation they extended for this study. We thank the Bangalore Water Supply and Sewerage Board (BWSSB), the Chief Engineer, B.R. Nagendra, and other staff members, and the Rajasthan Public Health Engineering Department and its Secretary, Bharat Meena, for their cooperation. Further, we acknowledge with thanks the support from the Lucknow Jal Sansthan (specially its Deputy Secretary, Raghuvendra Kumar) and UP Jal Nigam for their assistance with the data. We are indebted to the staff members of the Central Statistical Organisation (national accounts division, specifically Ramesh Kohli) for their assistance with the price indices. We thank the water supply departments of the six cities: Bangalore (D. Ramaiah in the Finance Division of BWSSB), Pune (Pramod Nirbhavne of Pune Municipal Corporation), Surat (J.K. Shah, Hydraulic Engineer, Surat Municipal Corporation), Jaipur (Agam Mathur, Chief Engineer, Rajasthan Public Health Engineering Department), Lucknow (Raghuvendra Kumar, Deputy Secretary, Lucknow Jal Sansthan), and Chandigarh (S.K. Bansal, Chief Engineer, Water Supply, Chandigarh Municipal Corporation) for clarifying the basis of their water tariffs in the second round of discussions with them.

We acknowledge with thanks the data we received from the Indian Meteorological Department, Pune. Finally, we are thankful for the assistance offered by the Mumbai-based International Institute of Population Sciences, especially the then Director, P.N. Mari Bhat, with population estimations. We would like to acknowledge the assistance of University Grants Commission, specifically Moolchand Sharma, who arranged for data on the number of people with bachelors' and masters' degrees from all universities of the six cities.

We thank Ralph Turvey for his comments regarding an earlier version of this work, although we were not able to address all of them. We appreciate the alacrity with which Amrit Pandurangi of PricewaterhouseCoopers responded to the questions we had regarding a study they did, upon which we draw here, as it relates to the norms regarding municipal roads and street lights.

The work in Chapter 5 was conducted by NIPFP with substantial research assistance from Sandeep Thakur. We gratefully thank him for his excellent research assistance with work on that chapter.

Chapters 8 and 9 are based on a study conducted by the NIPFP, which was funded by the Water and Sanitation Program (WSP) South Asia. Thanks are due to the WSP, particularly David Savage for his feedback and interest in the study. We also thank NIPFP and M. Govinda Rao for facilitating the study. We thank Navroz Dubash of Jawaharlal Nehru University (JNU) for his contributions to the chapter on Rajkot. We are grateful to Srinivas Chary, Administrative Staff College of India, for his comments regarding an early version as well as to Sandeep Thakur, Akshat Vipin, and Poulomee Basu for their assistance in field visits, summaries of facts, and preparation of tables pertaining to finances. Thanks are due to the then Municipal Commissioner of Ludhiana Municipal Corporation (LMC), S.K. Sharma, and his staff members, and the Punjab Water Supply and Sewerage Board (PWSSB) for taking out time to answer our questions and provide us with data. We thank LMC's former Municipal Commissioner, S.S. Sandhu, and the Chairman, Ludhiana Improvement Trust (LIT) for answering many questions. Further, we would like to thank the faculty of Punjab Agricultural University, specifically Sandeep Kapur; V.K. Goyal, CEO of Vardhman Mills, Ludhiana; and S.P. Karkara, former Commissioner, Ludhiana Municipal Corporation, and former member, Punjab's second State Finance Commission, who shed light on various aspects of service delivery. Thanks are also due to the Rajkot Municipal Corporation, the Municipal Commissioner and his staff members, especially one of the deputies who gave us his M.Phil thesis; the Councillors, Rajkot Urban Development Authority; and various other agencies which provided invaluable information on service delivery in Rajkot. We gratefully thank Public Affairs Centre for enabling the last rounds of revisions of the manuscript. Encouragement from Gopakumar Thampi, Director, Public Affairs Centre, is gratefully acknowledged.

Thanks are due to the anonymous reviewers of the manuscript for their comments on earlier versions. Finally, thanks are due to Oxford University Press for patiently monitoring the various stages of production of the book. The views in this manuscript do not represent those of the SANEI-GDN, WSP, PAC, or NIPFP. Any error remains our responsibility.

Abbreviations

2SLS	two-stage least squares
ADB	Asian Development Bank
AIC	average incremental cost
ARV	annual rateable value
BIMARU	Bihar, Madhya Pradesh, Rajasthan, and Uttar Pradesh
BDA	Bangalore Development Authority
BMTC	Bangalore Metropolitan Transport Corporation
BOT	build-operate-transfer
BWSSB	Bangalore Water Supply and Sewerage Board
CAA	Constitutional Amendment Act
CCF	City Challenge Fund
CEPT	Centre for Environmental Planning and Technology
CSO	Central Statistical Organisation
CTU	Chandigarh Transport Undertaking
DPC	District Planning Committee
EWS	economically weaker sections
FAR	floor area ratio
GDCR	General Development Control Regulations
GDP	gross domestic product
GEB	Gujarat Electricity Board
GIDB	Gujarat Infrastructure Development Board
GIDC	Gujarat Industrial Development Corporation
GoI	Government of India
GSDP	gross state domestic product
GTPUDA	Gujarat Town Planning and Urban Development Act
GWSSB	Gujarat Water Supply and Sewage Board

IBT	increasing block tariff
IDFC	Infrastructure Development Finance Corporation
IIR	India Infrastructure Report
INR	Indian Rupee
JNNURM	Jawaharlal Nehru National Urban Renewal Mission
kl	kilolitre
KSRTC	Karnataka State Road Transport Corporation
l	litre
LIG	Low Income Group
LIT	Ludhiana Improvement Trust
LMC	Ludhiana Municipal Corporation
lpcd	litres per capita daily
MC	municipal corporation
mld	million litres daily
MMRDA	Mumbai Metropolitan Regional Development Authority
MPC	Metropolitan Planning Committee
NDMC	New Delhi Municipal Council
NGO	non-governmental organization
NHAI	National Highways Authority of India
NIE	new institutional economics
NIPFP	National Institute of Public Finance and Policy
NIUA	National Institute of Urban Affairs
O&M	operations and maintenance
OLS	ordinary least squares
ORG	Operations Research Group
PAC	Public Affairs Centre
PDS	public distribution system
PHED	Public Health Engineering Department
PMT	Pune Municipal Transport
PWSSB	Punjab Water Supply and Sewage Board
RITES	Rail India Technical and Economic Services
RMC	Rajkot Municipal Corporation
RUDA	Rajkot Urban Development Authority
RWH	Rain Water Harvesting

SAP	Sutlej Action Plan
SANEI	South Asia Network of Economic Research Institutes
SANEI-GDN	South Asia Network of Economic Research Institutes and the Global Development Network
SEWA	Self-employed Women's Association
SME	small- and medium-scale enterprise
SWM	Solid Waste Management
TFC	Twelfth Finance Commission
UA	Urban Agglomeration
UIDSSMT	Urban Infrastructure Development Schemes for Small and Medium Towns
ULB	urban local body
ULCRA	Urban Land Ceiling and Regulation Act
UFW	unaccounted for water
UPSRTC	Uttar Pradesh State Road Transport Corporation
URIF	Urban Reform Incentive Fund
WDR	World Development Report
WPPI	Water Pricing Progress Index
WSP	Water and Sanitation Program
WTP	willingness to pay

CHAPTER 1

Urbanization and Infrastructure
An Introduction

BACKGROUND

The world population is expected to become two-third urban by 2025. While the urbanization phenomenon is widely accepted as being an inevitable by-product of development, there are many undesirable outcomes that have resulted from urbanization. With increasing population and demand for urban infrastructure services, the capacities of local governments in many countries are over-burdened. The Government of the Republic of Korea estimates that infrastructure shortages result in a gross domestic product (GDP) loss of as much as 16 per cent of its potential in the mid-1990s (see Singh and Ta'i, 2000). It is estimated that losses from traffic jams in Bangkok range from US$ 272 million to US$ 1 billion a year. Moreover, with respect to infrastructure such as water, Cole (2004) points out that there is a systematic relationship between water use and income, ascertaining that an inverted U-shaped relationship exists. Cole (2004) suggests that the levels of water use in developing regions will continue to increase for many years to come. Adequate infrastructure is not only necessary for increasing productivity, but also for raising the general quality of living.

The urbanization pattern in India also has been undergoing significant change, consistent with the world-wide phenomenon. The share of urban population in the total population of the country grew from 11 per cent in 1901 to 26 per cent in 1991. In 2001, the urban share of population increased to 29 per cent. The urban population in the country is expected to increase to about

500 million by 2021. While about 59 per cent of the increase in urban population in India during 1991–2001 was due to natural increase and only 22 per cent was due to migration, a comparison of the 2001 Census migration data with the 1991 Census shows high growth (32.9 per cent) in the number of total migrants by place of birth, which is more than the natural growth of the population (Census of India 2001b).

According to the 2001 Census of India, out of the total population that migrated within the country between 1995 and 2000, 36 per cent were migrants into urban areas (from rural as well as from other urban areas). More than 58 per cent of those who migrated to urban areas over this period were from rural areas. The migration data of 2001 Census indicate that 20.5 million out of the 283.6 million people enumerated in urban areas were migrants from rural areas who moved in within the last ten years. It may also be worth noting that rural–urban migration constitutes a significant component of inter-state migration (about 41.1 million as of 2001) taking place within the country. According to the 2001 Census, in terms of proportion of in-migrants to total population in urban agglomerations (UAs), Delhi UA was at the top, with in-migrants constituting 16.4 per cent of the total population of Delhi UA. Greater Mumbai (15.1 per cent) and Bangalore UA (13.4 per cent) followed. Further, as natural population increase slows, migration can play a dominant role in urban population growth—for example, if economic opportunities in urban areas expand rapidly while those in rural areas do not. Rural–urban migration is explained by the lack of suitable non-farm employment opportunity for youth in rural areas.

The by-products of urbanization have not been always positive. According to India's Union Urban Development ministry, 20 per cent of the country's urban households are denied access to safe drinking water, 58 per cent do not have safe sanitation, and more than 40 per cent of garbage generated is left uncollected for want of proper waste management.[1]

Tables 1.1 and 1.2, respectively, summarize the access to water supply and sanitation for all countries in South Asia. While none of the South Asian countries have universal access to a basic service like water supply even as of 2002, the access to this service is better in Iran, Maldives, and Sri Lanka than it is in India (Table 1.1). As far as sanitation is concerned, the condition is even worse, though countries such as Bangladesh and Bhutan provide much better population and household coverage with sanitation facilities (Table 1.2) as compared to that provided by India. When we view service delivery in a cross-national perspective, it becomes clear where we stand and it is necessary to explore whether municipal finances or pricing are the core of the service delivery problem in Indian cities. If not, what we can do to reform?

In fact, Delhi's Economic Survey 2003–4 (Government of Delhi, 2004) showed that Delhi's demographic profile had changed significantly due to migration. This survey reported that there had been a 50 per cent increase in migration into Delhi from other states since 2001. Further, this survey highlighted that the phenomenal increase in migration had exerted huge pressure on housing, water,

TABLE 1.1
Access to Water Supply in South Asian Countries

Country	Year	Population (%)		Water Coverage (%)	
		Total	Urban	Total	Urban
Afghanistan	1990	13,799,000	18	NA	NA
	2002	22,930,000	23	13	19
Bangladesh	1990	109,402,000	20	71	83
	2002	143,809,000	24	75	82
Bhutan	1990	1,696,000	5	NA	NA
	2002	2,190,000	8	62	86
India	1990	846,418,000	26	68	88
	2002	1,049,549,000	28	86	96
Iran (Islamic Republic of)	1990	56,703,000	56	91	98
	2002	68,070,000	66	93	98
Maldives	1990	216,000	26	99	100
	2002	309,000	28	84	99
Nepal	1990	18,625,000	9	69	94
	2002	24,609,000	15	84	93
Pakistan	1990	110,901,000	31	83	95
	2002	149,911,000	34	90	95
Sri Lanka	1990	16,830,000	21	68	91
	2002	18,910,000	21	78	99

Source: WHO-UNICEF, Joint Monitoring Programme, retrieved from the Water and Sanitation Program's website: http://www.wsp.org/, accessed on 18 May 2006.

TABLE 1.2
Access to Sanitation in South Asian Countries

Country	Year	Total	Urban Population	Urban Households
Afghanistan	1990	NA	NA	4
	2002	8	16	0
Bangladesh	1990	23	71	4
	2002	48	75	6
Bhutan	1990	NA	NA	NA
	2002	70	65	40
India	1990	12	43	25
	2002	30	58	18
Iran (Islamic Republic of)	1990	83	86	7
	2002	84	86	20
Maldives	1990	NA	100	99
	2002	58	100	99
Nepal	1990	12	62	NA
	2002	27	68	12
Pakistan	1990	38	81	41
	2002	54	92	52
Sri Lanka	1990	70	89	4
	2002	91	98	4

Source: WHO-UNICEF, Joint Monitoring Programme, retrieved from the Water and Sanitation Program's website: http://www.wsp.org/, accessed on 18 May 2006.

power, and other infrastructural demands in the city. In fact, that year, the Delhi government asked for extra funds from the Planning Commission for this, which were not granted due to resource constraints. Bangalore, which is also one of the selected cities for the marginal cost estimation of water in this manuscript, is another target of large-scale migration from the northern parts of the state and other states which are relatively poorer.

Out of a total of 761,485 migrants into the Bangalore UA in 2001, representing 13.4 per cent of the UA's population (of 5.7 million), 401,932 were from within the state and 353,156 were from outside. Bangalore is second next only to Greater Mumbai, in terms of the proportion of in-migrants to total population (13.4 per cent).

This book examines the provision of urban infrastructure services in India's urban areas, quite crucial for the sustainability of the urbanization that has been continually occurring.

OBJECTIVES

With increasing urbanization, rural–urban migration and the associated problems have received a lot of attention in the literature and policy circles. However, the question that remains unaddressed in a developing country like India is whether there are too many city immigrants (see Williamson, 1988). That is, is India over-urbanized in relation to the level of its development? If so, how can we identify this phenomenon more systematically?

It is important to answer these questions because they have implications for whether the problem is one of closing the cities to in-migration or correcting user prices being charged for urban infrastructure, as Williamson (1988) points out.

While the problems highlighted by India's Urban Development ministry imply that there are probably too many immigrants, the problems could well be due to the fact that migrants do not compensate for the social costs they create. One outcome with too many city immigrants could be that the change in the total cost of providing infrastructure services resulting from migration (the marginal cost) would be higher than the user prices actually charged. As Williamson (1988) points out, there has been no attempt to assess the quantitative relevance of this question. As other studies have also pointed out, there are no estimates of marginal costs for urban infrastructure services in India. However, this is crucial for efficient allocation of resources such as water supply and for answering the urbanization question.

The Expert Group on Commercialization of Infrastructure Projects (also called the India Infrastructure Report [IIR], 1996, or Mohan, 1996) appointed by the Government of India estimated, in respect of water supply, a requirement of US$ 17,418 billion to address the backlog till 1995. Besides, it estimated an additional investment of US$ 2,153 million during the period 1996–7 and investments of US$ 1,934 million during the period 2001–6. In the case of water supply, Suresh (1998) pointed out that the ratio between the water charges collected and expenditure incurred on operation and maintenance in some Indian states varies between 30 and 46 per cent. Similar requirements are estimated for sanitation (see Suresh, 1998).

While a number of factors underlie the levy of user charges for services such as water, gaps between the actual expenditure and what is collected may also partly be due to the costs created by migrants. Of course, pricing is only one aspect of the problem, albeit an important one. The solution for financing such expenditure might be to correct user charges for these services. Let alone marginal costs, there are no estimates of even costs required to attain a certain level of locally provided urban services such as solid waste, sanitation, sewerage, roads, and street lights.

Even if the above propositions are true, it is quite debatable whether finances really do affect service delivery in Indian cities. Therefore, in this book, we propose to answer the following specific questions:

1. What are the marginal costs of providing urban infrastructure services such as water in Indian cities? How do they compare with actual tariffs being charged? What are the pricing instruments most commonly used to charge for water in Indian cities?
2. With respect to urban services such as solid waste, sanitation, sewerage, street lights, and roads, what is the total expenditure required for ensuring a certain benchmark level of services? How does it compare with actual expenditures by cities on these services?
3. More generally, what are the challenges faced by Indian cities in reforming their service delivery? Are they primarily financial or are they institutional as well?

Each of these questions is answered in different chapters of the book. To answer the first question, we estimate the marginal cost (the change in the total cost resulting from a unit change in service) of providing water. Thereafter we are in a position to compare the costs with actual tariffs being charged for water supply.

There is a reason why marginal cost, not average costs, should be the basis of pricing for water supply. A city usually develops its least expensive water sources first; however, it normally becomes increasingly expensive to produce an additional unit of water as demand grows with increasing migration into the urban area. In such an instance, using the average cost of today would lead to an underestimation of the cost of water production in the future.

While in theory, costs should be the basis of pricing, in India, after independence, the public sector was assigned the primary responsibility for the provision of these goods which were substantially subsidized because of their essential nature. However, with a decade of economic liberalization in India, it is appropriate that private sector should participate in the provision of these services. If so, these projects should be made viable for the private sector, which calls for market-based mechanisms in the provision of these services. So part of this research (which deals with the marginal cost estimation of water) facilitates private sector participation in this important sector by providing information on marginal costs of water supply, which was obscure until now (see also *World Development Report*, World Bank, 2004). Thus, while the pricing itself is based on considerations of economic efficiency, the question is important for public policy because of their implications for providing sustainable levels of essential infrastructure services such as water supply.

In Chapters 2–5, we estimate marginal costs of water supply, and compare these marginal costs with the user prices actually charged in various Indian cities. Such an exercise can have invaluable policy implications as to whether cities should close their doors to in-migration or merely correct the pricing of services, as hypothesized by Williamson (1988). Even important national initiatives in India such as the Jawaharlal Nehru National Urban Renewal Mission (JNNURM) specify phased cost recovery for all important public services, primarily water supply, although they do not mention marginal costs.

To answer the second question we pose, for services other than water supply, namely sewerage, solid waste, roads, and street lights, we compare actual spending by cities against available benchmarks and study service levels, using measures and indicators developed by us in some cases. So, in Chapters 6–7, we study the total cost of providing other locally provided and financed services such as solid waste, sanitation, roads, street lights, and sewerage using available norms. We highlight under-spending by cities on these services, if any, and the extent to which they are under-spending, when compared against the available norms, to attain a certain level of each of these other services. We find here that under-spending in the case of several of these services might explain poor service delivery in Indian cities.

We make an attempt to answer the third question we pose in Chapters 8–9. Here we study challenges to reforming service delivery more generally in the context of developing countries, using case studies of Ludhiana in Punjab and Rajkot in Gujarat. It should be noted that our objective here is not to compare Ludhiana and Rajkot on a one-to-one basis as far as service delivery and institutional arrangements are concerned, but to address broader questions of what really are the challenges to service delivery, what are the bottlenecks to reform, and what could trigger changes to improving and reforming service delivery in these cities.

SURVEY OF PAST LITERATURE

While the literature on urban service delivery is vast, only relevant studies are summarized here. Given the importance of water supply, we find that a majority of studies on urban public services focus on water supply because it is the most important at the local level.

There are larger debates regarding the provision of and management of water and other 'public goods'. For instance, the *new public management theory* sees governmental institutions as undemocratic, unresponsive, inefficient, and failing in most other measures of what constitutes an effective organization. In addition, one of its remedies, the outsourcing of public services as a means to efficiency, has generated continuing debates that involve passionate proponents and critics alike. Another perspective, the *new institutional economics* (NIE), has its roots in Ronald Coase's fundamental insights about the critical role of institutional frameworks and transaction costs for economic performance. That is, states and institutions exist because of the transaction costs involved for individuals to negotiate. Further, various *theories of the state* hypothesize that the modern state is separate from and connected to civil society. While earlier thinkers, such as Thomas Hobbes emphasized the supremacy of the state over society, later thinkers, by contrast, tended to emphasize the points of contact between them. Last, not the least, there are important and dichotomous *debates regarding local government financing.* Some of these advocate fiscal decentralization and that a willingness to mobilize local revenue is the most allocative and efficient way of organizing public finance. More conservative views are in favour of restricting local government autonomy by advocating that central governments can achieve local economic efficiency through policies of fiscal equalization and redistribution (Tiebout, 1956).

While it is not possible to delve deep into all these debates here, we review the literature survey from the relevant perspectives.

Noll et al. (2000) analyse reforms of urban water systems in six developing countries that represent World Bank case studies of reforms. Their main finding is that, though conceptually rather simple to reform, water is quite different from other infrastructure so that 'appropriate' reform varies substantially across countries and is quite difficult, throwing doubts on the ability of the new public management theory to explain all phenomena.

Dinar (2000) discusses the political economy of water pricing reforms. This work addresses possible shortcomings of implementing normative economic approaches that may produce first-best pricing outcomes, which could supplement our findings here. The book answers questions relating to whether the water sector is different from other sectors, and whether reforms in the water sector should be designed and implemented differently than reforms of a similar type in other sectors. This book answers these questions by providing various analytical frameworks that allow comparisons across various conditions and by comparing reform processes under various circumstances in different countries. This further shows that the new public management theory advocating outsourcing might not be generalizable in the context of all countries.

Llorente and Zerah (2002) examine in India's context, formal and informal water suppliers in the water sector. The informal water suppliers such as bottled water and tanker companies became important in India in the post-1990 reform period. But these authors argue that in the actual regulatory context, the solutions these private operators provide are only peripheral ones. They conclude that the reform of the public monopoly in water is therefore inevitable.

Complementing these results, Raju et al. (2004) study the resources and management constraints in providing adequate and safe drinking water supplies in a medium-sized city, Kolar in (Karnataka) India. They find that (*a*) though 66 per cent of the city's households had piped water supply, 68 per cent of them had unauthorized connections, thus depriving the exchequer of its revenue; (*b*) the per capita supply was only one-third of the urban water supply norms; and (*c*) the city supplies were based on groundwater, which was quite contaminated, because of which the households had to depend on more expensive (Rs 100–500 per month) private tankers, while the public water fee was just Rs 45 per house per month. This study demonstrates how local government apathy often creates not a very optimal situation for the public in the case of water.

The perspective of the NIE is valid in both the above studies, since there is a need for the state to mediate in all cases, even when it is inefficient. The latter study also emphasizes the fact that civil society forms a public sphere, that is, a site of extra-institutional engagement with matters of public interest autonomous from the state and yet necessarily connected with it.

Shah et al. (2004) analyse a decade of water sector reforms in Mexico with the specific purpose of drawing lessons for Indian water policy. They find that Mexico's experience may not be a model for India, but it does suggest that changing the way in which a nation manages its water resources, frequently necessitates substantial changes in institutional structures, law, incentives, and commitment to reform the sector. This throws light on the NIE which stresses the important role of state and institutions when large transaction costs are involved. Thus, a number of studies agree that what constitutes reform varies significantly across countries and one country may not be a model for another.

A case study by the Water and Sanitation Program, South Asia (2000) speaks of the cancellation of the US$ 185 million Pune water supply and sewerage project. There are several reasons the case study cites were responsible for cancellation of the project, after great initial interest and enthusiasm. First, institutional structures were partly responsible, for example, when the Commissioner was transferred, the project was left without a local champion. Further, the estimated costs of the project were perceived by the local administration to be high, and were designed to ensure a high rate of return to the private operator at the expense of the consumer. Moreover, local contractors were averse to the idea of international firms being awarded the contract. The cancellation of this project thus highlighted how the lack of a well-informed public debate resulted in the cancellation of what may have been a model for other projects in the country. This study does initiate the debate of whether central government interference is desirable in implementing projects that have huge local importance. Fiscal decentralization has to result in a number of economic welfare gains, provided adequate institutional structures are in place for management of projects and programmes, as the NIE argues.

A study by the University of Birmingham (1999) corroborates this further. Being based on thirty-five urban centres in India, this study finds that private sector participation is unlikely to have a significant impact on delivery of public services such as water supply in the medium term, because of too many vested interests in the existing institutional patterns. Their research suggests that until there is a demand for institutional development from municipalities, which is, in turn, generated by demand for better service from customers, there can be no sustainable advances in service delivery. This study thus overshadows those theories of the state which suggest that state and civil society are indeed inter-related with each other, and that the prescription offered by the new public management theory in favour of outsourcing, is not a panacea.

These studies have implications for, and are consistent with, what we have to say in Chapters 8–9.

Link (2003) points out that the marginal cost of operating and maintaining infrastructure represents a component of optimal prices. His paper presents results for marginal infrastructure costs for different modes of transport (road, rail, airport, and seaports), employing different methodologies for estimating marginal costs, ranging from econometric approaches to engineering-based methods. This study summarizes the marginal cost of roads to be between €0.42 and €0.50 per vehicle kilometre in Switzerland for passenger cars. In fact, quite similar to the approach we take in this study, Tiina Idström (2004) estimates marginal rail infrastructure costs in Finland to be €0.13 per gross tonne kilometre, taking into account operations and maintenance (O&M) costs. These two studies are very similar to the exercise of marginal cost estimation we undertake in this book.

Expansion and improvement of public services is essential to improving the quality of life and productivity in all developing countries. Fox and Edmiston (2000) find how some African countries have been diligent in expanding the infrastructure necessary to provide public services, but unfortunately, most have not done a very good job of paying for them. They present a case study of water supply services in Egypt, which highlights the importance of user charges to enable expansion of coverage of water supply services, because taxes or inter-governmental revenues are less likely to provide a consistent funding source as competing uses can diminish available resources. Based on survey data from Lagos, Reedy (1986) found that many participants did not have access to public water supply because the supply authority could not afford to expand service delivery. This certainly does highlight the fact that transfer of finances to local governments (i.e., decentralization, as opposed to the view which advocates centralization of finances) is warranted for improvements in public service delivery.

Warford (1997) describes the general rationale for marginal opportunity cost pricing, illustrating it with reference to municipal water supply, and provides numerical examples. This paper then reviews the key issues involved in the implementation of marginal opportunity cost pricing.

Davis (2004) presents empirical evidence regarding the types and magnitude of corrupt behaviour in the provision of water supply and sanitation in South Asian countries. The study examines the strengths and weaknesses of strategies to reduce corruption among several public water and sanitation agencies. The study finds, based on interviews, focus group discussions with key informants, consumers, and staff, that where corruption is reduced, there is a shift in the accountability networks of service providers and a change in the work environment, natural for us to expect. This study certainly does lend veracity to the new public management theory which advocates outsourcing.

Turvey (1976) provided one of the earliest studies to explain the concept of the marginal costs of supplying water, which is a concept relevant only for pricing of metered supplies. This study presents a numerical example of how capital recovery factors may be computed for different components of capital expenditure because of the lumpy nature of the investments. In a similar spirit, Hanke and Wentworth (1981) analyse the marginal cost of municipal waste water services. They define and interpret marginal cost and then apply this to a hypothetical waste water system.

Roy et al. (2004) developed empirical measures of willingness to pay (WTP) by households for better water quality in Kolkata. This study estimates the average WTP as the investment made by households in purifying water, which it finds to be US$ 3.65 (INR 169) per month per household, based on a field survey of representative households in the city. This has implications for designing an appropriate and equitable water charge, since, as the study finds, monthly family expenditure (adjusted for family size) and educational attainment are also significant determinants of the WTP, at the household level.

Zérah (2002) reports findings from a household survey in Vijayawada (a city in Andhra Pradesh with a population of 800,000 in 2001). The survey indicated that 77 per cent of the city's households considered water to be cheap or very cheap. In the project zone, household WTP was, in fact, more than one and a half the average times the existing charges, testifying for the sustainability of water charges as a means of financing investment.

The above two studies demonstrate the relationship between the citizens and government, as do some theories of the state, and show that it is important for governments to tap consumer WTP for services rendered. More generally, the relationship between governments and the public has to be interactive, and there can be no unilateral governmental control over policy.

Given that water scarcity is likely to continue to be a major problem for many cities in developing as well as industrial countries, Saleth and Dinar (1997) investigate the kind of policy changes and institutional conditions necessary to ensure the economic viability of market-based solutions to inter-sectoral allocation problems in an urban context, similar to that advocated by the new public management theory. It provides a general framework for evaluating the effectiveness of water pricing that can be applied to other urban centres around the world. The main implication of this work is that although local level supply augmentation options cannot, by themselves, solve urban water deficit altogether, their exhaustion is admittedly a necessary condition for market-based inter-sectoral water transfers to be free of the damage to the incentive environment facing urban water sector. This is a study which we have found offers thumping support for the new public management theory.

The work in this volume goes a step further than the research above and argues that even water-deficient regions can solve their problems by getting water from a distant source and pricing it accordingly.

While most literature focus only on water supply, there are several studies of urban service delivery in general. Paul et al. (2004) assess the state of public services in India from a user perspective and offer a set of benchmarks for future comparisons. They have covered five services in their study—drinking water, health care, the public distribution system (PDS), public transport, and primary education. They assessed each of the services along four dimensions—access, use, reliability, and user satisfaction—using state-level data to compare the performance of different states with respect to these dimensions. They found that drinking water is accessible only to 55 per cent of Indian households within a distance of 100 m from home. They also reported absence of pucca roads by 60 per cent of the households in their villages, and the availability of public health facilities only to over 40 per cent of households within a distance of 1 km from their homes. Thus they found that while the levels of all public services was considered to be generally low by the surveyed households, drinking water fared better than the other services, with primary education being the lowest. This work has implications for those theories of the state which advocate active participation by the public and civil society, which ideally act as a check on public provision of services.

Rao and Aggarwal (1991) estimate unit costs of five public services—administrative services, police services, primary education, secondary education, and public health—and their expenditure needs in the Indian states. They find, based on their state-level analysis, that in order to ensure even average levels of the services they examine, a sizeable increase in transfers to poorer states would be required, supporting decentralization of finances to the local level.

For the purposes of this book, studies that detail efforts to improve service delivery in urban areas, and the possible reasons for their success or failure, focusing on the role of the availability of finance, are relevant. Bagchi (2001) examines various alternative and unconventional modes of financing basic urban infrastructure services in the country and their feasibility. Bagchi's study is a fallout of the lack of adequate decentralization of finances to the local governments we observe in India's federal system. Savage and Dasgupta (2006) demonstrate how more revenue and infrastructure do not mean better services, taking the case of Bangalore. Their data from the Water and Sanitation Program (2005) show significant revenue increases (accounting for inflation and population) during 1995–2003 for various service providers (Bangalore Mahanagara Palike, Bangalore Water Supply and Sewerage Board [BWSSB], and Bangalore Development Authority [BDA]). However, even with this, service outcomes have declined. They point out that there is need for a city-wide set of reforms that not only entail revenue, but also ensure effective expenditure management, new management approaches, and the need to focus on specific outcomes. This study thus dispels all ideas about mere outsourcing (advocated by the new public management theory), mere presence of a government or institution to make up for the transaction costs of a large number of individuals (suggested by the NIE), or theories of the state which advocate extreme state separation from civil society or their close relationships. The study also dispels the fact that mere decentralization of finances to the local government and agencies will do the trick.

Most recently, the India Infrastructure Report (IIR) (3iNetwork, 2006) on urban infrastructure examines the growth in urbanization in India in the last 100 years. This study examines the governance structure of urban local bodies (ULBs), the state of municipal finances, and developments in this sector. In IIR (2006), micro-level perspectives are covered with respect to urban services such as water supply, sewerage, municipal solid waste management, local transport, primary education, and energy management. While this is an invaluable resource on the existing state-of-the-art urban infrastructure-related issues and finances, it does not assess the quantitative relevance of the marginal costs of providing services such as water supply and the total costs of other urban services, along with actual expenditures made by cities. The work by us is an attempt to fill this gap.

Substantial investments in infrastructure have been made during the past decade by national, regional, and local governments; donors; private firms; and non-governmental organizations around the world. Differences exist across countries and services, but generally the universal delivery of infrastructure services continues to be plagued by problems that have existed for many years. The condition of infrastructure facilities is poor, the services provided are inferior, and the financing systems are inadequate. Fox (1994) identifies several broad areas for reform and recommends a series of actions to attain effective service delivery, similar to Chapters 8–9 of this book. In our research we focus on pricing for reforming water supply delivery and lack of adequate investment, capacity, and governance in the case of other urban services we study.

Summarizing, the literature reviewed here shows the need for government involvement and citizen participation in overseeing the provision of basic services, and that privatization is not a panacea, as argued by the new public management theory. The existing studies also confirm that user charges enable the provision of sustainable level of public services such as water supply, taking into account the investments required in developing countries to expand coverage, and offer strength to the view which advocates decentralization of finances to the local governments.

This book adds to this literature by

1. estimating the marginal costs of water supply in Indian cities and comparing them with actual tariffs being charged; reviewing pricing instruments used for charging water supply in several Indian cities and comparing them internationally;
2. evaluating the total costs of providing other local urban services against available benchmarks;
3. focusing on the issue of reforming local public services, and examining the bottlenecks and triggers of such reform, which have not been explored much in the literature, despite the wave of decentralization that has swept across the globe.

The answers to these questions have implications that can serve as input for service delivery reform in cities in many developing countries that are reeling under the negative impact of poor public services and are similar to Indian cities in many substantive senses.

In this work, we attempt to estimate the marginal cost of water, controlling for many characteristics that determine the costs and expenditure of water supply. This is something that has not been attempted in the literature, especially so for India, as is clear from the literature review presented above. Further, we make an attempt to compare other services such as sewerage, solid waste, street lights and roads, their actual expenditures with benchmark service levels and required expenditures. For sanitation, we are unable to compare physical levels of services due to problems with the quality and reliability of data. Finally, we attempt to understand what determines reforms in public service delivery, more generally.

SCOPE OF THE STUDY

One of the objectives of the book is to estimate marginal costs for water supply. That is, to estimate the additional burden of population on the supply and costs of this service. We examine short-run costs (O&M) of supplying water to residents. This means that we study costs of operation and maintenance for purposes of estimating short-run marginal cost. We do not attempt to perform estimation of long-run marginal costs, despite the availability and collection of data on capital expenditures by cities. This is because of the following reasons:

1. Capital costs are generally lumpy in nature, which means that they may or may not occur every year. It would be rarely appropriate to apply an econometric approach to such expenditures (see Turvey, 1976). However, O&M costs are continually occurring, and an econometric approach would be appropriate. Other literature on estimation of marginal costs for various modes of transport (Link [2003] for roads and Tiina Idström [2004] for rail infrastructure) use O&M costs as the basis for estimating short-run marginal costs.
2. For essential civic services, it may not also be desirable to recover the capital costs.

Given the data-intensive nature of marginal cost estimation and its relevance, we confine the marginal cost estimation to water. Note that in the case of other services—sewerage, sanitation, roads, street lights, and solid waste management—the best one can implement is a *quid pro quo* relationship, let alone charge on the basis of their marginal costs. In the instance of water supply, it is a feasible proposition. For these other core urban services, we attempt to capture the cities' actual expenditures on these services and compare them with benchmarks of the total expenditures required to attaining a desired level of service. This desired level could be, in the case of solid waste management, for instance, what it would cost the city to get rid of all garbage on the roads.

In the case of less obvious examples such as street lights, the actual expenditures are computed and compared in relation to benchmark service levels, which we define and measure. In the case of roads, we examine actual expenditures by cities and compare them with benchmark investments required. We attempt to examine if there is a discrepancy between the period for which the roads were *ideally* built and the period for which they *actually* last. The underlying assumption is that, among other factors, migrants could be responsible for the damage caused to roads, if they do not last for the entire period for which they were built. We explored from the cities, reasons for any discrepancy between the actual and ideal life of municipal roads.[2]

We did not examine physical norms for roads, but studied only financial norms or investment requirements and compared them with actual expenditures.

In the case of sewerage, we study various systems such as underground drainage (considered the best), open (covered and uncovered) soak pits, flush/septic tanks and institutional systems such as those used by universities or self-contained campuses. Note a caveat here—systems such as soak pits are usually privately provided for, and we do not account for the costs of privately provided services. We examine the costs of only publicly provided services. As with other services, we compare cities' actual expenditures on sewerage systems, examine their existing state of services, and compare these with benchmark levels of incremental investment required for acceptable level of services.

In the case of solid waste management, the appropriate cost question would be what it would cost the city to get rid of all garbage on the roads. Here we compare service levels and actual expenditures by cities and examine discrepancy between what is needed ideally and what is actually being spent.

In the case of sanitation, we would have liked to define the cost question as being what it would cost the city to get rid of open defecation completely. This has been motivated by the Maharashtra model for rural sanitation (*Economic Times*, 2005) which is a cash incentive scheme for creation of rural sanitation infrastructure. It is estimated that by announcing prize money worth US$ 1,429,190 (INR 66,000,000) per year, the Maharashtra government was able to create toilets worth US$ 43,308,792 (INR 2,000,000,000) every year. With this, Maharashtra has been able to declare about 350 villages in the state free of open defecation. However, we are unable to measure this adequately because our data allow us to measure access to public sanitation only, whereas open defecation is determined by the existence of private as well as public sanitation to a significant degree. So we confine ourselves to measures of public sanitation, actual expenditure by cities on this, and benchmark expenditures needed for 100 per cent sanitation coverage.

We do not study urban mass transport. The meticulous reader should note that the scope of our work is to study locally provided urban services which impose expenditure responsibilities on the local government. With the exception of a few cities, mass transport in most Indian cities is provided either by the state government or special purpose vehicles. While we can provide examples from other cities (Delhi, where DTC is offered by the state government of NCT of Delhi; Delhi Metro Rail Corporation (DMRC), a special-purpose vehicle, is a joint venture between the Government of India and the state government of the NCT of Delhi), in the context of several cities in the country (including several studied here), the status of public transport is as follows:

1. Jaipur: City buses are run by Rajasthan State Roadways.
2. Lucknow: UPSRTC (Uttar Pradesh State Road Transport Corporation, state agency) provides city road transport.

3. Chandigarh: Bus services provided by Chandigarh Transport Undertaking (CTU) which is an undertaking of the Union Territory of Chandigarh.
4. Bangalore: Bangalore Metropolitan Transport Corporation (BMTC), which is incorporated as a separate entity having been bifurcated from its parent body Karnataka State Road Transport Corporation (KSRTC, state government agency).
5. Surat: Public transport provided by the state government agency, Gujarat State Road Transport.
6. Pune: The Pune Municipal Transport (PMT) which is in a sorry condition, with an inadequate 900-odd fleet, with 50 per cent of the buses more than ten years old, resulting in nearly 15 per cent of the fleet being inoperable on any given day.

Based on the above examples, mass transport systems are not counted among those services which impose expenditure responsibilities on local governments, hence we do not study them here.

When we examine urban reform, we confine ourselves to questions relating to the broad challenges in improving public service delivery in Indian cities. We examine the role of finances and institutions in service delivery, taking the example of two case studies from north and western India—one each from Ludhiana (Punjab) and Rajkot (Gujarat). As discussed earlier, our objective is not to make one-to-one comparisons of these two cities with respect to service delivery. Water supply and sewerage are primarily dealt with in Ludhiana, the reader will be interested to know how Ludhiana, which is one of the richest cities of the country, performs or underperforms with respect to these basic services. The chapter on Rajkot contains information on a few other services including sanitation, drainage, solid waste, street lights, land use, and related institutional arrangements. This itself should not detract the reader from the value of these city-level case studies. These assessments of Ludhiana and Rajkot address broadly the need for urban reform, any potential bottlenecks, triggers for reform, and the reform agenda, which deserve attention in the context of these cities, quite representative of cities in many developing countries.

OVERVIEW OF THE BOOK

As described earlier, this book engages itself with three questions. The first one, related to the marginal cost estimations of water supply, is dealt with in Chapters 2, 3, 4, and 5. Chapter 2 describes the sample of cities and methodology of the study as relating to the marginal cost estimation, conceptual differences between costs and expenditure, and expectations regarding relationships in the marginal cost estimation of water supply.

Following this, Chapter 3 summarizes the data, sources, construction of variables, and their definitions required for the marginal cost estimation of water supply. Chapter 4 describes the findings from expenditures on water supply in the selected cities, and the marginal cost estimations of water supply. Chapter 5 describes the instruments and methods of water pricing, summarizing water pricing in few of the selected cities—Bangalore, Pune, along with that in Agra and Allahabad, where the Uttar Pradesh Jal Sansthan is entrusted with the responsibility of having to provide water supply, based on the authors' primary study of water pricing in these cities. This chapter also presents international practices in water pricing, relates pricing reforms with selected country characteristics, and sets out criteria which should serve as objectives of water pricing.

Chapters 6 and 7 deal with the second question related to the cost of other services which include solid waste management, sanitation, sewerage, roads, and street lights. Chapter 6 describes our research with solid waste management. This chapter explains the institutional, regulatory, and legal framework for solid waste collection, treatment, and disposal in India, costs and charging mechanisms that currently exist for solid waste management, and normative financing principles that should underlie the charges. Then the chapter goes on to report primary findings from expenditures on solid waste in the selected cities, comparing with norms, where relevant. Chapter 7 deals with our findings regarding the other important locally provided public services, namely, sewerage, street lights, sanitation, and municipal roads.

Chapters 8 and 9 address the challenges of reforming public service delivery in Indian cities. Chapter 8 debates the broader question of urban reform and studies whether finances really matter for improvements in public service delivery, by developing certain hypotheses, using the case study of Ludhiana as example. Chapter 9 makes an attempt to understand urban reform in the context of Rajkot, Gujarat. In these chapters, the potential bottlenecks to reforming service delivery, and triggers for reform in service delivery, if any, are examined. The final chapter, Chapter 10, summarizes the findings from all chapters, examines their implications for urban reform more generally, and provides the concluding remarks.

NOTES

1   These data are for urban areas in the country. It is possible that analogous, if not worse, problems exist in the rural areas regarding which reliable data are not available. However, if urbanization is an inevitable occurrence of growth, it is important to address these infrastructure problems in the urban areas. If such problems cannot be addressed in the urban areas, it would be much more difficult to address them in the rural areas.

2   Cities consist of different kinds of roads—access roads to houses, shopping streets, arterial roads, and state and/or national highways, for which state public works departments and the National Highways Authority of India (NHAI) are responsible. We confine ourselves to only those managed by the city.

CHAPTER 2

Sampling and Methodology for Marginal Cost Estimation of Water Supply

IMPORTANCE OF WATER

Urban water services are important to economic growth, productivity, and poverty reduction. The financial viability and sustainability of India's water supplying entities have been consistently emphasized in water policies enunciated in the successive five year plans. The Working Group set up to formulate the Ninth Five Year Plan for urban water proposed adoption of the principle of full cost recovery in order to enhance the financial viability of the water sector and full autonomy for institutions responsible for water supply in determining water tariff and tariff policy. It proposed that subsidies for the poorer sections should be selective, well-targeted, and transparent to ensure that there is no excessive cross-subsidization from other sectors like industry or commerce (see Ministry of Urban Affairs and Employment, 1996). Apart from laying emphasis on the financial aspects of urban water utilities and considering that urban water has important implications for productivity and quality of life, the Ninth Five Year Plan underlined the importance of universal coverage of population by water supply, adequacy in terms of water consumption norms, integration of water supply with liquid waste management, recycling of waste water and sewage, and privatization and participation of the community in the management of water supply systems (see Planning Commission,

1997). In a paper titled, *Urban Water Supply and Sanitation*, the World Bank made similar observations, stating that water tariff setting must increasingly focus both on economic efficiency and financial viability, without losing sight of social affordability (World Bank, 1999). Tariff rationalization, according to the paper, is an essential pre-requisite to the financial viability of agencies responsible for water supply and for increasing the financial flows into the sector.

The Tenth Five Year Plan (2002–7) has reinforced the water sector agenda as laid out in the Ninth Plan and other recent reports. While an assessment of issues relating to urban water supply is discussed elsewhere, it is important to reproduce the following quote from the Tenth Plan that sums up the water agenda: 'the unfinished tasks in water supply in urban areas may be summed up as augmentation to reach the prescribed norms, higher degree of reliability, assurance of water quality, a high standard of operation and management, accountability to customers and in particular special arrangements to meet the needs of the urban poor, and levy and recovery of user charges to finance the maintenance functions as well as facilitate further investment in the sector. The achievement of these tasks depends to a large extent on the willingness of the state governments and urban local bodies (ULBs) to restructure water supply organizations, levy reasonable water rates, take up reforms in billing, accounting and collection, and become creditworthy in order to have access to market funding' (see Planning Commission, 2002). It further observes that the 'reforms (in the water sector) relate to making the sector more professionally managed, with adequate autonomy and financial powers, and levy of user charges preferably determined by an independent regulatory authority. By the end of the Tenth Plan, the target would be to recover full O&M costs through levy of user charges' (Planning Commission, 2002). Financial sustainability has been emphasized in the Government of India's National Water Policy, as may be seen in the following quote (see Box 2.1).

This chapter describes our sampling considerations and methodology both for the marginal cost estimation of water supply and the cost of attaining a certain benchmark level of service, for the other services, in the cities of our study.

> ### Box 2.1
>
> Besides creating additional water resources facilities for various uses, adequate emphasis needs to be given to the physical and financial feasibility of existing facilities. There is, therefore, a need to ensure that the water charges for various users should be fixed in such a way that they cover at least the operation and maintenance charges of providing the service initially and a part of the capital cost subsequently. These rates should be linked directly to the quality of service provided. The subsidy on water rates to the disadvantaged and poorer sections of the society should be well targeted and transparent.
>
> National Water Policy, 2002
> Government of India

SAMPLING

For purposes of the marginal cost estimation and for studying other services, we chose six cities in the country:

1. Bangalore
2. Lucknow
3. Pune
4. Surat
5. Chandigarh
6. Jaipur

The sample of the cities was selected taking into account several considerations such as population size, variety in fiscal arrangements, institutional arrangements for provision of water, income, geography, data availability, and certain benchmark standards. While Bangalore, Pune, Jaipur, Lucknow, and Surat are million-plus cities, Chandigarh is a class I city, with 2001 population of 500,000.[1] The six cities cover the northern (Chandigarh), eastern (Lucknow), southern (Bangalore), and the western (Surat, Jaipur, and Pune) parts of the country.

The sample chosen represents a variety of fiscal arrangements. Pune and Surat continue to have the octroi, whereas Bangalore, Chandigarh, Jaipur, and Lucknow do not. Further, the sample we choose represents a variety of institutional arrangements for the delivery of public services, most importantly water supply. In Bangalore, the municipal corporation does not provide water, the city's utility, a parastatal agency, the Bangalore Water Supply and Sewerage Board (BWSSB) is responsible for water and sewerage services, whereas in Pune, the ULB is responsible for providing water supply. In Jaipur, water supply is not provided by the municipal corporation. Unlike in Bangalore, it is the responsibility of the Public Health Engineering Department (PHED), which is a state government department. In Chandigarh, water supply and sewerage have been the responsibility of the Municipal Corporation since 1996 (the municipal corporation in Chandigarh came into being only in 1994).

Tables 2.1 and 2.2, respectively, summarize the sources of drinking water for the six cities in the study, from the Census of India's 1991 and 2001 town directories. As summarized in the tables, most of the cities (except Lucknow) were dependent on tap water, in addition to tube wells and hand pumps in Surat and Jaipur, implying the existence of a water supply network. Further in Bangalore, note that while in 1991 tap was the only means of drinking water, in 2001 other sources such as wells, tube wells, and hand pumps had become important as well. This somewhat lends support to the idea that a city uses its least expensive sources of water supply first, and then resorts to increasingly expensive sources. We find a similar example in Jaipur which also started using tank water in 2001, in addition to taps and tube wells. Lucknow switched over to having a full-fledged water supply network in 2001, which was absent in 1991.

TABLE 2.1
Important Sources of Drinking Water in the Selected Cities, 1991

Name of Town	Tap Water	Well Water	Tank Water	Tube Well/ Hand Pump
Bangalore	√	–	–	–
Chandigarh	√	–	–	–
Jaipur	√	–	–	√
Lucknow	–	–	√	√
Pune	√	–	–	–
Surat	√	–	–	√

Source: Census of India 1991, Town Directory.

TABLE 2.2
Important Sources of Drinking Water in the Selected Cities, 2001

Name of Town	Tap Water	Well Water	Tank Water	Tube Well/ Hand Pump
Bangalore	√	√	–	√
Chandigarh	√	–	–	–
Jaipur	√	–	√	√
Lucknow	√	–	–	√
Pune	√	–	–	–
Surat	√	–	–	√

Source: Census of India 2001, Town Directory.

Further, Bangalore, Surat, and Pune are located, respectively, in the relatively high-income states, Karnataka, Gujarat, and Maharashtra.[2] Pune's population grew at a whopping rate of 51 per cent over 1991–2001, compared to its growth of 45 per cent over 1981–91. Chandigarh is a high-income Union Territory, whereas Jaipur and Lucknow are, respectively, in the states of Rajasthan and Uttar Pradesh (UP) that are generally known to be BIMARU (acronym for the states Bihar, Madhya Pradesh, Rajasthan, and Uttar Pradesh), that is, laggard and slow-growing. Besides, we had to ensure data availability for the data-intensive processes of marginal cost estimation.

Last, but not the least, Chandigarh and Surat in our sample serve as benchmarks for city planning, in general, and the provision of services such as sanitation/solid waste management, in particular. Chandigarh is a planned city, having been built from scratch. Designed by Le Corbusier, Chandigarh has been adjudged the best city in the country for the provision of services. The city has a well-planned underground network of pipes for the disposal of sewerage generated in the city. Further, the city has a well laid out underground storm water drainage system. The road network of the city of Chandigarh is based on a grid pattern, commonly found in cities in the west.

The city of Surat in India has also been rated quite highly since its transformation from the plague to one of the country's 'cleanest' cities that it has now become. The emergence of the powerloom industry in Surat has turned it into a million city, as Lahiri-Dutt and Samanta (2001) point out. In fact, if we examine the rate of growth of all million-plus cities during 1991–2001, Surat grew at the highest rate, with Nasik, Patna, Rajkot, Jaipur, Delhi, and Pune, occupying successive places. Broadly then, the costs in these cities for providing urban services should serve as benchmarks for those observed in other cities.

Thus the sample presents enough variety for local governmental responsibility and expenditure needs for the provision of the urban services we study here. These categories chosen are useful because we use them to report actual expenditures and service levels for all services we examine in the study.

METHODOLOGY AND DATA

As described, we estimate the marginal cost of providing water supply, which is summarized in Chapter 4. We compare these costs with user prices actually charged.

For this, we collected data on municipalities' capital and operating and maintenance expenditures on water supply. Further, we collected data on the actual volume of water supplied, along with data on other aspects such as leakages, revenues, and water tariffs. Next, we collected a variety of data pertaining to other factors that determine the costs of supplying water such as topography, rainfall, and price indices, along with the cities' octroi status and a description of institutional arrangements—whether or not municipality provides the service. Data on all these indicators that were used as explanatory variables are explained below.

For estimating the marginal costs of supplying water, we performed estimation of the total costs of O&M as dependent on the volume of service (water supply), which is endogenous (being determined by population or in-migrants), controlling several other factors that determine costs. The estimation tells us the incremental O&M costs of supplying every extra kilolitre of water.

The reader interested in details should note that it is important to separate out *capital* from *O&M* expenditures. There would be a set of O&M expenditures associated with every set of capital equipment. For instance, better quality capital expenditures (better equipment) would have lower O&M costs associated with them. While it may have been important, it was difficult to separate capital projects from their corresponding O&M expenditures in this case.

This is because we did not have disaggregated data on projects in the various cities where we visited, to enable us to determine which O&M were applicable to which capital projects. We estimate the O&M expenditures understanding that we could possibly be looking at short-run cost with changing capital.

Once we estimate the cities' marginal costs of providing an extra kilolitre of water supply, we compare them with the user prices charged in the cities. Water tariffs, in the event that household connections are not metered, are charged by cities based on the size of the piped connection. We obtained relevant data in the case of such cities. In the case of cities with metered connections, we obtained data on the slabs of tariffs for various levels of consumption. We get this heterogeneous data from cities/utilities/parastatal bodies on actual tariffs and compare them across cities.

The time period we chose for the study is 1991–2/2004–5.[3] This time period covers the post-liberalization (1991) period for the country, when major economic and political reforms started taking place. The timeframe we have chosen also includes the landmark year for local governments in India, the 74th Constitutional Amendment Act of 1992, which recognized ULBs as the third tier of government. We collected time-series data on primarily water supply as well as cross-sectional data, and where available, time-series data for the other services discussed for the six cities of the study. The research team visited each of the six cities with detailed questionnaires regarding each of the services for time-series data.

CONCEPTUAL DIFFERENCES: EXPENDITURE AND COSTS

Before we get into the details of the model, a few conceptual differences between what we observe and what we need are in order. From the beginning we were aware that what would be observed in the city's or service providers' budgets is actual *expenditure* on all the services, whereas what we are actually interested in is the *cost* of providing them, as pointed out by Chernick and Reschovsky (2004). Expenditure needs vary across local government jurisdictions in India as in the other countries (Reschovsky, 2006, surveys the various ways different countries that have attempted to measure expenditure needs) for several reasons:

1. Expenditure responsibilities are not the same for all local governments. As discussed earlier, in India, local governments in cities such as Bangalore, Delhi, and Chennai do not provide water supply and sewerage. In these cities, the Metro City Water Boards are responsible for development of the system including capital works, bulk supply, and operation/maintenance for water supply and related services. In the case of other cities (such as Pune and Chandigarh), the respective ULBs are responsible for these services. Such differences in responsibilities do cause a huge amount of variation in expenditure needs of local governments even within a single country. It means in any case that the expenditure responsibility of cities such as Pune and Chandigarh would be greater than what they would be in Bangalore, Delhi, and Chennai.

2. Further, expenditure needs could differ across local governments due to exogenous factors such as topography. The cost of providing water in elevated areas (such as Bangalore, which is 930 m above sea level) would be higher than that they would be in low-lying areas. Further, the relative dryness or wetness of an area (rainfall) is a determinant of expenditure on various urban services (especially water supply). Finally, the vector of relevant input prices a city is faced with, also determines the cost of providing services (for instance, the costs of electricity to pump up water from a low-lying source relative to the location of the city).

Quite understandably, there are distinctions between *costs* and *spending* on a public service, as the literature emphasizes. Actual spending (or expenditure) on a public service could be due to a number of different reasons, of which cost is just one. The costs of providing public services are determined by the price of inputs and exogenous factors such as topography which aggravate or reduce the costs of providing services, as highlighted above.

Actual *spending* on public services is determined by other factors, in addition to costs. Spending on local public goods is determined by their *desired* level, likely to be different for different income groups. See de Bartolome and Ross (2003) for an analytical frame-work that describes why this would be true. In general, this is also well-known from Tiebout (1956). Specifically, we expect willingness to pay (WTP) for local public goods such as water to increase with income and/or education.

Further, some local governments that are more efficient spend less for every unit of the public service delivered, when compared to less efficient ones. The size of the local economy could be a factor in determining scale economies for certain services. Other factors determining the efficiency of service provision are the degree of privatization in service delivery. Typically, private provision of services is known to have cut costs in many Indian cities. This is because public recruitment of personnel is expensive, and there is no explicit performance appraisal, making public provision of services inefficient.

Naturally, a big methodological challenge is to separate out that part of *expenditure* attributable to *preferences*, and that because of *costs* (this includes input prices, topography, and inefficiencies).

So, ideally, in reduced form, expenditure equations have to be estimated as a function of factors representing the various components—local preferences (measured by income or education), factors that determine efficiencies (scale economies, public–private partnerships) and those that influence costs (physical characteristics such as topography, temperate weather). This may be represented in the following equation for city i and time period t, as a study by the National Institute of Public Finance and Policy (2007) points out:

$$E_{it} = f(P_{it}, Z_{it}, F_{it}, \ldots) \tag{2.1}$$

The value E_{it} in Equation (2.1) refers to expenditure on water supply by the ith city at time period t. P_{it} refers to factors that denote *preferences* for local public services, such as income or education, again at time t. In the empirical work, we are unable to control for local preferences due to the unavailability of reliable data on income and lack of adequate data on education. Efficiencies (F_{it}) are determined by factors such as the level of the service, scale economies, expenditure responsibility, and revenue base of the local economy. The revenue base of the local economy could be considered endogenous, but in India's context, local governments' revenue bases determine their expenditure, but not vice-versa. While it is difficult to separate out cost and efficiency issues, factors that influence costs (Z_{it}) refer to physical characteristics such as topography, differences in temperature, and the relevant vector of input prices. So, in reduced form, expenditure equations are estimated as a function of factors representing the various components—preferences (where data were available), costs, and inefficiencies, over time.

Figure 2.1 shows these relationships and the econometric determination of expenditure and attempts to separate out factors that determine costs, inefficiencies, and preferences.

In the light of this discussion represented by Figure 2.1, we estimate the total O&M expenditure function for water supply for

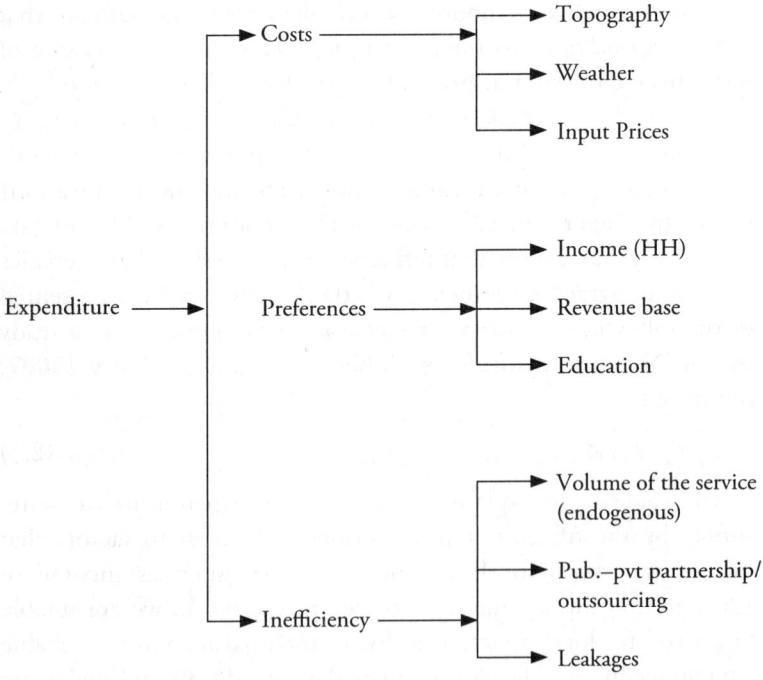

FIGURE 2.1: Econometric Determination of Expenditure on Water Supply
Source: Chernick and Reschovsky (2004) and authors' research.

city i and time period t, as shown in Equation (2.2), which is a reduced form of Equation (2.1):

$$Y_{it} = a_0 + a_{1it} \text{ volume of water supply} + a_{2it} \text{ rainfall} + a_{3it} \text{ altitude} + a_{4it} \text{ price index} + a_{5it} \text{ leakages} + a_{6it} \text{ octroi} + a_{7it} \text{ non-municipal body} + e_{it} \qquad (2.2)$$

The model in Equation (2.2) is self-explanatory, given the discussion above, regarding the impacts of various factors on the actual expenditures incurred on water supply by the municipal body or the parastatal utility (depending on who offers the service). Below we present our specific hypotheses regarding expectations of the impact of these various factors on expenditures incurred in the provision of water supply, in the light of the above discussion.

EXPECTATIONS REGARDING RELATIONSHIPS

The volume of water supply is the key variable we examine. The volume of water supply is clearly endogenous, so population is used as an instrument for this. All other factors remaining constant, the higher volume of water supply (necessitated by increasing population or migration) should increase expenditures. The coefficient on this variable will indicate how much we may expect the expenditures to increase as and when there is an increased supply of one kilolitre of water. This would be the estimate of *marginal expenditure*. We describe later how we come up with estimates of *marginal costs*, based on this marginal expenditure estimate.

We expect rainfall to have a positive effect on expenditure. All else remaining the same, the higher the extent of rainfall, the higher would be the quantity of water that is pumped out of the water source into the pumping station for treatment and distribution into the pipelines. The higher would be the expenditure because of this. Alternatively, if it were to be the case that rainfall reduces the distance between the water source and the distribution point, then it is possible that rainfall has a negative impact on expenditure on water supply. For this reason, the expected impact of rainfall on expenditure is ambiguous.[4]

A city's altitude has a positive impact on water supply expenditure. The higher the altitude at which a city is located, the higher would be the costs of having to 'pump up' water from a low-lying water source. Next, the vector of price indices has a positive impact on expenditure, for obvious reasons. If the prices of inputs were to increase, there is no way in which the expenditure on the service would be contained, assuming the same level of service as before.

Leakages from the water supply network are a sign of inefficiency in the system. While leakages in the previous year should have a positive impact on expenditure in the current year, leakages in the current year would be endogenous since the level of (O&M) expenditure also has some impact on leakages. For this reason, we included distance from the water source to the pumping station as an exogenous instrument for leakages. This way, we were able to control for the leakage's endogeneity. When controlled for its endogeneity, the current year's leakage should have a positive impact on expenditure. However, note that, if the volume of water supply used is net of leakages (which is what is used here), leakages could have no impact on expenditure, since the municipality does not incur extra expenditure to supply the leaked water to households or to the end consumer. They are most likely stolen or wasted.

Finally, given the buoyancy of a tax like octroi, however distortionary, we expect it to have a positive impact on expenditure. This is because octroi is highly liquid in form (providing cities with ready cash to spend) and hence provides every incentive for cities to spend readily. While the amount of octroi revenue could be endogenous with expenditure, we created an exogenous dummy (of 1) if the city had access to octroi, 0 otherwise.

Finally, to distinguish the impact on expenditure of municipal bodies from those in cities in which non-municipal bodies (such as parastatal agencies and other state-level agencies) provide water supply, we create a dummy (of 1) for non-municipal bodies, 0 otherwise. The way in which this is set up, we expected this to have an ambiguous impact on expenditure. This is because non-municipal bodies (such as parastatal bodies or commercial utilities) are known to be relatively more efficient than municipal entities in delivering the service, cutting on unit costs, but this does not in any way ensure that their total expenditure levels also would be lower or higher.

Based on the estimation in Equation (2.2), it is possible to construct a cost index for each local government i, assuming actual values of other factors. We construct a cost index for water supply by city.

MARGINAL COSTS

Having defined costs, and distinguishing them from expenditure, ideally, we would have liked to do an estimation of O&M expenditures on water supply for every city so that we can arrive at short-run marginal cost estimates. If done for every city, the marginal cost estimates would have implications for revision of water tariffs in each of the cities we study. However, the timeframe for which the data are available does not permit enough degrees of freedom to enable estimation for every city. If we were to do a pooled estimation of marginal costs for all cities, the degrees of freedom would not be a problem. Hence we were able to perform estimations of total expenditures for all cities, and for sub-samples of categories of cities, as we found relevant.

Note that our study also has implications only for the *average* tariff level in the cities. While *actual* water tariffs are somewhat different for various categories of users, the study is unable to throw light on what the *ideal tariff* levels should be for each of the categories of users—domestic, industrial, and commercial—of the system. This is because all cities' expenditures are reported only for total water consumption and not for consumption by use or category.

In the case of cities that have metering of water to record the volume of consumption, there is no problem in comparing marginal costs to water tariffs. In Chapter 5, we survey pricing mechanisms for water in various Indian cities. In the case of cities, however, that do not have metering but some other pricing mechanisms, we get some additional and different data to enable us to compare the marginal costs thus obtained to the average tariff level.[5]

While this chapter dwells upon the methodology, model, and relationships expected between the independent and the dependent variables, the next chapter describes the data, their sources (primary or secondary), and how we constructed the required variables for purposes of our econometric work and analyses for water supply.

NOTES

1. The Census of India's definition for various class size cities is as follows:
    Class I: Population > 100,000
    Class II: Population of 50,000–99,999
    Class III: Population of 20,000–49,999
    Class IV: Population of 10,000–19,999
    Class V: Population of 5,000–9,999
    Class VI: Population < 5,000.
2. Maharashtra, Karnataka, and Gujarat recorded more than 100 per cent growth of their per capita net state domestic product (at current prices) between 1993–4 and 2002–3, according to data from the Central Statistical Organisation (CSO).
3. While ideally the time period would have been historical, dating to the 1970s, such historical data has not been collected or systematically maintained by cities. Hence we had to satisfy ourselves to a relatively more recent time period.
4. It may be argued that if the impact of rainfall is ambiguous, and not actively explained through the data, the rainfall variable may as well be avoided. However, avoiding the variable is no solution since it will give rise to the omitted variable problem.
5. A question that one might like to answer is whether in cities that have metered connections and where tariffs reflect costs, the level and quality of services would be higher, or at least different from the others.

CHAPTER 3

Data, Sources, and Variable Definitions

In this chapter, we present the specific details of the data we have gathered through various secondary sources, our field visits to the cities, examination of budget documents, and discussions/clarifications with officials for purposes of obtaining data to enable us do the marginal cost estimation for water supply in the selected cities. We also describe in this chapter how all variables used in the econometric analysis for water supply and data analyses for other services in Chapters 6 and 7 were constructed.

The descriptive tables on (capital, O&M, and total) expenditures for water supply (as with solid waste, sanitation, sewerage, roads, and street lights in Chapters 6 and 7) are presented in the forthcoming chapter, in per capita terms, to get around the scaling issue. For this, we needed data on city population for a number of years. Data on population for the six cities for the census years (1991 and 2001) were readily available from the Census of India. For the intervening years, we estimated the population using a method recommended by the Mumbai-based International Institute of Population Sciences (IIPS).

POPULATION ESTIMATION

Data on population were fairly crucial to (recall Figure 2.1) the empirical work and estimation specifically as they related to water supply. First, note that while estimations for water supply expenditures were made of total (O&M) expenditure (in deflated terms), expenditure data were converted to per capita terms for purposes of enabling descriptive comparisons across cities.

For 1981, 1991, and 2001, census data were available on population. For the intervening years (1992–2000 and 2002–4), we used an exponential growth rate assumption recommended by the IIPS. The exponential growth rate is represented by the equation:

$$P_t = P_0\, e^{rt} \tag{3.1}$$

where P_t refers to population in the year t we are interested in estimating, P_0 is the base year (census year) population, t is the number of years from the base year for which we need to estimate P_t, and r is the growth rate of population from the base year to the tenth year.

We used r obtained from Equation (3.1) to estimate population for the intervening years. Based on Equation (3.1), we have

$$\frac{P_t}{P_0} = e^{rt} \tag{3.2}$$

It follows that

$$rt = \ln\left(\frac{P_t}{P_0}\right)$$

Solving for r gives us

$$r = \frac{1}{t}\ln\left(\frac{P_t}{P_0}\right) \tag{3.3}$$

Calculating the growth rate, r, as given by Equation (3.3), we estimated the population for the intervening years for all six cities, assuming the same growth rate within every decade.[1] Estimating population for the intervening years this way, we ensured that the final year's population (2001 population) we estimated was the same as what was reported in the Census for that year for all the cities. This way, we ensured confidence in our population estimation for the intervening years.

CONSTRUCTION OF PRICE INDEX

Recall from our earlier discussion (see Figure 2.1 in Chapter 2) that the vector of input prices that a city or region is faced with, along with other factors, determines the costs of providing water supply. Further, we needed data on price indices to convert the nominal expenditure into real terms. We used data on gross state domestic product (GSDP) at current and constant prices published and recommended by the Central Statistical Organisation (CSO) to deflate the nominal expenditure data to that in real terms. City-specific price indices are not available nor are published by the CSO. So we used price indices for states in which the selected cities were located.[2]

We needed the price index data from 1991 (in fact, from 1985 for a few cities—Bangalore and Surat—for which expenditure and other data were available and had been collected all the way since the mid-1980s) all the way up to 2004. The CSO has published data on components of GSDP by sector, in two series, at current and constant prices. The 'old series' covers the period 1980–1 to 1993–4 (for which 1980–1 is the base year) and the 'new series' covers the period 1993–4 to 2003–4 (for which 1993–4 is the base year) (http://www.mospi.nic.in/mospi_cso_rept_pubn.htm).

We used data on GSDP at current and constant prices for three sectors: electricity, gas, and water supply, construction, and other services. We used the new series data from CSO from 1994–5 onwards for these three sectors in their original form, since they had the desired 1993–4 = 100 as the base year. For the data from 1980–1 to 1993–4 (since they had 1980–1 = 100 as the base year), we used a scaling factor, according to the methodology recommended by the CSO, to convert all price indices comparable against the same base year (1993–4 = 100). The following procedure was followed in order to accomplish this objective:

1. First, for the six states in which each of our cities are located, the ratios of the respective state's gross state domestic product at current to constant prices were calculated. These were computed for the three sectors of interest (electricity, gas and water supply; construction; and other services) for all years (both old as well as new series).

2. A scaling factor was computed, for all three sectors, based on ratio of the GSDP for 1993–4 that had 1993–4 = 100 as the base, to the GSDP for the same year, 1993–4, which had 1980–1 = 100 as the base. These scaling factors were computed both for GSDP at current and constant prices for the three sectors and six states in which the selected cities are located.
3. Then, the GSDP for the years from 1980–1 to 1993–4 (that had 1980–1 = 100 as the base) were multiplied by the scaling factor computed in step (2), making their base 1993–4 = 100.
4. This way we converted all years' data (1980–1 all the way to 2003–4) to the same base year, 1993–4 = 100. With this, we had the entire range of state GSDP at current as well as constant prices for six states and three sectors, with the same base, 1993–4.
5. We took the ratio of current to constant GSDP for all years (for the three sectors and six states). This way, as we expected, we obtained a price index of 1 for 1993–4 for the three sectors and six states.

We used the deflator obtained in step (5) to deflate the nominal capital and O&M expenditures on all services to real terms. We used the deflators based on electricity, gas, and water supply for deflating expenditures on water supply and street lights. We used deflators we obtained for 'construction' to convert expenditures on roads and sewerage to real terms. Finally, we used deflators based on 'other services' to convert expenditure on sanitation and solid waste to real terms.

Rainfall and Altitude

As Figure 2.1 (in Chapter 2) shows, in addition to the price index, we used data on rainfall and topography (measured by altitude) to represent a city's natural cost disabilities in providing water supply. We obtained secondary data on rainfall from the Pune-based Indian Meteorological Institute and data on altitude (extent [in metres] to which a city is above the mean sea level) from the individual cities. The data on rainfall for the cities required over the period 1991–2003 were in monthly terms. Based on the monthly rainfall (for 12 months) of a particular year for a particular city, we computed the annual average rainfall (expressed in millimetres) by year for every city.

DEPENDENT AND OTHER VARIABLE DEFINITIONS

The water supply data we used in the estimation are in net terms (net of leakages). A caveat of course is that while the volume of water supply used is in *net* terms, the expenditure measure that we use refers to what the city incurs on the *gross* volume of water supply, including what eventually leaks out of the system.

We expressed the daily net volume of water supply (for all cities and years) in 1,000 l. Then we converted this quantity into annual terms (since the expenditure data are annual). We, of course, did have data on leakages in the supply of water in all cities, over time. We used this as a measure of inefficiency in the system.

As discussed earlier, the octroi is used as a measure of the revenue potential of the city (which could imply local *government* preferences), and it should be a significant determinant of expenditures. All cities with octroi (Surat and Pune in our sample) received a dummy of 1 and others with octroi having been abolished received a value of 0.

Since we expected cities in which non-municipal (or parastatal) bodies offer the service to be more efficient than municipal bodies, we included a dummy for whether it is a city in which a non-municipal body (such as Rajasthan's state department, Public Health Engineering Department [PHED], as in Jaipur, or a commercial utility such as the Bangalore Water Supply and Sewerage Board [BWSSB] in Bangalore) provided the service.

The forthcoming chapters summarize our findings from the research. First, in Chapter 4, we describe the expenditures on and physical level of the water supply by various categories of cities and then summarize the marginal cost estimations for water supply, and finally compare them with water tariffs, as we promised.

NOTES

1. This meant that for cities such as Surat and Bangalore for which we had data from the 1980s, we used the growth rate of population over 1981–91 to project data for the 1980s and used the growth rate of population over 1991–2001 to project population for the 1990s.

2. Recently according to guidelines of the Central Statistical Organisation, most states have been developing district-specific domestic products for all districts in their states. However, this is a very recent phenomenon (for instance, even in states such as Tamil Nadu, these district-specific domestic product estimates were not ready even until late 2007), hence at the time the work for this chapter was completed, state-specific domestic products were used. However, if there is indeed not much of a disparity between state- and district-specific indices, then it does not matter which one is used for deflation.

CHAPTER 4

Trends in Expenditure, Marginal Cost, and Pricing Structures

Findings from Data on Water Supply

In this chapter, we first describe the data on water supply in the cities of our visit, followed by the results from the marginal cost estimation of water supply. In our presentation of the descriptive data findings, we examine the expenditures on water supply as well as the physical levels of the service, for separate categories of cities, as we have deemed appropriate, that have been summarized earlier. The findings reported in the various tables in this chapter are based on our primary data gathered from the cities and budget documents. Where secondary sources such as the Census or others have been used, they are indicated.

DESCRIPTION OF DATA ON WATER SUPPLY EXPENDITURE AND SERVICE LEVELS

Tables 4.1–4.14 report descriptive statistics of the volume of expenditure and the level of service of water supply for various categories of cities, based on the primary data we obtained from our fieldwork in the cities. For the entire period covering our study, combining all the six cities, the average per capita capital expenditure is mostly lower than per capita O&M expenditure over the period in real terms (Tables 4.1 and 4.2). This does mean that cities spend less on creating assets than in operating and maintaining them, a trend that has been conventionally observed through the developing world.

TABLE 4.1

Capital Expenditure on Water Supply, All Cities

(Number of Cities = 6)

Year	Per Capita Expenditure (in Constant 1993–4 Prices, Rs)				Water Supply per Capita per Day* (Litres)	
	Average	Std Dev.	Max.	Min.	Average	Std Dev.
1991	50.34	51.72	107.14	0.46	206.13	99.65
1992	26.32	31.86	72.96	0.46	195.59	98.51
1993	21.70	18.47	43.87	0.46	239.98	148.26
1994	49.87	54.03	112.68	0.46	243.06	135.64
1995	44.79	30.02	84.97	0.46	257.54	147.88
1996	65.58	59.11	173.64	0.46	250.46	136.99
1997	48.49	37.87	102.52	0.00	246.11	130.14
1998	81.28	65.11	161.17	0.46	248.09	116.49
1999	110.83	122.38	321.41	0.00	248.13	103.73
2000	130.23	153.32	397.61	0.00	246.36	96.55
2001	102.52	170.87	447.02	0.00	244.56	96.48
2002	104.37	162.09	432.24	0.00	254.96	92.17
2003	55.42	43.87	120.99	0.46	248.48	84.61
Average	*68.60*				*240.73*	

Source: Chandigarh Municipal Corporation; Surat Municipal Corporation; Pune Municipal Corporation; Lucknow Jal Sansthan; Bangalore Water Supply and Sewerage Board; Public Health Engineering Department; Government of Rajasthan; and authors' computations and analyses.

Note: * The water supply data are net of leakages.

The volume of water supply per capita per day in the six cities varies between 196 and 260 l during the time period of the study. The maximum capital expenditure is Rs 447.24 per capita in 2001–2 while that for per capita O&M expenditure is Rs 473.52 (2002–3). The minimum per capita capital expenditure incurred is Rs 0.19 (1999) while the minimum per capita O&M expenditure is Rs 1.24 (1995). Thus, after the 74th Constitutional Amendment Act (CAA), while the spending continues to be low, cities have been continually increasing their spending on the provision of water supply.

Since our sample consists of cities and is based on several criteria, we make use of those classifications to study expenditures. As explained earlier, Chandigarh and Surat are our benchmark cities to demonstrate how much we can expect such cities to spend to offer a certain level of service.

TABLE 4.2
O&M Expenditure on Water Supply, All Cities
(Number of Cities = 6)

Year	Per Capita Expenditure (in Constant 1993–4 Prices, Rs)				Water Supply per Capita per Day (Litres)	
	Average	Std Dev.	Max.	Min.	Average	Std Dev.
1991	96.52	103.91	216.58	1.85	206.13	99.65
1992	99.75	109.91	249.37	1.39	195.59	98.51
1993	97.44	115.45	277.54	1.39	239.98	148.26
1994	119.61	158.86	381.91	1.39	243.06	135.64
1995	116.37	143.16	326.03	1.39	257.54	147.88
1996	149.16	157.47	395.30	1.39	250.46	136.99
1997	155.63	151.47	320.49	1.39	246.11	130.14
1998	166.25	160.71	350.97	1.39	248.09	116.49
1999	197.65	160.24	351.43	1.39	248.13	103.73
2000	215.20	182.41	425.32	1.39	246.36	96.55
2001	193.49	175.95	407.31	1.39	244.56	96.48
2002	203.19	195.80	473.35	1.39	254.96	92.17
2003	151.47	163.48	394.84	1.39	248.48	84.61
Average	150.90				240.73	

Source: Same as Table 4.1.

Across the years, on average, we find that both per capita capital and O&M expenditures incurred by the benchmark cities are higher than that of non-benchmark cities, as we expect (Tables 4.3 and 4.4). Further, over time, benchmark cities supply greater quantity of water (265.18 l per day per person) than the non-benchmark cities (which supply only 228 l per capita per day). This finding emphasizes that better access of water supply in terms of volume supplied per capita per day should be associated with substantially higher O&M and capital expenditures.

Next, we studied expenditure patterns on water supply by cities in which the municipal corporations supply water to residents vis-à-vis those in which non-municipal bodies such as parastatal (for instance, the Bangalore Water Supply and Sewerage Board [BWSSB] in Bangalore) and other state-level bodies offer the service. While non-municipal bodies (including state-level and parastatal bodies) are also governmental agencies, they may have incentives to be commercially viable, similar to a private company.

Our findings are interesting. We find that on average, both per capita capital and O&M expenditures for the cities in which

TABLE 4.3

Capital Expenditures on Water Supply, Benchmark and Other Cities

| Year | Benchmark Cities (Number of Cities = 2) | | | | Non-benchmark Cities (Number of Cities = 4) | | | |
| | Per Capita Expenditure (in Constant 1993–4 Prices, Rs) | | Water Supply per Capita per Day (Litres) | | Per Capita Expenditure (in Constant 1993–4 Prices, Rs) | | Water Supply per Capita per Day (Litres) | |
	Average	Std Dev.	Average	Std Dev.	Average	Std Dev.	Average	Std Dev.
1996	103.44	98.83	267.71	216.78	46.64	33.25	241.84	123.76
1997	74.81	39.71	266.99	210.17	30.94	30.48	235.67	114.30
1998	104.37	80.35	268.72	181.32	69.27	66.04	237.77	105.99
1999	192.57	182.41	284.14	134.29	69.73	85.43	230.13	103.08
2000	132.54	130.69	285.43	108.38	129.30	182.87	226.82	100.47
2001	55.42	35.10	294.10	108.90	126.07	214.74	219.79	95.43
2002	50.80	13.85	289.83	98.96	131.61	202.27	231.72	100.34
2003	92.36	40.18	280.70	89.00	30.94	28.17	227.01	92.88
Average	*100.79*		*279.70*		*79.31*		*231.34*	

Source: Same as Table 4.1.

TABLE 4.4
O&M Expenditures on Water Supply, Benchmark and Other Cities

Year	Benchmark Cities (Number of Cities = 2)				Non-benchmark Cities (Number of Cities = 4)			
	Per Capita Expenditure (in Constant 1993–4 Prices, Rs)		Water Supply per Capita per Day (Litres)		Per Capita Expenditure (in Constant 1993–4 Prices, Rs)		Water Supply per Capita per Day (Litres)	
	Average	Std Dev.	Average	Std Dev.	Average	Std Dev.	Average	Std Dev.
1996	122.84	102.06	267.71	216.78	162.09	193.03	241.84	123.76
1997	178.25	176.41	266.99	210.17	144.08	165.32	235.67	114.30
1998	207.81	202.27	268.72	181.32	145.47	166.25	237.77	105.99
1999	268.77	96.98	284.14	134.29	162.09	186.11	230.13	103.08
2000	288.16	135.31	285.43	108.38	178.72	210.12	226.82	100.47
2001	267.38	198.11	294.10	108.90	156.09	181.95	219.79	95.43
2002	250.30	183.33	289.83	98.96	179.64	224.90	231.72	100.34
2003	263.69	185.64	280.70	89.00	76.20	122.84	227.01	92.88
Average	*230.90*		*265.18*		*150.55*		*231.34*	

Source: Same as Table 4.1.

non-municipal bodies offer the service are, in fact, lower than they are in municipality service provider cities (Tables 4.5 and 4.6). This could be either a reflection of the fact that non-municipal bodies are more efficient in the delivery of their services or that they spend too little per capita. There appears to be greater support for the latter since the average per capita per day volume of water supply is also higher in the municipality service provider cities than in the non-municipal counterparts. But, water supply is also more volatile in municipality provider cities than that in non-municipal service provider cities.

We slice the cities in another way to distinguish the impact of octroi-levying cities from those that do not levy octroi. Historically, it is well-known that the octroi, while being a distortionary tax, is a buoyant source of revenue for cities. Hence cities that have access to this revenue, no matter what, should be spending more than the cities that do not have access to this revenue source (because their states have abolished it). In our sample of cities, as described earlier, Surat and Pune continue to have the octroi whereas Bangalore, Lucknow, Jaipur, and Chandigarh do not.

Aggregating the O&M and capital expenditure across all the years, we find that the octroi-levying cities indeed spend higher per capita on water supply than their non-octroi counterparts (Tables 4.7 and 4.8). The per capita per day supply of water in the octroi cities is also, on average, higher than that in the non-octroi cities, a finding that again reinforces the relationship between spending and level of service in the case of water supply. While spending may or may not translate into higher levels of service, it is possible that where cities are efficient (for instance, those that ensure minimal leakages) in their provision of the service, higher spending does result in higher volume of the service.

Further, we made a distinction between cities whose populations rapidly grew in the 1990s and those that grew more slowly during this period (Tables 4.9 and 4.10).[1] Surprisingly, the slow-growth cities spent more (capital as well as O&M) per capita on water and were able to supply higher volume of water per capita. We noted that Bangalore, which is the highest spender on water in absolute terms, was a slow-growing city during the 1990s. So it is possible that the findings in Tables 4.9 and 4.10, of the slow-growing cities

TABLE 4.5
Capital Expenditures on Water Supply, Non-municipal and Municipal Provider Cities

Year	Non-municipal Provider Cities (Number of Cities = 3)				Municipal Provider Cities (Number of Cities = 3)			
	Per Capita Expenditure (in Constant 1993–4 Prices, Rs)		Water Supply per Capita per Day (Litres)		Per Capita Expenditure (in Constant 1993–4 Prices, Rs)		Water Supply per Capita per Day (Litres)	
	Average	Std Dev.	Average	Std Dev.	Average	Std Dev.	Average	Std Dev.
1991*	62.80	55.42	149.69	34.30	12.47	0.00*	262.56	118.72
1992	29.56	38.33	149.00	41.48	17.09	0.00*	242.18	126.60
1993	19.86	22.17	168.00	42.95	27.25	0.00*	311.97	193.82
1994	40.64	62.34	184.39	42.37	76.66	0.00*	301.72	184.04
1995	31.40	26.78	184.15	37.90	64.65	29.09	330.92	192.55
1996	39.25	36.48	181.62	34.91	92.36	72.50	319.30	177.43
1997	30.94	30.48	180.03	32.03	74.81	39.71	312.19	167.97
1998	54.49	72.04	189.15	51.68	108.06	56.80	307.02	144.35
1999	70.19	104.37	183.56	54.08	151.47	147.31	312.71	107.07
2000	141.77	222.13	181.46	52.91	119.14	95.13	311.25	88.73
2001	156.09	252.14	177.80	55.48	48.49	27.71	311.33	82.58
2002	164.40	234.13	182.83	76.12	44.79	14.32	303.05	73.63
2003	18.47	25.86	183.53	76.88	80.35	35.10	291.79	65.80
Average	66.14		176.55		70.58		301.38	

Source: Same as Table 4.1.

Note: *For 1991–4, the capital expenditures are just for Surat, hence the standard deviation is 0. Pune did not supply data on capital expenditures for those years and Chandigarh became a municipal corporation only in 1996.

TABLE 4.6

O&M Expenditures on Water Supply, Non-municipal and Municipal Provider Cities

Year	Non-municipal Provider Cities (Number of Cities = 3)				Municipal Provider Cities (Number of Cities = 3)			
	Per Capita Expenditure (in Constant 1993–4 Prices, Rs)		Water Supply per Capita per Day (Litres)		Per Capita Expenditure (in Constant 1993–4 Prices, Rs)		Water Supply per Capita per Day (Litres)	
	Average	Std Dev.	Average	Std Dev.	Average	Std Dev.	Average	Std Dev.
1991	70.66	111.76	149.69	34.30	135.77	114.06	262.56	118.72
1992	85.89	141.77	149.00	41.48	120.53	82.20	242.18	126.60
1993	95.59	157.94	168.00	42.95	100.67	57.73	311.97	193.82
1994	129.30	218.43	184.39	42.37	104.83	69.73	301.72	184.04
1995	110.83	186.11	184.15	37.90	124.22	112.68	330.92	192.55
1996	134.38	226.28	181.62	34.91	163.94	101.60	319.30	177.43
1997	108.98	182.87	180.03	32.03	202.27	131.61	312.19	167.97
1998	110.83	185.18	189.15	51.68	221.66	145.01	307.02	144.35
1999	118.68	201.34	183.56	54.08	276.62	69.73	312.71	107.07
2000	144.54	242.91	181.46	52.91	286.32	95.59	311.25	88.73
2001	130.23	213.35	177.80	55.48	256.30	141.31	311.33	82.58
2002	160.24	271.08	182.83	76.12	246.14	129.77	303.05	73.63
2003	5.54	6.00	183.53	76.88	248.45	133.92	291.79	65.80
Average	*108.13*		*176.55*		*191.36*		*301.38*	

Source: Same as Table 4.1.

TABLE 4.7
Capital Expenditures on Water Supply for Cities with and without Octroi

Year	Cities with Octroi (Number of Cities = 2)				Cities without octroi (Number of Cities = 4)			
	Per Capita Expenditure (in Constant 1993–4 Prices, Rs)		Water Supply per Capita per Day (Litres)		Per Capita Expenditure (in Constant 1993–4 Prices, Rs)		Water Supply per Capita per Day (Litres)	
	Average	Std Dev.	Average	Std Dev.	Average	Std Dev.	Average	Std Dev.
1995	64.65	29.09	230.84	184.75	31.40	26.78	25.44	24.28
1996	121.45	73.43	226.18	170.55	37.87	30.02	34.24	36.33
1997	102.52	NA	221.56	157.28	35.10	26.32	29.33	30.78
1998	138.08	32.79	220.89	140.92	52.65	58.65	64.93	67.98
1999	195.34	178.25	229.73	124.87	68.35	85.43	91.81	95.06
2000	158.40	94.21	234.12	118.15	116.37	187.95	195.27	198.72
2001	57.73	31.86	229.29	110.90	124.69	215.20	220.93	223.58
2002	36.94	6.00	226.12	100.39	138.54	198.11	210.18	216.30
2003	60.03	5.54	220.30	92.43	52.65	61.88	60.97	60.26
Average	*103.91*		*226.56*		*73.07*		*85.03*	

Source: Same as Table 4.1.

TABLE 4.8
O&M Expenditures on Water Supply, Cities with and without Octroi

Year	Cities with Octroi (Number of Cities = 2)				Cities without Octroi (Number of Cities = 4)			
	Per Capita Expenditure (in Constant 1993–4 Prices, Rs)		Water Supply per Capita per Day (Litres)		Per Capita Expenditure (in Constant 1993–4 Prices, Rs)		Water Supply per Capita per Day (Litres)	
	Average	Std Dev.	Average	Std Dev.	Average	Std Dev.	Average	Std Dev.
1991	135.77	114.06	205.75	93.92	70.66	111.76	206.31	116.66
1992	120.53	82.20	183.62	107.16	85.89	141.77	201.57	110.47
1993	100.67	57.73	296.37	271.43	95.59	157.94	211.79	94.33
1994	104.83	69.73	283.87	256.58	129.30	218.43	222.65	83.98
1995	124.22	112.68	275.98	236.73	110.83	186.11	248.31	132.01
1996	148.24	138.08	268.45	217.83	149.62	187.03	241.47	123.04
1997	151.47	139.00	260.48	200.96	157.47	178.25	238.93	120.65
1998	157.01	130.69	262.06	171.90	170.87	193.03	241.10	112.13
1999	246.14	64.65	279.51	127.74	173.18	197.65	232.44	107.28
2000	237.37	62.80	285.84	108.96	204.58	231.82	226.62	100.10
2001	181.03	75.74	281.44	91.00	199.50	222.59	226.12	106.74
2002	179.18	83.12	274.67	77.53	215.20	247.06	241.82	115.48
2003	175.02	60.03	265.87	68.03	135.31	224.90	236.90	107.24
Average	*158.58*		*263.38*		*146.00*		*228.92*	

Source: Same as Table 4.1.

TABLE 4.9
Capital Expenditures on Water Supply, Cities by Population Growth

Year	Fast-growing Cities (Number of Cities = 3)				Slow-growing Cities (Number of Cities = 3)			
	Per Capita Expenditure (in Constant 1993–4 Prices, Rs)		Water Supply per Capita per Day (Litres)		Per Capita Expenditure (in Constant 1993–4 Prices, Rs)		Water Supply per Capita per Day (Litres)	
	Average	Std Dev.	Average	Std Dev.	Average	Std Dev.	Average	Std Dev.
1991	6.47	8.31	199.80	67.20	94.21	18.47	212.45	142.09
1992	8.77	11.55	187.59	76.09	43.87	41.10	203.58	135.21
1993	13.85	18.93	242.15	213.68	29.56	19.86	237.82	96.35
1994	38.79	54.03	234.40	200.64	60.96	73.43	251.71	74.24
1995	42.95	42.49	230.84	184.75	47.10	2.77	284.23	135.64
1996	80.82	87.28	226.18	170.55	50.34	19.86	274.75	126.74
1997	51.26	72.50	221.56	157.28	46.64	15.24	270.66	125.67
1998	91.90	82.66	220.89	140.92	70.19	57.73	275.28	108.86
1999	130.23	169.02	229.73	124.87	90.97	88.20	266.53	101.45
2000	105.75	113.14	234.12	118.15	155.16	210.12	258.59	94.32
2001	38.33	40.18	229.29	110.90	166.25	243.37	259.83	101.35
2002	24.48	21.70	226.12	100.39	184.26	214.74	298.22	87.08
2003	40.18	34.64	220.30	92.43	78.97	59.57	290.76	74.78
Average	*51.83*		*223.31*		*86.04*		*260.34*	

Source: Same as Table 4.1.

TABLE 4.10

O&M Expenditures on Water Supply, Cities by Population Growth

Year	Rapid-growth Cities (Number of Cities = 3)				Slow-growth Cities (Number of Cities = 3)			
	Per Capita Expenditure (in Constant 1993–4 Prices, Rs)		Water Supply per Capita per Day (Litres)		Per Capita Expenditure (in Constant 1993–4 Prices, Rs)		Water Supply per Capita per Day (Litres)	
	Average	Std Dev.	Average	Std Dev.	Average	Std Dev.	Average	Std Dev.
1991	90.97	111.76	199.80	67.20	207.81	12.01	212.45	142.09
1992	80.82	90.05	187.59	76.09	213.81	49.87	203.58	135.21
1993	67.88	70.66	242.15	213.68	209.66	96.05	237.82	96.35
1994	70.66	77.58	234.40	200.64	268.31	160.71	251.71	74.24
1995	83.12	106.68	230.84	184.75	265.07	86.36	284.23	135.64
1996	99.29	129.30	226.18	170.55	278.93	104.37	274.75	126.74
1997	101.60	131.15	221.56	157.28	290.93	36.48	270.66	125.67
1998	105.29	128.84	220.89	140.92	308.02	52.65	275.28	108.86
1999	164.40	148.24	229.73	124.87	326.95	31.40	266.53	101.45
2000	158.86	143.16	234.12	118.15	363.90	73.89	258.59	94.32
2001	120.99	116.84	229.29	110.90	339.42	92.36	259.83	101.35
2002	120.07	118.22	226.12	100.39	363.90	118.68	298.22	87.08
2003	117.30	108.98	220.30	92.43	306.17	125.15	290.76	74.78
Average	*106.25*		*223.31*		*287.91*		*260.34*	

Source: Same as Table 4.1.

spending more per capita than the fast-growing ones, are influenced by Bangalore.

Finally, we distinguished between cities that are located in the BIMARU (Bihar, Madhya Pradesh, Rajasthan, and Uttar Pradesh) states with those in the non-BIMARU states (Tables 4.11 and 4.12). We find, as we would expect, on average, that the O&M and capital expenditure across the years for the non-BIMARU cities are higher than that of BIMARU cities. Noticeably, the per capita per day average of water supplied for non-BIMARU cities is also much higher than that for BIMARU cities, as we would expect, again demonstrating a strong relationship between spending and service levels with respect to water supply in the cities.

RESULTS FROM ESTIMATION

The literature (McNeill and Tate, 1991; World Bank, 1994) widely acknowledges that marginal cost pricing of water is efficient. Technically we know that the marginal cost is determined by taking the first derivative of the total cost (understanding the distinction between cost and expenditure) curve with respect to the volume of water supplied. As McNeill and Tate (1991), Link (2003), and Tiina Idström (2004) point out, the marginal cost is equal to the marginal operating cost, which includes variable costs. As Turvey (1976) points out, the capital costs required to meet incremental demand for water tend to be lumpy and cannot be determined statistically. Others (e.g., Warford, 1997) also generally accept that for capital expenditures, a statistically determined function would be rarely appropriate. So we do not attempt to calculate or estimate marginal cost for capacity expansions, based on capital expenditures.

The first step in our analysis develops a cost (expenditure) function based on the city's/utility's budgets for O&M expenditures. As we know, more generally, the cost function shows the relationship between the water supplied and the costs incurred.[2] Further, other factors such as topography, input prices, and expenditure responsibilities of local government determine expenditure/cost levels.

Tables 4.13–4.21 show the results of various regressions we estimated for purposes of obtaining the marginal cost of supplying 1000 l of water. We estimate Equation (2.2) of Chapter 2 by

TABLE 4.11

Capital Expenditures on Water Supply, Cities by State

Year	BIMARU Cities (Number of Cities = 2)				Non-BIMARU Cities (Number of Cities = 4)			
	Per Capita Expenditure (in Constant 1993–4 Prices, Rs)		Water Supply per Capita per Day (Litres)		Per Capita Expenditure (in Constant 1993–4 Prices, Rs)		Water Supply per Capita per Day (Litres)	
	Average	Std Dev.	Average	Std Dev.	Average	Std Dev.	Average	Std Dev.
1991	40.64	56.80	154.77	46.88	59.57	66.96	231.81	114.81
1992	7.39	10.16	155.71	56.32	44.79	39.71	215.53	116.31
1993	7.85	10.62	174.93	58.31	35.56	12.01	272.51	176.84
1994	4.62	6.00	172.63	52.54	94.67	25.40	278.27	157.42
1995	24.48	34.17	174.98	48.67	58.19	23.09	298.82	169.83
1996	22.63	31.40	173.82	45.53	87.28	60.03	288.78	157.21
1997	15.70	22.17	174.02	42.84	70.19	29.09	282.16	149.72
1998	13.39	18.93	190.2	73.05	114.99	48.49	277.03	132.25
1999	10.16	13.85	184.25	76.47	161.17	121.92	280.08	109.1
2000	13.85	19.40	183.48	74.66	188.88	159.32	277.79	98.62
2001	10.62	14.78	180.29	78.22	148.24	200.88	276.7	96.67
2002	30.48	42.49	182.83	76.12	141.77	193.96	303.05	73.63
2003	18.47	25.86	183.53	76.88	80.35	35.10	291.79	65.8
Average	16.94		175.8		98.90		274.95	

Source: Same as Table 4.1.

TABLE 4.12
O&M Expenditures on Water Supply, Cities by State

| Year | Cities in BIMARU States (Number of Cities = 2) | | | | Cities in Non-BIMARU States (Number of Cities = 4) | | | |
| | Per Capita Expenditure (in Constant 1993–4 Prices, Rs) | | Water Supply per Capita per Day (Litres) | | Per Capita Expenditure (in Constant 1993–4 Prices, Rs) | | Water Supply per Capita per Day (Litres) | |
	Average	Std Dev.	Average	Std Dev.	Average	Std Dev.	Average	Std Dev.
1991	6.47	6.47	205.75	93.92	157.01	88.67	206.31	116.66
1992	4.16	3.69	183.62	107.16	163.48	94.67	201.57	110.47
1993	4.16	4.16	296.37	271.43	159.78	109.91	211.79	94.33
1994	3.23	2.77	283.87	256.58	197.19	167.17	222.65	83.98
1995	3.69	3.23	275.98	236.73	191.65	140.85	248.31	132.01
1996	3.69	3.23	268.45	217.83	221.66	142.23	241.47	123.04
1997	3.23	2.77	260.48	200.96	231.82	122.84	238.93	120.65
1998	3.69	3.23	262.06	171.9	247.06	129.30	241.1	112.13
1999	2.31	1.39	279.51	127.74	295.09	68.35	232.44	107.28
2000	4.16	3.69	285.84	108.96	320.95	104.83	226.62	100.1
2001	6.93	7.85	281.44	91	286.32	130.23	226.12	106.74
2002	4.16	3.69	274.67	77.53	302.94	155.63	241.82	115.48
2003	5.54	6.00	265.87	68.03	248.45	133.92	236.9	107.24
Average	*4.26*		*263.38*		*232.57*		*228.92*	

Source: Same as Table 4.1.

ordinary least squares (OLS) and two-stage least squares (2SLS) because of the endogeneity of the volume of the service.[3] The number of observations for the estimation is based on time-series data (during 1991–2003) for the six cities described earlier.

When all cities are taken into account (Table 4.13), the amount of water supply (net of leakages) does not have a significant impact on expenditures. This implies that when all cities are included, the volume of water supply does not impose any extra costs on the system. But if the expenditures are themselves very low (which they were in the case of two BIMARU cities, Lucknow and Jaipur; see later discussion for estimates of how low their expenditures were compared to the other four cities studied), this finding does not mean much (for instance, see Table 4.23 which compares the costs and expenditures by the cities).

As Table 4.13 summarizes, the altitude of the city and the price index it is faced with for water, gas, and electricity make a big difference to its cost of providing water supply. Specifically, for every 1 m that the city is located above the mean sea level, there is an increase in expenditure on water supply to the extent of Rs 1,355,690.[4] This is reasonable to expect given the average expenditure of the cities on water supply (Rs 346,469,375 in real terms, see Table 4.23). This result is also reasonable because of the costs of having to pump up the water from a low-lying water source. In fact, this is the reason why Bangalore's O&M costs of providing water are quite high. In the next chapter, we present further details of the disaggregation of costs for many cities including Bangalore.

Further, Table 4.13 shows that if the price index faced by the city is high, the cost of providing water supply is also high, reasonable to expect. Leakages in the system have a negative impact on expenditure. Note that, since the volume of water supply used is net of leakages, the leakages could have a negative impact on expenditure, as the municipality does not incur extra expenditure to supply them to households or to the end consumer. Here the magnitude of the estimate implies that for every one percentage point leakage (water not supplied to the end-consumer), there is a reduction in expenditure to the extent of US$ 213,230 (Rs 9,846,940).

With a view to adjusting for the time availability of the water supply (e.g., whether random supply in some part of the day, or

TABLE 4.13

Estimation of Expenditure on (Net) Water Supply

(Dependent Variable: Operations & Maintenance Expenditure, All Cities [Deflated in 1993–4 Prices])

Variable	OLS Estimates			2SLS Estimates			Variable Mean
	Coeff.	Std Err.	T-ratio	Coeff.	Std Err.	T-ratio	
Constant	-409392000*	218210000	-1.8761	-409392000**	204117000	-2.0057	
Rainfall	1090410	1023420	1.0655	1090410	957319	1.1390	66.61
Altitude	1355690***	157051	8.6322	1355690***	146908	9.2282	350.88
P_Index	2360240***	880440	2.6808	2360240***	823576	2.8658	132.48
Nwslitann	0.39	1.12	0.3456	0.3883	1.0512	0.3694	118,240,560
Leakages	-9846940*	5299500	-1.8581	-9846940*	4957230	-1.9864	25.88
Octroi	242468000	160781000	1.5081	242468000	150397000	1.6122	0.38
Parastat	66006300	143749000	0.4592	66006300	134465000	0.4909	0.58
Dependent variable mean	371,780,893						
Adjusted R²	0.79						

Source: Same as Table 4.1.

Notes: Number of observations = 64.

*** Statistically significant at the 1 per cent level.

** Statistically significant at the 5 per cent level.

* Statistically significant at the 10 per cent level.

uninterrupted), we obtained time-series data from each of the individual cities on the duration of the water supply in terms of annual average of the daily number of hours of water supply. As one can imagine, this is a very rough measure of the time availability of water supply since it irons out seasonal variations (across summer, winter, and rainy months) and across-the-year (drought, normal monsoon, or flooding years) variations. Nevertheless, this was the only quantitative measure we could come up with, and we included this as another exogenous regressor to examine its impact on costs. Table 4.14 presents these estimates. This table shows that a city's altitude and the price index continue to be the factors that most significantly affect the costs (expenditures) of providing water to its residents. The volume of water supply or its duration does not have any impact on the expenditures.

Table 4.15 presents estimates of the expenditure on water supply, assuming a double log form [log of expenditures (the dependent variable) and log of the net water supply]. First, note that the double log form provides a much better fit than the estimates in Table 4.13. The adjusted R^2 is a distant 0.92 for the double-log model (compared with 0.79 for the linear model). It shows that for every 1 per cent increase in net water supplied to residents, there is a more than 1 per cent increase in expenditure incurred to supply the water, consistent with expectation. Altitude has the expected positive impact, and leakages continue to exhibit the negative impact as in the previous specification. Non-municipal bodies spend less than municipal bodies on water bodies, because they are more efficient in delivering per unit of the service, or they spend less because of the fact that they operate like commercial entities.

Because of differences in the spending patterns for municipal and non-municipal entities providing the service, we performed estimations of expenditure on water supply by institutional arrangement. We performed separate estimations for cities in which the municipal body provides the service and those in which other entities such as parastatal agencies or other state-level agencies provide the service.

Tables 4.16 and 4.17, respectively, summarize the results for non-municipal bodies and municipal entities. The volume of net water supplied on expenditure is unanimously positive in both

TABLE 4.14

Estimation of Expenditure on (Net) Water Supply, Controlling for Water Supply Duration
(Dependent Variable: Operations & Maintenance Expenditure, All Cities [Deflated in 1993–4 Prices])

Variable	OLS Estimates			2SLS Estimates			Variable Mean
	Coeff.	Std Err.	T-ratio	Coeff.	Std Err.	T-ratio	
Constant	−337056000	261870000	−1.29	−337056000	242244000	−1.39	
Rainfall	1254560	1142480	1.10	1254560	1057730	1.19	66.69
Altitude	1573830***	171535	9.17	1573830***	158811	9.91	362.76
P_index	2820880***	941505	3.00	2820880***	871664	3.24	134.84
Nwsann	−1.06	0.83	−1.28	−1.06	0.77	−1.38	116136130
Leakages	−8732970	6330150	−1.38	−8732970	5860580	−1.49	26.51
Octroi	237953000	200904000	1.18	237953000	186001000	1.28	0.38
Parastat	74654800	173730000	0.43	74654800	160843000	0.46	0.57
Wshours	−15932000	15026100	−1.06	−15932000	13911500	−1.15	4.35
Dependent variable mean	407,709,732.80						
Adjusted R²	0.82						

Source: Same as Table 4.1.

Notes: Number of observations = 63.

*** Statistically significant at the 1 per cent level.

TABLE 4.15
Estimation of Expenditure on Water Supply, Using Double Log Form
(Dependent Variable: Log of Operations & Maintenance Expenditure, All Cities [Deflated in 1993–4 Prices])

Variable	OLS Estimates			2SLS Estimates			Variable Mean
	Coeff.	Std Err.	T-ratio	Coeff.	Std Err.	T-ratio	
Constant	-1.5000	5.1785	-0.2897	-4.7291	5.9797	-0.7909	
Rainfall	0.0055*	0.0030	1.8225	0.0048*	0.0029	1.6496	66.61
Altitude	0.0058***	0.0004	13.6956	0.0056***	0.0004	13.1020	350.88
P_Index	0.0030	0.0026	1.1641	0.0025	0.0025	0.9862	132.48
Log of net annual water supply	1.1425***	0.3051	3.7453	1.3341***	0.3531	3.7782	18.49
Leakages	-0.1113***	0.0153	-7.2900	-0.1136***	0.0145	-7.8113	25.88
Octroi	0.6921	0.4542	1.5240	0.5939	0.4393	1.3520	0.38
Parastat	-2.7948***	0.4125	-6.7755	-2.8754***	0.3968	-7.2458	0.57
Dependent variable mean	18.17						
Adjusted R^2	0.92						

Source: Same as Table 4.1.

Notes: Number of observations = 64.

*** Statistically significant at the 1 per cent level.

* Statistically significant at the 10 per cent level.

regressions. The magnitude of the estimate implies that municipal bodies incur greater expenditures (Rs 3.39) per kilolitre of water supplied than the non-municipal entities (Rs 2.53); this has been discussed earlier. As expected, altitude has a positive impact on expenditure in the case of both institutional arrangements. Leakages have a positive impact on expenditure in the case of non-municipal entities, demonstrating that these problems are attended to and are fixed. Such proactive behaviour in fixing O&M problems (maintenance of a leaking pipe, for example) has a positive impact on expenditure. However, leakages do not have a discernible impact on expenditure of municipal bodies most likely because they are not fixed, at least not regularly. The only other difference is that in the case of municipal bodies, rainfall has a negative impact on expenditure. This most likely occurs because in the case of rainy years, the municipal bodies spend less, even after controlling for the water supplied, because it is likely that consumption of water for various purposes is obtained from rainwater. This is specially so if households are aware of and use rainwater harvesting effectively.

A few of the cities (the BIMARU cities, Lucknow and Jaipur) had unduly low expenditures (both capital as well as O&M). Lucknow's average (in constant 1993–4 terms) annual O&M expenditure on water supply during the period of the study was Rs 13,885,443, and Jaipur's average (again in constant terms, with 1993–4 = 100) O&M expenditure on this service was only Rs 2,823,760, compared with an average annual O&M expenditure of Rs 515,526,740 for all cities excluding these two during the period of study. Hence we removed the two low-spenders and re-estimated the regressions. When we did this, we find several interesting results, as shown in Table 4.18. This table shows that the volume of water is statistically significant in determining expenditure. Specifically, the magnitude of the estimate shows that for every 1 kl of water supplied by the city, it incurs an additional cost of Rs 2.62. We discuss more regarding this in the section on policy insights.

When the low-spending cities are excluded, leakages have a positive impact on expenditures, as we expect. Specifically, for every one percentage point more of leakages in the distribution system, the city spends Rs 31,132,200 on O&M, reasonable to expect, because leaking pipes have to be fixed. Altitude has a

TABLE 4.16

Estimation of Expenditure on (Net) Water Supply for Non-municipal Bodies
(Dependent Variable: Operations & Maintenance Expenditure [Deflated in 1993–4 Prices])

Variable	OLS Estimates			2SLS Estimates			Variable Mean
	Coeff.	Std Err.	T-ratio	Coeff.	Std Err.	T-ratio	
Constant	-1049370000***	107787000	-9.7356	-1049370000***	98661200	-10.6361	
Rainfall	44125	789464	0.0559	44125	722624	0.0611	67.78
Altitude	1079310***	99483	10.8491	1079310***	91061	11.8526	395.09 metres
P_Index	17985	653323	0.0275	17985	598009	0.0301	134.86
Nwsann	2.5273***	0.8100	3.1202	2.5273***	0.7414	3.4088	116,902,220
Leakages	30721700***	4498710	6.8290	30721700***	4117820	7.4607	23.46%
Dependent variable mean	398,800,236.80						
Adjusted R^2	0.96						

Source: Same as Table 4.1.

Note: Number of observations = 37.

TABLE 4.17
Estimation of Expenditure on (Net) Water Supply for Municipal Bodies
(Dependent Variable: Operations & Maintenance Expenditure [Deflated in 1993–4 Prices])

Variable	OLS Estimates			2SLS Estimates			Variable Mean
	Coeff.	Std Err.	T-ratio	Coeff.	Std Err.	T-ratio	
Constant	213755000	251400000	0.8503	213755000	221714000	0.9641	
Rainfall	-1370080*	788454	-1.7377	-1370080*	695351	-1.9704	65.01
Altitude	580232*	326998	1.7744	580232*	288385	2.0120	290.28
P_Index	991955	768470	1.2908	991955	677727	1.4637	129.21
Nwsann	3.3912***	0.9923	3.4176	3.39***	0.88	3.8752	120,074,570
Leakages	-16916800	11465200	-1.4755	-16916800	10111300	-1.6731	29.19%
Dependent variable mean	334,754,384						
Adjusted R^2	0.68						

Source: Same as Table 4.1.
Note: Number of observations = 27.

TABLE 4.18

Estimation of Water Supply Expenditures, Low-spending Cities Excluded
(Dependent Variable: Operations & Maintenance Expenditure [Deflated in 1993–4 Prices])

Variable	OLS Estimates			2SLS Estimates			Variable Mean
	Coeff.	Std Err.	T-ratio	Coeff.	Std Err.	T-ratio	
Constant	-398399000***	146249000	-2.7241	-398399000	130389000	-3.0555	
Rainfall	-1160020	804080	-1.4427	-1160020	716882	-1.6182	71.96
Altitude	-1033960***	257338	-4.0179	-1033960***	229431	-4.5066	487.12
P_Index	1634950**	796399	2.0529	1634950**	710034	2.3026	128.64
Net water supply	2.6200**	0.9782	2.6785	2.6200**	0.8721	3.0043	135,764,470
Leakages	31132200***	6012290	5.1781	31132200***	5360300	5.8079	28.42
Octroi	-36646500***	11991400	-3.0561	-36646500***	106910000	-3.4278	0.62
Parastat	1187610000***	138763000	8.5586	1187610000***	123715000	9.5996	0.31
Dependent variable mean	605,248,321.90						
Adjusted R²	0.93						

Source: Same as Table 4.1.

Notes: Number of observations = 39.

*** Statistically significant at the 1 per cent level.

** Statistically significant at the 5 per cent level.

negative and significant impact on expenditure in this specification, when, in fact, we expect a positive effect. This is due to the fact that when low-altitude and low-spending cities such as Lucknow and Jaipur are excluded, relatively low-altitude cities such as Surat that spend more remain in the sample and dominate the results. A similar case holds good for octroi. Table 4.18 shows that octroi revenue has a negative impact on O&M expenditure, contrary to expectation. However, note that the highest spender on water supply is Bangalore which does not have octroi. This dominates the results shown in Table 4.18. Finally, note that in cities in which non-municipal bodies supply water, on average, the absolute O&M expenditures are higher. However, in *per capita* terms, note that such cities spend less on water supply than their municipal service provider counterparts (see Table 4.6).

To control for the time availability of water supply when the low-spending cities are excluded, we re-estimated the regressions in Table 4.18 by including the duration of water supply in the cities. These results are summarized in Table 4.19. As in Table 4.18, the price index for water, gas, and electricity has the expected positive impact on the costs. Leakages and octroi continue to have the same impacts on costs as in the earlier regression. The duration of water supply has a negative impact on the costs.

This implies that the longer the duration of supply, the lower are the marginal costs. Foster (2006) in fact points to the hidden costs of intermittent water supply, and the fact that well-managed continuous water supply turns out to be far cheaper than intermittent supply. For example, intermittent (lower duration) water supply systems are vulnerable to absorption of contaminated water during periods of low pressure and actually suck in raw sewage during periods of negative pressure, and the costs of treating it are higher. Further, if cities are committed to delivering a certain quantity of water to their residents, the shorter the duration, the greater the extent to which water pipes have to be larger. The cost of maintaining pipes in a shorter duration regime is also higher because of frequent turning off and on. For all these reasons, it is possible that the cities that supply water to their residents for a shorter duration incur higher costs/expenditures than their counterparts that are able to supply for a longer duration.

Table 4.19
Estimation of Water Supply Expenditures (Controlling for Water Supply Duration), Low-spending Cities Excluded (Dependent Variable: Operations & Maintenance Expenditure [in 1993–4 Prices])

Variable	OLS Estimates			2SLS Estimates			Variable Mean
	Coeff.	Std Err.	T-ratio	Coeff.	Std Err.	T-ratio	
Constant	403246000**	188088000	2.14	403246000**	167691000	2.40	
Rainfall	−725718	1031570	−0.70	−725718	919701	−0.79	72.15
Altitude	−48787	265291	−0.18	−48787	236522	−0.21	501.23
P_Index	2755060***	992242	2.78	2755060***	884639	3.11	132.45
Net water supply	−0.62	0.60	−1.03	−0.62	0.53	−1.15	131001910
Leakages	39387600***	8109960	4.86	39387600***	7230480	5.45	29.41
Octroi	−909550000***	170240000	−5.34	−909550000***	151779000	−5.99	0.62
Number of hours of water supply	−136936000***	17592000	−7.78	−136936000***	15684300	−8.73	4.06
Dependent variable mean	653,821,675.3						
Adjusted R²	0.92						

Source: Same as Table 4.1.

Notes: Number of observations = 39.

*** Statistically significant at the 1 per cent level.

** Statistically signifcant at the 5 per cent level.

We did separate regressions for fast-growing and slow-growing cities. Table 4.20 shows that fast-growing cities incur greater marginal costs of supplying water than their slow-growing counterparts. Specifically, the fast-growing cities incur Rs 5.05 for every additional kilolitre of water they supply. This implies that these cities need to recover a greater extent from consumers than the other cities, consistent with expectation.

This finding makes sense when we recall that our fast-growth and slow-growth cities are classified in terms of their population growth. So whether or not migration makes a difference to a city's expenditures for producing a certain service, its population does. The only other factor that has a significant impact on expenditures in this specification is altitude, and it has a negative impact. This result is again dominated by Surat because it is located in a relatively lower altitude, is a high-spender, and grew rapidly during the 1990s.

Table 4.21 shows the regression results for slow-growing cities. Here the volume of water supply is not a significant factor anymore in explaining expenditure, consistent with our expectations and hypotheses. The other significant factor explaining expenditure is altitude, which has the right sign, and is largely driven by Bangalore, which is a high-altitude, high-spending city.

Overall, the model chosen to represent O&M expenditures is a fairly good one, since the adjusted R^2 ranges above 0.80 in all cases.

COMPARISON OF MARGINAL COSTS AND WATER TARIFFS

We are answering the following question in the study: Given that the cities have spent a certain amount on O&M expenditures for water over a period of time, what should their tariffs be? During our field visits, we collected water tariffs from all cities, prevalent at the time of the survey. Tables 4.22 and 4.24 summarize the water tariffs for the six cities and tariffs for non-domestic uses in Surat Municipal Corporation, respectively, as of 2006 when work for this book was completed.

We checked with the individual cities as to what criterion their actual current tariffs were based upon. For a basic service like water,

TABLE 4.20

Expenditure Regressions for Fast-growing Cities

Variable	OLS Estimates			2SLS Estimates			Variable Mean
	Coeff.	Std Err.	T-ratio	Coeff.	Std Err.	T-ratio	
Constant	−352761000*	203387000	−1.73	−352761000*	186168000	−1.89	
Rainfall	−1048110	725246	−1.45	−1048110	663843	−1.58	56.24
Altitude	−715109*	398242	−1.80	−715109*	364525	−1.96	246.75
P_Index	−541579	569928	−0.95	−541579	521675	−1.04	129.86
Net water supply	5.05***	0.76	6.65	5.05***	0.69	7.27	158,519,210
Leakages	12265800	10236500	1.20	12265800	9369780	1.31	28.10
Dependent variable mean	218,216,083						
Adjusted R²	0.77						

Source: Same as Table 4.1.

Notes: Number of observations = 37.

*** Statistically significant at the 1 per cent level.

* Statistically significant at the 10 per cent level.

TABLE 4.21
Expenditure Regressions for Slow-growing Cities

Variable	OLS Estimates			2SLS Estimates			Variable Mean
	Coeff.	Std Err.	T-ratio	Coeff.	Std Err.	T-ratio	
Constant	-1052430000***	124751000	-8.4363	-1052430000***	110020000	-9.5658	
Rainfall	213324	837460	0.2547	213324	738570	0.2888	81.21
Altitude	1125800***	85795	13.1219	1125800***	75664	14.8788	505.17
P_Index	294778	673557	0.4376	294778	594021	0.4962	136.16
Net water supply	0.32	0.88	0.3619	0.32	0.78	0.4103	136,525,070
Leakages	41460500***	5494390	7.5460	41460500***	4845600	8.5563	23.28
Dependent variable mean	582,221,557						
Adjusted R^2	0.97						

Source: Same as Table 4.1.
Notes: Number of observations = 27.
*** Statistically significant at the 1 per cent level.

the primary criterion the cities have used to charge water is nothing more formal than a vague concept of affordability, even though they systematically maintain data on operations, maintenance, and capital expenditures (which they perceive to be the same as costs). Cities such as Jaipur have always kept the price of their water low and affordable for major sections of the population. Political considerations play a major role there, and no cost or expenditure considerations are taken into account. In Lucknow, the water tax is set at 12.5 per cent of the annual rental value of the property, so it is primarily related to consumption (of water) which is assumed to depend on the size and other characteristics of property. No considerations of coverage of capital or O&M expenditures or costs are taken into account by the Lucknow Jal Sansthan. Similarly, in Pune, the water tax is set at a certain proportion of property taxes which are based on the annual rental value of property.[5] This is based on the assumption that consumption of water is related to the carpet area of the household. Hence while the cities relate water tariff to the consumption of the good, most are unable to recover their actual costs or expenditures of supplying water due to concerns of affordability or political considerations.

On the other hand, in Bangalore, the tariff is set on the basis of proportionate increases in the electricity expenditures which account for nearly half of the total expenditures. The tariffs thus devised are sent to the state government for approval, which in turn revises them to ensure affordability. Surat also switched over to a system of metered connections in March 2008 (Table 4.22 is based on 2006 data from cities). In this system, consideration is paid both to expenditures and usage of the good. This is because the water tariffs are based on the O&M expenditures of supplying water, and the carpet area of the household for which the connection is given. The cost (expenditure) of salaries of the employees and water treatment are covered by the water tariff. Currently Surat is able to recover about 70 per cent of its O&M cost (expenditure) through the tariff. By 2011, as required by the Jawaharlal Nehru National Urban Renewal Mission (JNNURM), the city will be covering 100 per cent of O&M expenditures through its water tariffs. However, the city is not covering depreciation charges in its water tariff. Similarly, our discussions with the Chandigarh

Municipal Corporation revealed that it has attempted to cover nearly 80 per cent of its operating and maintenance costs through the tariff. For instance, on average, about Rs 65 crores is incurred annually on O&M costs, out of which nearly Rs 50 crores is recovered through the tariff. Further revisions to the water tariff are held up by the state government due to political considerations.

Beyond the issue of tariffs, note that a city's household income does not have any impact on the government's cost of providing water supply. Alternatively, income may have some impact on the *expenditures* on water supply. Since it is a measure for affordability, it indicates local preferences. Had income data been available at the city level, it would have been possible for us to say whether the presence of high-income households encourages the city to spend more or less on water supply or vice-versa. This would have also enabled us to examine the impact of affordability of households on expenditure by the service provider, holding other things constant. However, as explained earlier, income at the city level in India is available at best only for a single year, but certainly not for a time-series that the data set developed here requires. A city's income, if available, may have been used as the basis of tariff fixation, and not estimation of marginal costs.

Remember that the estimates obtained here represent only the O&M expenditures. Because of this, they appear to be lower than the international evidence regarding marginal costs of providing water. A World Bank (1994) study finds that in Lima, the *long-run* marginal costs of providing water supply was US$ 0.45 per cubic metre (i.e., per kilolitre) whereas the actual tariffs were only around US$ 0.28 per cubic metre. We have arrived at *short-run* marginal cost estimates in this study. Recall that for purposes of computing *long-run marginal costs*, we have to get data on expenditures by projects, disaggregated by civil works, and plant and equipment, on which we did not get any information from the cities. If we had access to such disaggregated data, then we could have attempted computation of long-run marginal cost, using the approach suggested by Turvey (1976). This hinges upon the use of discount rates and arriving at different capital recovery factors for plant and equipment vis-à-vis civil works.

TABLE 4.22

Current Water Tariff Structure for Metered Water Connections

City	Rate of Water Tariffs (Rate per Kilolitre)*		
	Duration	Domestic	Non-domestic
Chandigarh	From 31.3.2002 till now	1–15 kl @ Rs 1.75 per kl 15–30 kl @ Rs 3.50 per kl 30–60 kl @ Rs5.00 per kl above 60 kl @ Rs 6.00 per kl Weighted average: Rs 5.01 per kl	Institutional: Rs 9 For government and semi-government offices: Rs 12. For industrial, semi-industrial, and commercial establishments: Rs 11
Surat		All unmetered monthly Rs 240 (not consumption-based)	13.0**
Pune	1.4.2000 to 31.3.2005	Rs 3.00 per kl	Rs 16.00
	From 1.4.2005 till now	Rs 3.00 per kl	Rs 21.00
Bangalore	Current	Rs 19.44 per kl	Rs 6 to Rs 60.00
Jaipur	From 1.6.1998 till now	Up to 15 kl @ R. 1.56 per kl 15–40 kl @ Rs 3.00 per kl Above 40 kl @ Rs 4.00 Weighted average: Rs= 3.39 per kl	Limit — Non-domestic — Industrial Up to 15 kl — Rs 4.68 — Rs 11.00 15–40 kl — Rs 8.25 — Rs 13.75 Above 40 kl — Rs 11.00 — Rs 16.50
Lucknow	Current	Rs 2.45 per kl	Non-domestic: Rs 12.25 Commercial: Rs 7.35 Government: Rs 4.90

Source: Same as Table 4.1.

Notes: * These tariffs are current as of 2006, when this work was originally completed.

** For non-domestic uses, depending on the purpose, various tariff rates apply, the highest being applicable for industrial uses (Rs 24 per kl), and the minimum (of Rs 4 per kl) for use in educational institutions. What is reported here is the average of the non-domestic rate for various purposes. The full schedule of rates for non-domestic uses is summarized in Table 4.24.

For a moment, assume that the estimates in Table 4.20 (for the fast-growing cities) represent the upper range for *short-run marginal costs* (Rs 5.05) per kilolitre. Table 4.22 summarizes the actual water tariffs in the six cities. Note that all cities except Surat have metered connections. In the case of Chandigarh and Jaipur, we computed weighted average tariff based on the quantities and rates for various categories. This weighted average tariff turns out to be Rs 5.05 per kilolitre in Chandigarh and Rs 3.39 per kilolitre in Jaipur. Based on the estimates in Table 4.20, Jaipur and Pune (both of which are fast growing) are clearly under-charging their water, especially so if capital costs were taken into account. Chandigarh might be just another case of under-charging if capital costs were taken into account. Currently, based on just marginal O&M costs, it is just about right. On the other hand, Bangalore is over-charging. The results do not have implications for Surat which has all unmetered connections. If the direct outcome of what we have highlighted here is that an additional kilolitre of water supply imposes some burden on the city (which is statistically significant in the case of fast-growing cities in which Surat is counted), only a volumetric consumption regime (i.e., metering of existing household connections) will be able to fix the problem. Finally, Lucknow spends very little on water supply and for this reason an additional kilolitre of water might not impose much burden on the city. However, as we see below (see Table 4.23), Lucknow and Jaipur spend even less than what their cost factors require them to spend. So spending better

TABLE 4.23
Predicted Expenditures, Costs, and Actual Expenditures

	Predicted Expenditure (in Rs)	Predicted Costs (in Rs)	Actual Expenditure (in Rs)	Expenditure as Per Cent of Costs
Bangalore	1,112,490,054	1,233,245,120	1,160,988,429	94.14
Chandigarh	245,392,716	477,419,369	265,347,001	55.58
Lucknow	79,174,409	162,945,899	13,885,449	8.52
Jaipur	33,332,401	175,134,556	2,823,768	1.61
Pune	634,002,449	708,297,618	484,399,661	68.39
Surat	422,231,360	345,152,276	151,371,852	43.86
Average	*421,103,898*	*517,032,473*	*346,469,360*	*45.35*

Source: Same as Table 4.1.

TABLE 4.24
Schedule of Water Tariffs for Non-domestic Use, Surat Municipal Corporation

Type	Number	Purpose of Usage	Rate (Rs per 1000 Litres)
A	1	Premises for public institutional services like bus, railway, Gujarat Electricity Board, Surat Electricity Company, and banks	12
	2	General industries power looms/diamond/jari, kasab/workshop	8
	3	Temporary water connection for non-commercial and individual construction purposes	10
B	1	For halls used for social functions	8
	2	Properties like dispensary, hospitals, nursing homes, maternity homes, chemists, and those related with medical services	8
	3	Photo studios	10
	4	Dhobi ghat	8
	5	Private swimming pools	15
	6	Gymkhana and sports clubs	15
	7	All types of restaurant and canteens (inclusive of tea/snack shops)	10
	8	Properties like nursery, plantations activity used for commercial use	8
	9	Properties used for residential use for private/limited company	10
	10	Guest houses	15
C	1	Soft drinks/soda manufacturing organizations	15
	2	Ice cream/ice manufacturing organization	15
	3	Cold storage plant	15
	4	Central air condition plant	15
	5	Cinema/theatre	15
	6	Film processing/sound studios/film laboratory	15
	7	RCC/PCC materials and marble mosaic tiles manufacturing works	15
	8	Temporary water connection for commercial purposes and construction	15
	9	Temporary water connection for public fair, function, exhibition	15
	10	All types of hotels—up to three stars	15
D	1	Dyeing and printing houses	16
	2	Four-star/five-star hotels	16
	3	Water parks/amusement parks	16
E	1	Commercial purpose/shops other than mentioned above	6

(cond..

Table 4.24 (*cond...*)

F	1	For educational institutions (above 1.5 " size connection)	4
G	1	For residence purposes, outside city area	10
	2	For commercial purposes, outside city area	20
	3	For industrial purposes, outside city area	24
		Average rate per kilolitre	*12.87*
		Maximum rate per kilolitre	*24*
		Minimum rate per kilolitre	*4*

Source: Surat Municipal Corporation Website, http://www.suratmunicipal.gov.in/content/hydraulic/tariff.shtml.

and charging consumers for the additional burden might be the solution for better service delivery.

Frequently, price hike policies are viewed as the logical outcome of deregulation and break-even cost. This need not necessarily be the case. Over and above the issue of pricing, it is important for the cities to be efficient in their management. For instance, reduction of leakages, thefts, and unaccounted for water (UFW), in the distribution system, will reduce expenditures. As we have observed in the case of most of the cities, leakages account for nearly one-third of the total water supplied. Needless to say that greater efficiency in management of the distribution will result in better service to consumers while containing the costs and the tariffs.

On the basis of the estimates in Table 4.13 (estimation for all cities), we arrive at predicted expenditures and predicted costs (based on cost factors including topography [altitude], price index, and rainfall). We compare these with actual average expenditures incurred by these cities on water supply. Table 4.23 summarizes this. This table shows that with the exception of Surat, we may expect all cities to incur costs (based on exogenous factors such as topography, price index, and rainfall outside of their control) consistently higher than their expenditures on water supply. This implies that the marginal expenditure estimates presented here should be viewed as conservative estimates of marginal costs. This also suggests why the estimates here are low compared to marginal costs computed internationally. Table 4.23 also shows that in the case of Lucknow and Jaipur, the actual expenditure as a proportion of costs predicted on the basis of various factors is shockingly low, being less than 10 per cent! Bangalore is the one that spends most appropriately in accordance with its cost conditions.

The next chapter summarizes the instruments and methods of water pricing in a few of the selected cities, so we may understand and evaluate the feasibility of marginal cost pricing.

NOTES

1. We used the average growth rate of population during 1991–2001 for the six cities to distinguish between fast-growth and slow-growth cities. Based on this, cities that grew relatively rapidly during the 1990s were Surat, Jaipur, and Pune. Bangalore, Chandigarh, and Lucknow were classified as being the slow-growth cities.

2. What determines this volume of water supply (or of any other service considered here) is of course subject to debate—migration, increasing population, or simply demand. We do not have data to determine the demand schedule for water for which micro, household-level data on water tariffs paid and quantity of water consumed would be necessary. Education is a normative characteristic, which could affect the preference for water. But that may not necessarily affect the actual expenditure/cost incurred, at least not so in India's context. If education affects the demand for water, then it must be the case that the highest water spending municipalities should also be the ones with an educated population since that indicates water demand. We did attempt to get data on the proportion of population with bachelors' and masters' degrees in the six cities of our study over the entire time period. This was available only for a few years, which substantially reduced the size of our already small sample.

    In alternative specifications, we were exploring the possibility of using average household income in the city as an exogenous determinant of the level of expenditure on water supply, which is a different variant of the education characteristic. But that may not be necessary or desirable. That will be mixing positive and normative issues. Further, income data at the city level in India are rarely collected; for a single year we could use data published by the National Council of Applied Economic Research (NCAER). But in no case are they available in a time-series fashion, as required for the study. So, effectively, we were unable to adequately control for local preferences for public services in determining expenditures.

3. The instruments we used in the 2SLS estimations were population and average of the temperature difference between the maximum and minimum for various cities, along with the endogenous variables. Population determines the volume of water supplied and is exogenously

determined. Further, temperature differences in any given city (between the summer and winter months) are exogenous and could affect the expenditure through its impact on rainfall. Finally, we use the distance from the water source to the pumping station as an instrument for leakages, as discussed earlier.

4. The regressions were performed on data in deflated Indian Rupees (INR), hence the coefficients are to be interpreted in terms of INR.

5. For instance, for annual rental value ranging from 0 to 3,000, the water tax is Rs 1,000 a year (see Sridhar and Bandyopadhyay, 2007).

CHAPTER 5

Instruments and Methods of Water Pricing

Setting appropriate prices is indispensable to providing adequate water to India's growing urban population. We have learned from Chapter 4 that water in most Indian cities and towns is under-priced, with damaging long-run consequences for households who have limited and poor quality water services and for water-supplying entities that are unable to invest in and expand water coverage. Let alone coverage of marginal costs or even average costs of supplying water, most water-supplying entities—be these the Public Health Engineering Department (PHED), state- or city-level water boards, or municipal governments—are run at a loss and cover the loss—defined as the gap between revenues from the sale of water and cost of water provision—from government subsidies and accelerated depreciation of capital. The result is a low-level equilibrium: low tariff, poor services, and constraints on access, especially of poor households. While the need for appropriate pricing of urban water has been long stressed in the earlier chapters and is widely recognized as central to broader urban sector reforms, what constitutes water price reform remains an elusive and emotive issue. Moreover, the goals and objectives of water pricing are often conflicting. Using city-level experiences of water pricing, particularly in respect to the size of the consumer base, multiple instruments of charging, price discrimination between different water-user groups, and price-cost linkages, going beyond the marginal cost issue, this chapter provides a framework that spells out key areas of reform, objectives that may govern water pricing, and parameters of tariff rationalization.

The Importance of Urban Water Pricing

How is it that water which is so useful that life is impossible without it, has such a low price; while diamonds, which are quite unnecessary, have such a high price.

Setting appropriate prices is central to the reform of the urban water sector in India, and it enables water quality move to a higher level equilibrium (see Box 5.1: ADB's Water Pricing Policy).[1] Current levels of water pricing in most Indian cities and towns are deficient in several respects.

1. The price of urban water is low in relation to the cost that is incurred on its provision. Although firm estimates in respect of water price and costs are sparse, and estimates of marginal costs are hard to obtain, on average, prices or recoveries from the sale of water and other charges relating to water provision are approximately 22–5 per cent lower than the O&M costs. Recent city-specific studies of Bangalore, Chennai, and Hyderabad (see Raghupathi and Foster, 2002; World Bank, 1995) show that the typical price charged for water for residential use is about Rs 1.5 per cubic metre which is one-tenth of the O&M costs actually incurred, raising serious concerns about the financial viability and sustainability of urban water utilities. Annual losses on account of operating and maintaining the urban water supply systems are conservatively estimated at Rs 50,000–60,000 million, placing an enormous burden on water-supplying entities.

2. Under-pricing has resulted in poor service and reduced incentives to expand the spatial coverage of services. Although most cities and towns have been able to reach a reasonably high level of access to safe water—of the 90.01 per cent according to the Census of India, 2001, only about 50 per cent of the urban households have 'tap water within premises'. Access to tap water within premises is as low as 27.1 per cent in Bihar, 29.3 per cent in Kerala, and 34.9 per cent in Tamil Nadu. Most

households face limited hours of service, and water services are uniformly sub-standard. The cost of intermittent water supplies for households is said to be high; according to a recent paper, the average capital cost for installing pumps, water filters, tanks, and other equipments is estimated at Rs 2,620 per household (see Rana, 2003). In Delhi, the annual cost of reducing water supply unreliability is placed at Rs 844 per household (see Zérah, 2000). The Government of India and the World Bank recently reported that urban water systems in India 'deliver on average 50 to 60 per cent of their capacity to end-users, compared with 80 to 85 per cent in other countries. Poor, and sometimes non-existent, management leads to waste and inefficiency, with the resultant large claim on resources that could be redeployed for service improvements.'

Tariff adjustments to achieve cost recovery are central to the water sector. Most water supplying entities in India operate at a loss. They finance the shortfall between tariff revenue and costs through operating and capital subsidies from the government and through depreciation of capital. The result is a low level equilibrium characterized by low tariff, poor service and limits on access, especially of poor households.

3. The objective of large-scale subsidization of water on grounds of lack of affordability by the poor has not been achieved. Much of the evidence points out that the poor pay more, often two-to-three times, if coping costs were included, and the price subsidy meant for them and built into tariff structures, for example, in increasing block tariff (IBT), is appropriated by the non-poor households. Subsidies on private taps are poorly targeted, as no more than 30 per cent of the beneficiaries are poor. Moreover, a large proportion of urban poor households do not have private connections and are, therefore, unable to benefit from water subsidies. Such regressivity in the distribution of subsidies when poor do not have access to subsidized piped water service is a common phenomenon in Indian cities and towns.

4. Under-pricing has affected the finances of state governments who have either absorbed the losses of urban water utilities or adjusted the losses by reducing the capital account support to them for capacity expansion. Although the macroeconomic

consequences of low water prices are difficult to assess, urban water services could cost the state governments the equivalent of 0.3 to 0.4 per cent of their gross domestic product (GDP).

When water tariffs are lower than the cost of provision, there is little incentive to expand the service, and fewer resources are allocated to water than would be optimal.

This chapter is in response to the need to further advance the above-stated agenda. The present position where the water-supplying entities—be these the parastatal organizations or the municipal governments—run into losses by selling water below the cost and where their losses have to be either written off or adjusted against future grants or absorbed by the states or merely allowed to be kept on books is unsustainable. Under-pricing of urban water, it is widely agreed, has not only affected the financial health of water supply undertakings, but resulted in wasteful usage of water, and as referred to earlier, impeded the expansion of water services and reduced the coverage of urban poor households.

Although the need for *getting the prices right* appears obvious and compelling, what is, in fact, an appropriate charge is neither straightforward nor easy to determine. As reviewed in Chapter 2, the literature suggests at least three sets of pricing mechanisms: (*a*) long-run marginal cost, (*b*) short-run marginal cost, and (*c*) average costs. As the discussion of our findings in the earlier chapters show, information on costs do help a water-supplying entity in determining an appropriate charge for water which requires addressing a host of questions: What costs are incurred in water provision? What is the nature of costs? What are the different ways in which costs are possible to be recovered? What instruments are possible to be used? Who should pay for the lost water, and the like.

The agenda of appropriate urban water pricing as enunciated in the successive five year plans and other initiatives requires that the following issues be specifically examined and analysed:

1. Instruments of water charging: In what alternative ways is urban water charged, and to what extent do these instruments meet the contemporary principles of water charging.

2. Existing pricing structures: What pricing structures are currently in use? What objectives and principles underlie them? What are these based on?

3. Price-cost linkages: What part of the cost is recovered by prices? What is the impact of non-revenue water and implicit subsidies on cost recovery?

We examine these issues in this chapter using the data drawn from Bangalore, Vadodara, Allahabad, and Agra, as also the data from other on-going studies on the financial structures of municipalities and city-specific parastatal agencies responsible for water provision. It lays out a framework for pricing reforms in the water sector. This chapter emphasizes the need to gather information about the structure of supply costs and consumer preferences. By understanding the latter, it is expected that water utility companies will be able to offer price and service options to consumers that are efficient than the existing systems.

This chapter is laid out in four sections. The second section presents the key instruments of urban water charging and water pricing structures. In the third section, we analyse the experiences with urban water pricing in four cities and supplement the same with other examples. In particular, this section examines the structure of costs in supplying water and the different charging instruments and the outcomes in terms of revenues and expenditures. The fourth section provides a framework for urban water charging together with a brief explanation of objectives that water price much aims to achieve.

Urban Water Pricing: Instruments and Methods

Instruments of Urban Water Charging

Three types of instruments are generally used for charging water. One is a connection fee or a fixed access charge. Such a fee is levied to provide the user a connection to a municipal (public) water supply system. A connection fee or charge is based on the size of the plot or holding, the size of connection and ferrule, or a combination of plot size and the size of the ferrule. It is unclear if the connection fee is designed to contain an element of capital cost that is involved in laying out the distribution network.

Box 5.1
ADB's Water Pricing Policy

Conservation of water and its sustainable use are increasingly critical factors in managing a scarce resource. Governments and civil societies need to see water as an economic good. Financial incentives for optimizing water use will be strengthened through a mix of water charges, market-based instruments, and penalties. Public awareness programmes will reinforce the incentives. The incentives include water use rights, licenses and charges, tradeable permits, effluent charges, water treatment fees, access fees, environmental liabilities, and tax incentives. Managing water demand is a function of efficient pricing, effective regulation, and appropriate reduction and awareness. ADB will promote tariff reforms through its water-related projects and programmes to modify structures and rates so that they reward conservation and penalize waste.

ADB will consistently advise governments of the need to adopt cost recovery principles in their water policies and strategies. The expansion of access to water and the improved provision of water services require that capital costs be funded mainly from within the sector by accessing debt market and developing appropriate tariff structures. Consumers will be expected to meet the full operation and maintenance costs of water facilities and service provision in urban and rural water supply and sanitation schemes subject to subsidy considerations. ADB will also promote the inclusion of environmental externalities and the recovery of resources management cost in tariff systems adopted by Developing Member Countries (DMCs).

Subsidies are a controversial issue in the water sector. ADB will support subsides for water services in the following circumstances: (*i*) where treated water uses have beneficial external effects in preventing health problems, (*ii*) where the transaction costs of measuring usage are very high, and (*iii*) where a limited quantity of treated water for the poor is regarded as a basic human need.

Source: 'Water for All', The Water Policy of the Asian Development Bank, 2001.

A second type of charging instrument is a water tax for which provision exists in most municipal legislations. It is a tax which is unrelated to water use or consumption. It forms a part of property taxation, is leviable on the annual rateable value of land and property, and is meant to essentially serve as a general tax. Conditions under which a water tax may be levied are prescribed in municipal legislations which, among others, include categories of water users who may be exempted from payment of water taxes, those who might be subject to a ceiling on the rate at which water tax may be levied, and the use to which receipts from such a levy may be applied. For example, the Uttar Pradesh Municipalities Act lays down that a water tax may not be levied on properties which have an annual (rateable) value of less than Rs 300; the Uttar Pradesh Municipal Corporation Act, 1959 lays down that the proceeds of water tax (along with that on drainage and conservancy taxes) may be pooled and used for purposes connected with the construction, maintenance, extension, and improvement of the service. The Maharashtra Municipal Act 1965 provides for a general water tax as a part of the consolidated tax on property and a special water tax for water supplied by the municipal council. It further lays down that a municipal council instead of imposing a special water tax may fix rates for supply of water by measurement. The Bombay Municipal Corporation Act provides for a water tax if the premises are not charged for water by measurement, and a water benefit tax which is in addition to water tax or water charges on all residential properties in Greater Bombay. Water tax and water benefit taxes are applied to the annual rateable value of premises, with the tax rate discriminating between residential and non-residential properties (Table 5.1).

TABLE 5.1
Water Tax on Annual Rateable Value: Brihanmumbai Mahanagarpalika

Nature of Premises	Water Tax Rate (%)	Water Benefit (%)
(1)	(2)	(3)
Residential	20	10
Non-residential	45	20

Source: Brihanmumbai Mahanagarpalika.

A third pricing instrument used is a water charge. Conceptually designed as a charge on consumption, it is an ubiquitous instrument for charging both metered and unmetered water supplies. Overall, in addition to the three types of pricing instruments discussed earlier—a connection fee, a water tax, and a water charge—there are minor instruments such as a meter rent, a license fee, a water cess, a meter maintenance charge where meters are provided by the water supplying agency, development charges,[2] and fixed charges for capital renovation[3] of the water system which are used for operating water supply systems. Many of the instruments yield little revenue, raising questions about the purpose for which they are being retained on statute.

Water Pricing Structures

As we have discussed thus far, marginal cost pricing is an indispensable aspect of water pricing rules (see American Water Works Association, 1991). A basic premise for the creation of autonomous water boards, for instance, was that they will be able to set tariff equal to the marginal cost of providing services to each category of consumers. However, few water-supplying entities have control over price fixation. Further, as must be clear from Chapter 4, implementing marginal cost pricing for water does prove to be difficult on account of the problems in using historical accounting data, estimating external costs, apportioning joint costs, and addressing equity-related concerns. These problems have impeded the use of marginal cost pricing by water agencies.

Water pricing structures in India are extremely complex and often even clumsy. At one level, price structures distinguish between metered connections and unmetered connections as also bulk provision from non-bulk, discrete provision. At another level, price discrimination is common with (*a*) categories of water users which comprise not only the principal categories of domestic users and non-domestic users but also the assorted categories consisting of water use for washing motor vehicles, cattle sheds, stables, and the like, and (*b*) income groups of households, assumption being that low-income households use less quantities of water and high-income households have higher consumption levels. Water pricing may differ with the quality of water supplies, for example, filtered, unfiltered, tube well supplies, and the like. Cross-subsidy is central to the principle of price discrimination. As would be seen later, non-domestic users subsidize the domestic sector. High-income households using larger quantities of water subsidize low-income households, raising questions about the desirability of overloading certain categories of water users.

Water pricing structures are either volumetric or non-volumetric. Volumetric structures rely in one way or another on the volume (quantity) of water, and are used only under conditions of metered supplies of water. Non-volumetric structures are applied to other measures (such as the size of the pipe or ferrule used) that are proxies to water consumption.

A tariff structure is a set of procedural rules that determine the service conditions and charges for various categories of water users. As stated earlier, charges for water are based on two components: the volume of water consumed and a set of factors other than water use. Conceptually, it is possible to use one of the two components. Thus, water can be charged on the basis of the value of property (water tax) rather than the level of consumption. Alternatively, water can be charged on the basis of water use multiplied by the unit price. A variant which is more common is to use a mix of the two, that is, a fixed monthly charge and a charge based on consumption.

Several types of water tariff are in use in Indian cities and towns. These are discussed in the following sections.

INCREASING BLOCK TARIFF (IBT)

An IBT is a series of prices that increase in steps as consumption rises. The key feature of IBT is that it contributes to equity by allowing low-income households to pay lower rates for water than other households. An IBT structure is based on the volumetric component. A water user in a particular category, such as residential, is charged a relatively low price per unit for consumption up to a specific amount. This amount defines the size of the initial block. A user whose consumption exceeds the size of the initial block faces a higher price per unit for the additional consumption until the user exhausts the second block, and then a still higher price until reaching the top block in the increasing block structure.[4]

To construct an increasing block tariff, three parameters are needed: (*a*) the number of blocks, (*b*) the size of the block in terms of water use, and (*c*) the price per unit in each block. The case for IBT is argued on several grounds. First, IBT provides equity as high-income households tend to subsidize the water usage of low-income households. It is based on the assumption that the consumption levels of water among high-income households is greater, and because a greater percentage of their water use occurs in the higher blocks they pay a higher average price for water. Second, IBT can promote water conservation and sustainable water use. This is because in this regime, the water price increases with water use, and it discourages wasteful water use. Third, an IBT is needed to implement marginal cost principles. This is so because with marginal costs rising with total water use, prices should rise accordingly with individual household use. This has been the main justification for multi-block structures.

Thus, for an increasing and decreasing block tariff structure, a water bill could be calculated as under:

Let Q^* = amount of water sold to a specific consumer.

Q_1 = maximum amount of water that can be sold in the first block at price P_1.

Q_2 = maximum amount of water that can be sold in the second block at P_2.

Q_3 = maximum amount of water that can be sold in the third block at P_3.

If $Q^* < Q_1$, then the consumers bill = $(Q^*)\,P_1$.

If $Q_1 < Q^* < Q_2$, then the consumer water bill = $P_1 Q_1 + (Q^* - Q_1)\,P_2$.

If $Q_1 + Q_2 < Q^* < Q_3$, then the consumer's water bill = $P_1 Q_1 + P_2 Q_2 + [Q^* - (Q_1 + Q_2)]P_3$.

Water utilities in Delhi and Hyderabad use block tariffs for domestic and non-domestic supplies in combination with other price structures. Delhi uses four blocks of 10 kl each, and the price per unit of water in the terminal block is 8.6 times that in the initial block (see Table 5.2). Hyderabad uses four blocks of unequal sizes, and the price per unit of water in the fourth block is set 3.7 times higher than the price in the first block. What is important to note is that the size of the first block—be it 10 kl or 15 kl, is well above what would be a true 'lifeline' block to meet basic human needs.[5] This implies that the revenue elasticity of water usage with respect to the rates in the higher blocks would be relatively lower, and depends on the distribution of households in each of the use categories.

TABLE 5.2
Increasing Block Tariff for Domestic Use

City	Size of the Initial Block (kl)	Number of Blocks	Water Tariff/kl Rs
(1)	(2)	(3)	(4)
Delhi	<=6	4	Free for the first block, rising to Rs 10 per kl for the fourth block.
Hyderabad	<=30	4	Rs 6 per 1,000 l, rising to Rs 25 per kl for the fourth block.

Sources: Delhi Jal Board (DJB) and Hyderabad Metropolitan Water Supply and Sewerage Board (HMWSSB).

IBT is commonly used in non-domestic metered supplies. Compared with domestic supplies, the price structure for non-domestic supplies is several times higher, although on account of the differences in the size of blocks, comparisons are difficult to arrive at. In Delhi, the non-domestic tariff is placed at Rs 10 per kl (for commercial uses) and Rs 15 per kl (for industrial purposes) up to a ceiling of 50 kl beyond which the tariff rate is Rs 30 per kl. In Hyderabad where the size of the initial block is 30 kl, the water tariff for the initial block is Rs 6 per kl.

UNIFORM VOLUMETRIC CHARGE

A uniform volumetric charge forms an important part of water price structures in several Indian cities and towns. It is a fixed charge per unit of water consumption, which may vary with the category of users. Thus, water charge may be fixed at Rs 2 per kl for domestic users and at another rate for commercial or industrial users. Like the IBT, a uniform tariff is commonly used in cities such as Kanpur, Indore, Surat, and Madurai (see Table 5.3). The main merit of uniform tariff lies in its simplicity. At the same time, it provides no incentive to consumers to affect savings on water use, and may, in fact, violate the principle of water conservation, given that the rate remains the same across households with varying consumption levels.

TABLE 5.3
Uniform Water Tariff

| City | Uniform (Rs/kl) Tariff | |
| | Domestic | Industry |
(1)	(2)	(3)
Kanpur	2.0	10.0
Indore	2.0	22.0
Surat	NA*	13.0**
Madurai	5.0	20.0

Source: Various municipal corporations.

Notes: * Surat does not have metered connections for domestic use. The charges there are a flat rate of Rs 240 per annum per connection per family. Refer to Table 4.22, Chapter 4.

** For non-domestic uses, depending on the purpose, various tariff rates apply, the highest being applicable for industrial uses (Rs 24 per kl), and the minimum (of Rs 4 per kl) for use in educational institutions. What is reported here is the average of the non-domestic rate for various purposes.

LINEAR WATER CHARGE

This is a charge which rises with consumption, not in blocks as is the case with IBTs, but every discrete unit of water consumption. Thus, a consumer in Kerala is required to pay a monthly charge of Rs 22 for consumption not exceeding 10 kl, the charge increases to Rs 25 for connection level of 11 kl, and rises in tandem, until it reaches 100 kl for which the charge is Rs 550 (see Table 5.4).

TABLE 5.4
Linear Water Charge, Kerala

| Kl Connection/kl | Charge including Meter Inspection Charge (Rs) |
(1)	(2)
10	22
11	25
12	28
13	31
25	67
50	182
100	550

Source: Kerala Water Authority.

TWO-PART TARIFF

A two-part tariff where under there is a minimum charge for a fixed quantity of water beyond which the charge may either follow an IBT structure or a uniform tariff. Conceptually, a minimum charge is in the nature of a rent payable by all users having a water connection, whether or not water is used. The minimum charges are so fixed that they are lower than the tariff rate laid down for the initial block, giving advantage of lower tariff to low water consuming households. An example of a two-part tariff is given in Table 5.5.

TABLE 5.5
Two-part Tariff, Hyderabad

Part	Rs
(1)	(2)
PART 1	
Minimum/month	90
PART 2	
<30 kl	6.0
30–200 kl	10/kl
>200 kl	25/kl
>500 kl	25/kl

Source: HMWSSB.

TARIFF FOR UNMETERED SUPPLIES

Price structures commonly used for unmetered supplies are either annual fixed charges as shown in Table 5.6 or charges that vary with the size of water connection. Separate pricing structures are applied to standpoint connections where such charges are provided for under the rules.

The above examples and illustrations demonstrate the complex nature of water price structures in Indian cities and towns (see Box 5.2 for information regarding water tariffs in Latin American Countries). Variations are far too large to be able to test their adequacy with respect to the objectives that underlie designing pricing systems and structures. Most pricing systems, particularly those where the provision of water is the municipal corporation's responsibility, are historically driven with little change having been effected in their format and structure. A typical example here is of

TABLE 5.6
Pricing Structures of Unmetered Supplies at Current Prices

| City | Annual Flat Rate (Rs/year) | | Annual Ferrule based Prices | | |
	Domestic	Industrial	Ferrule Size	Domestic	Non-domestic industrial
(1)	(2)	(3)	(4)	(5)	(6)
Vijayawada	480	–			
Surat	240	–	*	NA	*
Belgaum	–	–	1 "	1,155	10,375
Gwalior	720	1,440			
Nagpur			½ "	300	1,200
			¾ "	600	2,400
Patiala	20@	60**			
Kanpur++			½ "	360–1200	
Gorakhpur			¾ "	540–1800	

Source: Various municipal corporations.

Notes: * In Surat, all religious/educational water connections, which are unmetered up to 1½ " connection are charged at a flat rate of Rs 240 per annum per connection.
** Per tap.
@ For the first tap; for the second and subsequent taps the rate declines.
++ In Kanpur, the annual tariff depends on (*a*) ferrule and (*b*) annual rateable value.

the Kolkata Municipal Corporation where users have been divided into forty-nine categories for the levy of a connection fee. These categories comprise, among others, stables, cooling plants, flushing purposes in the market areas, fire fighting, medical practitioners, film actors and painters, owners of newspapers, estate agents, race horse jockey, persons engaged in profession of loading and unloading and the like. Attempts have, in recent years, been made to simplify the pricing structures and to periodically adjust them in line with costs. In Bangalore, tariffs have been revised six times between 1999 and 2000; the Bangalore Water Supply and Sewerage Board (BWSSB) is endowed with powers to adjust the tariff if it is warranted on account of an increase in power tariff rates; for adjustment of tariff on account of other factors like salary increase or additional maintenance costs, approval of the government is essential. The Chennai Metropolitan Water Supply and Sewerage Board has also taken steps to simplify the tariff system. Many progressive municipal corporations like Mumbai have also adjusted the tariff structure in order to meet the rising cost of water provision, although it retains the historically complex pricing regime.

Box 5.2
Water Tariffs in Latin American Countries

In the systems studied in various Latin American countries, the structure of the domestic water tariff has the following characteristics:

- There is a fixed minimum volume which is charged regardless of whether or not water is consumed. This is 15 m^3 in most places; in Panama it is 30 m^3 for residential consumers and lower amounts for low-income areas.
- The marginal per-metre charge for consumption above the minimum is a progressive function of the total volume consumed. In El Salvador there were three ranges; in Nicaragua there were nine; in Panama five; and in Venezuela four. The degree of progressiveness related to volume varies considerably from place to place.
- There are regional variations, which aim to capture differences in costs and/or in social conditions. These normally specify a higher tariff for the metropolitan system. In Venezuela there were seven 'types' of tariff; in El Salvador there were two (metropolitan and other); in Nicaragua there were two geographical distinctions within the capital city according to the distance from an historically important source and the regions paid less than the capital; in Panama there were four regional or spatial variants in the tariff.
- There was normally a special tariff for 'social' cases. Sometimes this only applies to standpipes (El Salvador); in other cases it applies generally to informal settlements (Managua, Panama, and Venezuela).
- In all these systems, the coverage of micro metering is relatively low; in some of them, it is simply non-existent. In such conditions, the water company's discretionary estimates of each user's water consumption are crucial to tariff setting. This discretion is often used with the intention of trimming the bill to what the company thinks each part of the market will bear.

Source: Ian Walker, ibid.

WATER PRICING EXPERIENCES: A FOUR-CITY SURVEY

Urban water in India is a state subject; the central government's responsibility in respect of water which is defined in River Board Act, 1956 and Inter-State Water Disputes Act, 1956, is limited to the regulation and development of inter-state rivers and river basins and provision of support for such programmes as the accelerated urban water supply, low-cost sanitation, and establishment of water monitoring systems. The functions in respect of this sector stand allocated to the PHED, for example, in Rajasthan; a state-level agency with state-wide jurisdiction like the Kerala Water Authority and Delhi Jal Board; state-level parastatals such as those in Karnataka and Uttar Pradesh (Karnataka Water Supply and Sewerage Board and Uttar Pradesh Jal Nigam); metropolitan-level agency like in Bangalore, Chennai, and Hyderabad; and municipal corporations and municipalities in such states as Gujarat, Madhya Pradesh, and Maharashtra (see Table 5.7 for an illustration).

TABLE 5.7
Institutional Set-up for Operating Urban Water Systems, Illustrative

Institution	Example	Spatial Jurisdiction
Public Health Engineering Department (PHED)	Rajasthan	State-wide
State-level parastatal agency	Kerala, Delhi	State-wide (excluding NDMC)
Metropolitan agency	Bangalore, Chennai,	Metropolitan-wide Hyderabad
City-level specialized agencies	Uttar Pradesh Jal Sansthans	Lucknow, Varanasi, etc.
Municipal corporations Municipalities (small)	Gujarat, Maharashtra Andhra Pradesh, Uttar Pradesh, Tamil Nadu	Mumbai, Ahmedabad, etc.

Sources: Various state agencies and municipal corporations.

It is not uncommon to find existence of arrangements wherein capital works are dealt with by a state-level agency (PHED), and the O&M of water supply systems being conducted by a city-level agency or municipality, as in Punjab. In Ludhiana, for example, the capital works for water supply are dealt with by the Punjab Water

Box 5.3
Private Sector Participation

Depending upon the specific situations, various combinations of private sector participation in building, operating, leasing and transferring water resources facilities may be considered.

Source: National Water Policy.

Private sector participation will be encouraged in various aspects of planning, investigation, design, construction, development and management of water resources projects for diverse uses, wherever feasible. Private sector participation will help introducing corporate management in improving service efficiency and accountability to users. Depending upon specific situation, various combinations of private sector participation in building, owning, operation, leasing and transferring of water resource facilities will be considered.

Source: Karnataka State Water Policy.

Supply and Sewage Board (PWSSB), whereas O&M projects are the responsibility of the Ludhiana Municipal Corporation (LMC) (see Chapter 8).

> For the reason that urban water is a state subject, institutional arrangements for its provision and management and systems of pricing including price structures vary across states.

Participation of the formal private sector (excluding the production of bottled water) in urban water provision and management is negligible, although several cities in India have witnessed the emergence of small-scale water providers (see Box 5.3 for the role of the private sector envisaged in the national water policy and the water policy of Karnataka). Small-scale providers are engaged in providing water to slum and squatter settlements who are unserved by public supplies.

The sample cities we studied for work in this chapter, namely, Agra, Allahabad, Bangalore, Pune, and Vadodara, two of which are included in the marginal cost estimations, display the same diverse arrangements; the municipal corporations are responsible for water provision in Pune and Vadodara, while this function is discharged by the Uttar Pradesh Jal Sansthan in Agra and Allahabad. A Water

Supply and Sewerage Board provides and maintains the water supply system in Bangalore. It also maintains the responsibility for capital expansion of the system (see Table 5.8).

TABLE 5.8
Institutional Framework for Water Provision

City	Institution
Agra	Uttar Pradesh Jal Sansthan/Jal Nigam
Allahabad	Uttar Pradesh Jal Sansthan/Jal Nigam
Bangalore	Bangalore Water Supply and Sewerage Board
Pune	Pune Municipal Corporation
Vadodara	Vadodara Municipal Corporation

Sources: Uttar Pradesh Jal Sansthan/Jal Nigam; Bangalore Mahanagara Palike; Pune and Vadodara Municipal Corporations.

Water provision comprises the following: (*a*) capital improvement work and asset creation; (*b*) O&M; and (*c*) billing, levy, and collection of water charges. Capital improvement works include source development, installation of plants and pumping stations, laying the distribution networks, and the like. O&M functions relate to the running and maintaining the system and ensuring a proper distribution of water. Minor capital works include repairs to the system which also form a part of the O&M expenditure. Levy and collection of charges for providing access to water and selling water constitute an important responsibility of water-supplying entities.

Pune and Vadodara Municipal Corporations and the BWSSB hold responsibility for all functions relating to the provision of water. On the other hand, the Agra Jal Sansthan and Allahabad Jal Sansthan are responsible for the operations, billing, and collection of charges, while the responsibility for capital works rests with the Uttar Pradesh Jal Nigam.

Water Provision: Key Features

The sources of water supply to the sampled cities comprise rivers in the case of Agra which draws water from the river Yamuna, and Allahabad which also draws water from the same source combined with water from nearly 130 tube wells, dams, and borewells. Agra and Allahabad do not have any assessment of water demand; demand is assumed to be co-terminus with the quantity of water that is released from the system. The BWSSB is able to supply close to 90 per cent of water demand, and Vadodara Municipal Corporation is also reported to be meeting 98 per cent of the city's water requirements. Bangalore is supplied water from Cauvery river, Arkavatty-T.G. Halli, and Hessaraghatta rivers with a capacity of 540 mld, 140 mld, and 25 mld, respectively. Pune also has three sources namely, Khadkwasala dam, Pavana dam, and Pashan lake each with a capacity of 160 mgd, 5 mgd, and 5 mgd, respectively. In some instances, cities do provide an estimate of water demand based on the standard recommended by the National Commission on Urbanization, and scale these estimates to the size of their population. However, the absence of actual data on effective water demand and its sensitivity to price change remains an important handicap in formulating appropriate water pricing policy.

Other aspects of water supply relate to the installed capacity, water released, volume of water charged, and distribution losses. It is common to observe differences, on the one hand, between water released and installed capacity (few cities would release the entire volume of water held in the system) and, on the other hand, between water charged and water released. The water charged is usually less than the water released on account of (a) free water that many cities provide and (b) distributional losses. In recent years, the quantity of non-revenue water has risen enormously.[6] Key statistics in respect to these features are given in Table 5.9.

Our survey results show that the distributional losses are, on average, 30 per cent, which is roughly twice the norms and standards. Free water supplied via public standposts accounts for 15 per cent

TABLE 5.9
Water Provision in Sampled Cities

Features	Agra	Allahabad	Bangalore	Pune
(1)	(2)	(3)	(4)	(5)
Installed capacity (mld)	280	230	705	790
Water released (mld)	250(89%)	210(91%)	645(91%)	NA
Distributional losses (mld)	75(30%)	63(30%)	213(33%)	176(22%)
Free water (mld)	37.5(15%)	58.8(28%)	NA	NA
Water charged	137.5(55%)	117.6(56%)	432(67%)	517(65%)

Sources: Uttar Pradesh Jal Sansthan; BWSSB; Pune Municipal Corporation; and authors' computations.

in Agra and 28 per cent in Allahabad, whereas in Bangalore, the city corporation buys water from the BWSSB for free distribution among urban poor communities. The water charged ranges between a low of 55 per cent in Agra and 56 per cent in Allahabad and a high of 65–7 per cent in Bangalore and Pune. These facts, as we show later, have an important bearing on the financial viability of water-supplying entities.

Metered versus unmetered water supplies are another important aspect that impinge on the pricing structures and consequently upon the overall financial health of water-supplying organizations. In Agra, of the 110,000 connections, 80 per cent are reported to be non-functional with the result that water billing is done on a minimum annual charge basis. This is a particular characteristic of domestic meters; non-domestic meters are reported to be functional where it has been possible to bill on the basis of water consumed.[7] However, in view of the fact that domestic supplies account for 80 per cent of the total water consumption in Agra which carries a fixed annual charge, stagnancy is observed in the revenues earned from water sales.

The position in Allahabad resembles that in Agra: of the 86,000 water connections only about 55 per cent are metered, and of these, 90 per cent of the metered connections are not in working condition. In other words, 5–6 per cent of the households in Allahabad have working metered connections, who pay according to the tariff fixed for them. In Pune, properties connected to metered connections account for 41 per cent of the total number of properties and properties with unmetered connections account for 27.7 per cent. A noteworthy feature of Pune Municipal Corporation lies in water connections among slum households (see Table 5.14).

CHARGING INSTRUMENTS IN SELECTED CITIES

As indicated earlier, there are different ways in which water is charged. In Agra and Allahabad, five instruments are used for charging water:

1. A water tax using the annual rateable value (ARV) as the base
2. Water charge on all metered and unmetered water connections

3. Meter rent on metered water connections
4. Development charge/fee for connections which is akin to a connection charge
5. Service and supervision charge on all connections

Standposts are not charged in Agra and Allahabad. An important feature of the charging system in Agra and Allahabad is that the charges discriminate between different categories of consumers: thus, the charges vary between domestic consumers and non-domestic consumers, with non-domestic consumers being further categorized into special industry categories (Rs 15 per kl), business (Rs 7.5 per kl), government and semi-government institutions (Rs 6.0 per kl), army cantonment board (Rs 4.5 per kl), and municipal works (Rs 3.0 per kl).[8] Charge for special industry is five times that of water for domestic users. Rate structures are given in Tables 5.10–5.16.

Pricing policies usually do not distinguish between access and usage. Subsidies are generally on prices on water, but access charge (at least in some cities) tend to be high as when they are linked to possession of built-up space. As a result, the subsidies are perverse and anti-poor.

The BWSSB makes use of a connection fee which differs with the floor numbers (high for upper floors in comparison with ground floors), and also with the users where the domestic users pay a lower fee as compared with the non-domestic users; a water consumption charge where domestic consumers in high-rise apartment buildings and government institutions are charged at bulk rates and others according to rates for different slabs; and meter hire charges. In Pune where water provision is the responsibility of Pune Municipal Corporation, water charging instruments comprise a water connection charge, a water tax, a water benefit tax, volumetric water charge, and fixed charges for new unmetered connections in slum settlements. Thus, water is charged in different ways, consisting of (*a*) a one-time charge, invariably for a connection; (*b*) an annual charge or a tax, often leviable on the ARV, and also a meter rent, leviable generally once a year; and (*c*) a water consumption charge collected on a monthly, bi-monthly, or an annual basis.

A water charge from unmetered household is more in the nature of a fee, rather than a charge. It promotes inefficient consumer behaviour.

TABLE 5.10
Water Connection Charge at Current Prices, Pune

Diameter of the Pipe (in Inches)	Charges (Rs) 1999–2000
(1)	(2)
0.50	500
0.75	1,000
1.00	2,500
1.00–2.00	5,000
2.00–3.00	7,500
3.00–4.00	10,000

Source: Pune Municipal Corporation.

TABLE 5.11
Water Connection Charge at Current Prices, Bangalore

Type	Fee (Rs)
(1)	(2)
Domestic (ground floor)	1,620
Domestic (ground and first floors)	2,220
Domestic (ground and two floors)	2,820 + prorata charges @ Rs 70/sq. metre
Non-domestic	1,050 + prorata charges @ Rs 120/sq. metre

Source: Bangalore Mahanagara Palike.

TABLE 5.12
Annual Water Benefit Tax, Pune
(Rs in Current Prices)

Basic	1996–7	1999–2000
(1)	(2)	(3)
Annual rateable value	2%	2%

Source: Pune Municipal Corporation.

TABLE 5.13
Water Charge for Metered Connections at Current Prices, Pune

Type	1996–7	1999–2000
(1)	(2)	(3)
Domestic	2.00	2.50
Non-domestic	10.00	16.00

Source: Pune Municipal Corporation.

TABLE 5.14
Annual Water Charge for Slum Settlements at Current Prices, Pune

Year	Rs
(1)	(2)
1996–7	175.0
1999–2000	250.0

Source: Pune Municipal Corporation.

TABLE 5.15
Volumetric Domestic Water Tariffs at
Current Prices, Bangalore, 1999–2000

Consumption Slab (kl)	Tariff Rs/kl*
(1)	(2)
<15	5.00
15–25	6.50
25–50	10.00
50–75	25.00
75–100	30.00
>100	30.00

Source: Bangalore Mahanagara Palike.
Note: * A minimum payment of Rs 75 per month for each apartment
in a high-rise building.

TABLE 5.16
Water Charges for Domestic Use in Agra and Allahabad
(Rs in Current Prices)

Annual Rateable Value	Size of Meter Connection					
	15 mm		20 mm		25 mm	
	Agra	Allahabad	Agra	Allahabad	Agra	Allahabad
(1)	(2)	(3)	(4)	(5)	(6)	(7)
<360	360	480	540	720	840	1080
360–2000	720	900	1080	1080	1620	1200
2001–3500	1080	1080	1620	1200	2400	1680
3501–5000	1380	1200	2040	1680	3060	2040
>5000	1800	1680	2700	1800	3600	2400

Source: Uttar Pradesh Jal Sansthan/Jal Nigam.

STRUCTURE OF COST

Water provision, which includes production and distribution of
water, entails costs. These comprise, in the main, establishment cost

which includes salaries and wages; electricity charges; chemicals for treatment of water; general repairs and maintenance of plant and machinery; cost of raw water where applicable; and interest payments. For the reason that water is drawn from different sources and distances, the structure of costs varies between different cities, often even widely, as we have discussed in principle already in Chapter 2. We summarize the structure of costs for five sample cities, during a couple of years in Tables 5.17 and 5.18.

TABLE 5.17
Structure of Cost Incurred on Water Provision,
Per Cent of Total Cost, 1995–6

Structure	Agra	Allahabad	Bangalore	Pune	Vadodara
(1)	(2)	(3)	(4)	(5)	(6)
Establishment	50.2	65.7	17.7	22.1	18.0
Electricity	18.8	4.0	56.9	44.6	20.4
Chemicals	13.7	10.4	–	2.2	–
General repairs	4.3	8.5	7.8	10.0	29.8
Raw water	–	–	–	16.4	–
Interest payments	–	–	17.6	4.6	31.4
Others	13.1	11.3	–	–	0.4
Total	100.0	100.0	100.0	100.0	100.0

Sources: Uttar Pradesh Jal Sansthan/Jal Nigam; Bangalore Mahanagara Palike; Pune and Vadodara Municipal Corporations; and authors' computations.

TABLE 5.18
Structure of Cost Incurred on Water Provision,
Per Cent of Total Cost, 1999–2000

Structure	Agra	Allahabad	Bangalore	Pune	Vadodara
(1)	(2)	(3)	(4)	(5)	(6)
Establishment	48.6	78.7	20.1	19.0	24.2
Electricity	14.8	1.2	59.5	47.8	48.5
Chemicals	19.5	4.5	–	1.9	–
General repairs	2.3	9.6	7.6	8.8	13.9
Raw water	–	–	–	16.3	–
Interest payments	–	–	12.8	6.2	13.3
Others	14.9	6.1	–	–	0.1
Total	100.0	100.0	100.0	100.0	100.0

Source: Uttar Pradesh Jal Sansthan/Jal Nigam; Bangalore Mahanagara Palike; Pune and Vadodara Municipal Corporations; and authors' computations.

Tables 5.17 and 5.18 display great heterogeneity in the structure of cost of water provision across cities, which reflects the joint effect of local factors such as geography, system and operational inefficiencies, which we have discussed at length in Chapter 2. In Agra and Allahabad, establishment costs account for anywhere between 50 and 70 per cent of the total cost; the same, however, is only about 17–20 per cent in Bangalore, Pune, and Vadodara.[9] Electricity costs are a major cost in Bangalore, Pune, and Vadodara, and negligible in Allahabad. Electricity has become an important component of cost in the production and distribution of water. Energy costs are particularly high in Bangalore on account of sources that are distant and because energy is spent on abstraction, diversion, and transport. Also, electricity costs are exogenous to the water-supplying entities.[10]

> *Energy costs reflect the three-dimensional arrangements of water source, reservoirs, and treatment plants in a given topography, and abstraction, and recharge.*

Table 5.19 shows the per unit costs of water production and distribution. We show the per unit (kl) cost to be varying between a low of Rs 3.22 in Pune, Rs 2.67 in Allahabad, and Rs 3.69 in Agra, and a high of Rs 12.98 in Bangalore. The per unit costs for Agra and Allahabad are inclusive of unpaid electricity charges. Of these, as shown earlier, electricity is the principal cost item in Bangalore[11] and Pune, and establishment being the main cost item in Agra and Allahabad. Most costs on a unit basis have risen over time, with the rates of rise in electricity costs being greater compared to other cost items.

RECOVERIES FROM THE WATER SECTOR

The instruments of water charges and charging methods have been stated in the preceding section. The water-supplying entities recover the cost incurred on water provision in different ways including a connection charge, water tax, fees, charges, and so on, as discussed above. The recoveries in the case of the sampled cities are shown in Table 5.20.

While per unit per kl recoveries from the sale of water in 1999–2000 were Rs 3.1 in Agra, Rs 2.28 in Allahabad, Rs 13.79 in

TABLE 5.19
Per Unit/kl Structure of Cost in Water Provision, 1999–2000
(Rs in Current Prices)

Structure	Agra	Allahabad	Bangalore	Pune
(1)	(2)	(3)	(4)	(5)
Establishment	1.54	1.66	2.61	0.61
Electricity	0.47	0.03	7.72	1.54
Chemicals	0.62	0.10	–	0.06
General repairs	0.07	0.20	0.99	0.28
Raw water	–	–	–	0.53
Interest payments	–	–	1.66	0.20
Others	0.47	0.13	–	–
Subtotal	3.17	2.11	12.98	3.22
Total (including outstanding electricity charges)	3.69	2.67	12.98	3.22
Water installed capacity (mld)	280	230	705	790

Sources: Uttar Pradesh Jal Sansthan/Jal Nigam; Bangalore Mahanagara Palike; Pune Municipal Corporation; and authors' computations.

Bangalore, and Rs 2.40 in Pune, over a four-year period, in 1995–6, per unit recoveries rose at an annual rate ranging between 9.9 per cent in the case of Pune, 13.5 per cent in Bangalore, and 18.1 and 14.5 per cent in the case of Allahabad and Agra, respectively. An important point to note is that the recovery from water sales has risen at a faster rate over the 1995–6 to 1999–2000 period compared to expenditure on water provision, perhaps signalling that price adjustments have found acceptance as a necessary tool for achieving financial viability among water-supplying entities.

The price of water as manifest in recoveries, however, does not cover the cost incurred in water provision in Agra, Pune, and Vadodara. In these three cities, the price is able to cover 97.9 per cent, 48.3 per cent, and 74.4 per cent of the cost, respectively, in Agra, Vadodara, and Pune. On a per capita basis, annual losses are Rs 2.69 in Agra, Rs 64.5 in Pune, and Rs 121.1 in Vadodara in 1999–2000 (Table 5.21). Although the losses have declined, the position is still unsustainable. Pune is the only one that has increased its recovery during 1995–6 to 1999–2000, both in per capita terms as well as in terms of kilolitres (Tables 5.21 and 5.22).

TABLE 5.20
Water Account Recoveries at Current Prices

Recoveries	1995–6 Per Unit/kl, Rs				1999–2000 Per Unit/kl, Rs			
	Agra	Allahabad	Bangalore	Pune	Agra	Allahabad	Bangalore	Pune
(1)	(2)	(3)	(4)	(5)	(6)	(7)	(8)	(9)
Sale of water	1.61	0.94	7.75	1.56	2.94	1.90	13.29	2.27
Other receipts	0.13	0.17	0.30	0.05	0.16	0.38	0.59	0.12
Total	1.74	1.11	8.04	1.61	3.10	2.28	13.79	2.40

Sources: Uttar Pradesh Jal Sansthan/Jal Nigam; Bangalore Mahanagara Palike; Pune Municipal Corporation; and authors' computations.

Table 5.21
Water Price-Cost Linkage (Expressed in Per Capita
Rs Terms, Current Prices)

Cities	Recoveries from Sale of Water		Cost Incurred on Water Provision*		Recoveries as a % Water Provision	
	1995–6	1999–2000	1995–6	1999–2000	1995–6	1999–2000
(1)	(2)	(3)	(4)	(5)	(6)	(7)
Agra	65.98	128.46	84.02	131.15	78.53	97.94
Allahabad	52.75	101.45	63.11	93.91	83.59	108.03
Bangalore	349.58	537.11	387.07	505.35	90.32	106.29
Pune	146.40	187.63	158.24	252.15	92.52	74.41
Vadodara	61.63	112.90	187.00	233.91	32.95	48.26

Sources: Uttar Pradesh Jal Sansthan/Jal Nigam; Bangalore Mahanagara Palike; Pune and Vadodara Municipal Corporations; and authors' computations.
Note: * Unpaid dues for electricity not included in costs.

TABLE 5.22
Water Price-Cost Linkage (Expressed in Per Unit/kl
Rs Terms, Current Prices)

Cities	Recoveries from Sale of Water		Cost Incurred on Water Provision		Recoveries as a % Water Provision	
	1995–6	1999–2000	1995–6	1999–2000	1995–6	1999–2000
(1)	(2)	(3)	(4)	(5)	(6)	(7)
Agra	1.74	3.10	3.04	3.17	57.2	97.8
Allahabad	1.11	2.28	1.86	2.11	59.7	108.0
Bangalore	8.04	13.79	8.91	12.98	90.2	106.2
Pune	1.61	2.40	1.74	3.22	92.5	74.5

Sources: Uttar Pradesh Jal Sansthan/Jal Nigam; Bangalore Mahanagara Palike; Pune Municipal Corporation; and authors' computations.

The following are a few summarizing observations:

1. Urban water is charged in many ways—a connection charge is a one-time levy; tax and other rents like meter rents are payable annually, while other consumption charged are either paid every month or at a pre-determined time. For this reason, the accounting of revenues of water-supplying entities assumes a complex character, particularly when the life of the water system is unstated or unspecified.

2. On the cost structure, fixed costs are shown in the form of interest payments or debt charges for those cases where a water

supply system has been upgraded or augmented. Thus, in Agra and Allahabad which have not added any new capacity, these do not form a constituent of cost. Further, a perusal of cost structure shows that, on the one hand, there are non-discretionary expenditures in the form of salary payments and interest and debt charges, and, on the other hand, it consists of electricity charges that are determined exogenously by different agencies and topographical factors.

3. With the exception of Bangalore where tariff revisions have led to a marginal surplus, other water-supplying entities run into losses with the usual consequences for service delivery, expansion of water networks, and the like. It means that the most basic requirement of any water tariff, that is, to raise enough revenues to cover the cost of service provision is simply not met in most Indian cities. Also, since most households in cities which use an IBT fall into the first or second block, end up receiving large subsidy on water.

4. High proportion of non-revenue water is a common feature in Indian cities and towns. It should be evident that to the extent it cannot be brought down, non-revenue water will impede any attempt to rationalize water tariff structures.

WATER PRICING: SETTING THE STAGE FOR REFORMS

A Framework for Reforms

Pricing of urban water as also other urban infrastructural services is a key failing in India (see Box 5.4 on the comparative capacities of paying for water across India and France). Apart from their legendary inadequacy, both in quality and quantity, the prices that are charged for them constitute a relatively small proportion of the long-run marginal costs,[12] even when its adverse consequences are widely recognized. First, the institutions responsible for the provision of such services do not receive enough revenues to improve and maintain them adequately, thereby resulting in poor service for those served and reduced incentives to extend water to additional population. Second, cheaper services encourage those with easy access to use them excessively. Third, such policies adversely affect

---

Box 5.4
What is Capacity to Pay for Urban Water?

A household in France spends approximately 1.4 per cent of income or five days of income on water. It is nearly 1 Euro per day for consumption level of 120 m³ per year or 10 m³ per month.

In India, below an income level of Rs 2,000 per month, the per cent of income for water expenses would be significantly higher than in the developing countries. In Rajkot, on the basis of an average monthly income of Rs 5,000, the costs are approximately 4 per cent of income, with an average consumption of 65 lpcd. In Vijaywada, the water budget is 5.2 per cent and the average consumption is 100 lpcd.

Source: Alain L. Dangeard, Dematedee, mimeo, undated.

---

distribution, as low-income and poor households pay a higher price than other higher-income households.

Financial viability and tariff-setting are linked throughout the country's water sector. Current approach to tariff-setting has resulted in tariff levels often far below the basic O&M levels, let alone full cost recovery. Tariff reforms are also constrained by lack of rational tariff structures which match the costs and charges in relation to the incidence of benefits; low current tariff levels in most cities make a transition to full cost recovery politically difficult, due to the high initial revision requirements; lack of customer consultation in service planning which is needed to link investment decisions to effective demand; inadequate accounting systems which do not make it possible to assess the real costs of services; and lack of a system of indexation which would enable revenues to keep up with the rising cost of inputs.

The existing pricing system and structures are thus inadequate and unsustainable. Price reform under these circumstances would seem not only desirable but essential. An efficient system of urban infrastructural services is crucial for the economy of the cities as well as the national economy. Cities hold the key to economic growth. The competitiveness of nations, as evident from many developing countries shows, depends on the competitiveness of cities. Price reform of urban water and city bus transport is thus a crucial agenda.

The issue is: *what should price reform in respect of these two services consist of*?

Past work in India on water pricing is limited and focused on (*a*) the adequacy of water tariff and (*b*) issue of leakages. In the case of water, the merits of intermittent supply versus a regular supply have also been examined along with the cost of metering. An upward revision of water tariff to the point of full cost recovery and an indexation mechanism to allow for general price increase, reduction of leakages, change over from unmetered to metered supplies in the case of urban water, and greater efficiency in revenue collection have been highlighted in the agenda for improving the operations of water services. These are important components in the financial viability of urban water utilities.

The limited analysis of the finance data of urban water utilities undertaken in this chapter has discerned several areas which, in a way, point to some directions in developing a framework for reform. Five areas are underlined here. The first is of primary importance and relates to the relevance and effectiveness of the existing pricing system and structures. The pricing structures, especially of urban water, are in several parts, which are differentiated according to the nature of users, quality, quantity, and several other factors. Apart from the clumsiness of structures which was demonstrated by giving an example from the schedule of water rates of the Kolkata Municipal Corporation, what tariff rate is appropriate for which part or sub-part, and which charging instrument is appropriate for which part stands neglected in most earlier work on pricing matters. It needs to be emphasized that the existing pricing structures do not make it possible to assess if they can achieve full cost recovery or even partial cost recovery. The pricing structures are obsolete and need to be replaced with structures that are simple, easy to apply, and transparent.

A second issue which has received surprisingly scant attention is concerned with the user or consumer base which is limited, which is narrow, and which is possibly over-exploited. Only 30–40 per cent of urban households pay for water and other similar services; and if this proportion is held in other urban areas as indeed appears to be the case, the likelihood of any price reform to achieve financial sufficiency and economic efficiency would be dim. Expanding the user base is an important component of water reform agenda.

A third issue is linked to the unbalanced revenue base of water utilities, with much of the burden currently being borne by the non-domestic sector. The finance data of urban water utilities has clearly brought out the extent of cross-subsidies that exist in the water sector. It has two adverse impacts: (*a*) the non-domestic users, mainly industry and commerce, pass on the costs associated with higher tariff to domestic users in the form of higher prices of their products and (*b*) lower prices for households mean larger wastage of water. It is imperative for water utilities to move towards a more rational pricing structure which may mean price increases for the domestic users and price decreases for the non-domestic sector. A rational structure may yield a positive net benefit as the non-domestic users may be expected to pass on the cost savings associated with lower water prices in the form of lower output prices. Fourth, a necessary condition for establishing efficient prices for goods such as water is the complete accounting of their costs. Although this chapter has utilized finance data, there exists uncertainty as to whether all costs attributable to service have been accounted for, in the light of our discussion in Chapter 2. Further, many cost components are indivisible.

Finally, there is the complex issue of metering of urban water. While the merit of metering is accepted as it is said to allow households to determine how much water they are prepared to pay for, the issue is: how much difference does metering make to revenues in practice. In countries where these have been empirically examined, metering is said to have reduced consumption among some, relatively better-off households; in others, particularly low-income groups where consumption levels were low, consumption registered an increase reflecting the unmet demand of the period when water was unmetered and rationed. Experiences of other countries suggest that metering should form an integral part of the overall price reform agenda, rather than being taken up in isolation.

Metering should be promoted on the basis of fairness and as a means of improving operating efficiency and lowering costs.

INTERNATIONAL PRACTICES

Examples of 'best practice' in this sphere are fewer than in other areas such as decentralization and private sector participation. From the available limited evidence, there appears to be some attempt at rationalization of tariffs in developing countries. Protection of the poor has been attempted through a life-line block which is cross-subsidized by other higher consumption blocks. In order to overcome the problem of high rate revisions required for full cost recovery, a phased introduction of full cost pricing is adopted as was done in Guinea. The service delivery in Guinea was a commercial operation exercised by a private operator. Politically feasible increases in tariffs were made possible through external credit which was phased, in order to recover full costs from customers over a pre-determined period.

Innovative examples of infrastructure charges for provision of block-level distribution and collection networks are available from Brazil, where under a condominial financing system, 'households pay for the on-lot costs, block pay for the block sewers and decide what level of service they want from these'. Policymakers in Brazil are considering developing water markets to allocate water. Water markets are uncommon in Brazil, but it has existed in Cariri region. While the Cariri market is a small isolated system, it provides indications of the value of water, the possibilities of allocating and enforcing water rights, and the willingness of water users to pay and cooperate to assure a secure water supply.

A World Bank (1997) study of water pricing experiences classifies countries as high, medium, and low according to what it calls a Water Pricing Progress Index (WPPI). It prepared the index using two criteria, viz., current pricing practices and current mode of funding. Those countries which used some economic pricing method, or at the very least, recovered full O&M costs, or a portion of capital costs from users were grouped in high progress category. Countries which financed water systems with governmental resources were categorized as low progress countries. The findings of the study are shown in Table 5.23.

Other overseas experiences suggest that, in some circumstances, it is possible to charge for actual usage at levels higher than at the individual household. In others, participation of stakeholders, to

TABLE 5.23

Relationship between Pricing Reforms and Selected Country Characteristics

	Rank	High	Medium	Low
Gross National Product				
WPPI	High	Australia, France, New Zealand, Spain, United States	Botswana, Namibia	
	Medium	Israel, Italy, United Kingdom	Brazil, Portugal, Tunisia	Madagascar
	Low	Canada		India, Pakistan, Tanzania, Uganda
Water Availability				
WPPI	High	Australia, Botswana, New Zealand	France, Namibia, Spain, United States	
	Medium	Brazil	Italy, Portugal, United Kingdom, Madagascar	Israel, Tunisia
	Low	Canada	India, Pakistan, Tanzania, Uganda	
Budget Deficit				
WPPI	High	Australia, France, Namibia, Spain, United States	Brazil	Botswana, New Zealand
	Medium	Israel, Italy, Portugal, Tunisia, Madagascar	United Kingdom	
	Low	Canada, India, Pakistan, Tanzania, Uganda		

Source: The World Bank, 1997, 'Water Pricing Experiences: An International Perspective', World Bank Technical Paper No. 386.

decide on standards and investment priorities in relation to cost and prices, is found to be useful in water resource planning. In recent concession contracts for water services, participation of the private sector has helped to also reduce the average tariff levels. This is largely due to the significant efficiency improvements which have been possible with the entry of the private sector. In Manila, the tariff proposed by the winning bid for half of the city was almost a fourth of the existing tariff. This clearly highlights the link between efficiency improvements and financial viability with acceptable tariff levels, all three criteria of which much be satisfied for the tariff structure to be effective.

Objectives of Water Pricing

Setting water tariffs requires striking a balance between four main objectives (adopted from Whittington, 2002):

1. Revenue sufficiency: From the point of view of water-supplying entities, the main purpose of tariff is cost recovery. The revenue from water users should be sufficient to pay the O&M cost of water utility's operations, to repay loans undertaken to replace and expand the capital stock, and to provide a return on capital at risk. The revenue stream must thus be adequate to attract both equity capital and debt financing. Ideally the revenue stream should be relatively stable and not cause cash flow or financing difficulties for the utility.

2. Economic efficiency: Economic efficiency requires that prices be set to ensure that consumers face the avoidable costs of their decisions. In other words, water prices should signal to consumers the financial and other costs that their decisions to use water impose on the rest of the society. From an economic efficiency perspective, a tariff should create incentives that ensure, for a given water supply cost, that users obtain the largest possible aggregate benefits. This means that volumetric water charges should be set equal to the marginal cost of supplying water. In this work, in Chapter 4, we have shown that it is indeed possible to estimate and compute marginal costs for water supply, although in a rough manner. In practice it is commonly assumed that the marginal cost of supplying water

can be approximated by the average incremental cost (AIC), that is, the average cost of water from the next water capacity expansion project. Alternatively, the AIC of additional water may be the unit cost of reducing unaccounted for water (UFW).

3. Equity: Equity means that the water tariff treats similar customers equally and that customers in different situations are not treated the same. This would usually be interpreted as requiring users to pay monthly water bills that are proportionate to the costs they impose on the utility by their water use. Inequities can result when water consumption is not metered. For instance, until March 2008, in Surat, water was being provided at a flat rate of Rs 240 per year per connection for all the domestic connections, with the result that low users of water were cross-subsidizing high users of the good. However, now a volumetric consumption regime and a more equitable one has made way, with various slabs of consumption charged at different rates (for instance, for monthly consumption of up to 25,000 l, the water and sewerage charges are Rs 3 per kl, and Rs 12 per kl beyond 25,000 l of monthly consumption).

4. Poverty alleviation: Water services are often seen as a 'basic right' and their access as necessary regardless of whether or not people can pay. This objective leads many people to recommend that water services be provided free, at least to the poor. Providing water free through private connections can conflict with the objectives of cost recovery and efficient water use. However, some mix of differential pricing for high- and low-income users of the service should be possible, as we explain below. In these ways, water pricing can become an instrument of poverty alleviation.

Tariff Restructuring

Given the objectives, the first step in rationalizing tariff structures is to establish a link between tariff and cost by introducing separate charges for the following:

1. Connections: (a) a connection fee to cover the direct cost of connecting to the municipal mains; in the case of a multi-

storeyed system at the block level, it may include the cost of on-site networks; and (*b*) a charge for management, billing, and metering, which may cover the fixed cost of maintaining the connection;

2. Distribution systems: an infrastructure development charge to cover the cost of developing or augmenting the secondary and tertiary distribution systems;

3. Consumption: (*a*) a consumption charge for water, on a volumetric basis to cover the cost of creating and maintaining water abstraction capacity and the primary distribution system, and (*b*) the economic costs of water procurement and operating cost of supply. Other charges would be of no revenue significance.

The key to pricing, however, is consumption charge for water. What charging method would ensure compatibility with the objectives? It is necessary to underscore the role of the 'equity' objectives in water tariff fixation. Second, acceptable tariffs require that adequate service levels are provided and maintained for the poor within their affordability limits. Typically, it has meant fixing lower than optimal levels of pricing, ignoring the financial viability considerations. Instead of lower tariffs, it is useful to base tariff levels on financial viability criterion and then manage affordability issues through mechanisms such as the following:

1. A life-line block in the tariff structure for consumption-related tariff

2. Providing explicit subsidies to the poorer sections for connection and infrastructure development charges (Under the existing system, subsidies for slum settlements and special social groups are available from the state and central government plan allocations. It is essential that such subsidies are made explicit, pooled, and allocated in relation to the overall size of the problem.)

3. Developing and using appropriate credit systems to spread the payment for infrastructure and connection charges over time

4. Separation of water supply accounts and budgets and a complete assessment and valuation of all its assets (such provisions already exist in Maharashtra as per the Section 95 of the

Maharashtra Amendment pursuant to the 74th Constitution Amendment Act)

5. Clear guidelines and objective criteria on the cost to be included in determining the different charges

6. Measurement of UFW and collection efficiency of different charges with a clear indication of their (a) impact on average tariff levels and (b) measures to reduce inefficiencies

7. Indexation of average tariff.

An important decision in respect of tariff restructuring is to make a choice between a two-part tariff and an IBT structure. The IBT structure has been questioned on the ground that it gives households with private connections much more water than what is needed at a very low price.[13] To the extent initial block can be fixed at levels which correspond to a level equal to a household's essential water needs, an IBT structure is an effective method of water charging.

Financial viability requires that, over time, revenues equal expenditure, both operating and capital. It is essential to recognize and reduce inefficiencies related to excess manpower, poor collection of revenues, and high levels of water leakages in the system. It is imperative that strong incentives are introduced to reduce these inefficiencies. A critical aspect in sustaining financial viability over time is to introduce indexation of charges so that the revenues keep up with increases in cost of those inputs which are beyond the utility's control. In addition, it is important to structure tariffs in ways which do not create disincentives for metering. One alternative would be to introduce group meters in specific settlements. It is likely that, given the historically low level of tariffs, many cities will be able to achieve financial viability only over time. Such a timeframe needs to be determined and, in the interim, subsidies provided to support the transition process as is implied in the Jawaharlal Nehru National Urban Renewal Mission (JNNURM).

Another important aspect concerns the possible externalities from water and sewerage services. The environmental and health benefits, especially from improved water quality and sewage collection and treatment, generally accrue to larger groups and are more public in nature. Subsidies may be necessary to achieve these benefits. Any such subsidies should be internalized at appropriate levels, such as a city, and group of cities. Ideally, these groups need to jointly decide on appropriate service levels, investment, and resultant tariff levels. This requires that the level of subsidies be predictable and allocated in a transparent manner.

The need for price reform in water is evident and compelling. The implications of water under-pricing are well-understood, but more needs to be learned about the structure and distribution of demand, the cost structure, and the magnitude of external costs associated with urban water supply. This is a perspective that goes beyond pricing of services.

The forthcoming Chapters 6 and 7 focus attention on other important locally provided public services, respectively, solid waste in Chapter 6, followed by sewerage, street lights, sanitation, and municipal roads in Chapter 7.

NOTES

1. Water price reform is an important agenda in many developing countries. See the following quote. 'The reformulation of tariffs and subsidy policies is central to the reform of water and sanitation services in developing countries. The traditional model of service provision has coupled public ownerships with tariffs that are set well below the cost of the service, justifying this in terms of the importance of water services for the health status of the poor. However, results have often been unsatisfactory. Service quality and coverage remain inadequate in many countries, and subsidies directed at public water companies have often benefited the middle classes rather than the poor, who remain unconnected to the public network. Reformers have proposed to break out of this low level equilibrium through a combination of private sector provision, full cost tariffs, and better targeting of subsidies' (Ian Walker, 'Pricing, Subsidies and the Poor', mimeo, undated).

2. Development charges are meant to cover the cost of water and sewer lines, and are payable by plot holders. See the schedule of rates of the Delhi Jal Board, available at http://www.delhijalboard.nic.in/

3. Fixed charges for capital valuation are a feature of the water charging system in Rajasthan. See the Notification of the Rajasthan Public Health Engineering Department, dated the 28 May 1998.

4. In a survey of Asian countries, the Asian Development Bank (ADB) found that twenty out of a sample of thirty-eight countries used increasing block tariff.

5. A family of five using 40 l per capita per day for 30 days requires 6 kl in a month; most first blocks are higher than this (see Foster, 2001).

6. Non-revenue water comprises free water, distributional losses, and unaccounted for water (UFW) , euphemism for water that is drawn illegally.

7. It should appear that low tariff is a disincentive to keeping the meters in a working condition. The government requires that water be supplied even when meters are not in a working condition.

8. Figures in parenthesis are the per kl charge for each category in Agra.

9. Data on the quantity of electricity used for water production and distribution are not known.

10. Low component of electricity charges in Agra and Allahabad may be explained, in part, by non-payment of electricity charges by the two corporations and, in part, by easy access to water from river sources like Yamuna.

11. This makes sense when we consider Bangalore's altitude, being located 930 m above mean sea level, a fact which we emphasize in Chapter 2, as contributing to the *costs* (rather than the expenditures) of providing water supply in such cities.

12. The Bangalore Water Supply and Sewerage Board recently estimated the long-run marginal cost of water to be supplied by Cauvery at Rs 43 per kl. Recall that our marginal cost estimates in Chapter 4 are based on all cities, not just on Bangalore. As against this, the weighted monthly average tariff is about Rs 14.

13. Of the 17 water utilities in an ADB's data set that use increasing block structures, only two had a first block of 4–5 m^3 per month or less. Most of the others had initial blocks of 15 m^3 per month or more.

CHAPTER 6

Solid Waste Management
Institutions, Financial Mechanisms, and Expenditure

In the case of other services, as discussed in the earlier chapters, we did not attempt to estimate marginal costs, but examined expenditures and the level of the service with a view to determining the expenditure required to ensure a certain benchmark level of service, as for instance, the requirement for ensuring 100 per cent solid waste collection efficiency. Focusing on solid waste, this chapter explains the institutional, regulatory, and legal framework for solid waste collection, treatment, and disposal in India, costs and charging mechanisms that currently exist, and normative financing principles that should underlie the charges. Then the chapter goes on to report primary findings from the field visits with respect to expenditures on solid waste in the selected cities, comparing with norms, where relevant. Additionally, in this chapter, we describe the physical service levels of solid waste, by comparing solid waste collection efficiencies across cities with various spending patterns.[1]

Solid waste is a major source of environmental pollution in Indian cities and towns. It is estimated that anywhere between 30 and 35 per cent of the total waste remains uncollected from the city roads; similarly, the waste disposal services in most cities and towns are archaic and inadequate and carry high environmental risks. The combined effect of the inefficiencies in collection and inadequate and unsafe disposal is evident in widespread insanitation, contaminated water, and high incidence of chronic respiratory and communicable diseases found in Indian cities. Further, there is evidence to suggest that the overall environmental quality in Indian cities and towns may be worsening on account of the pressures of growing urbanization and unregulated growth of cities.

Attempts to address solid waste-related environmental problems in Indian cities and towns have focused largely on improving waste collection, enhancing the frequency of waste collection, increasing trucking capacity, and introduction of mechanized cleaning of city garbage. In a few isolated cases, new institutional arrangements with the participation of non-governmental organizations and the private sector have come into being for solid waste collection and management. The financing aspects of solid waste services have received little or no attention in the country. No systematic use has also been made of the economic and fiscal instruments for understanding their impact on the quantum of waste. There exists neither an incentive for waste reduction nor a penalty for excessive waste generation or its indiscriminate dumping on roads, kerb-sides, or even at the designated landfill sites.

This chapter enables a better understanding of the cost structure and the pattern of financing solid waste services in Indian cities and towns. It explores the options for redesigning the charging system in a way that it impacts the pattern of household consumption, and consequently, the quantum and volume of waste. An effective charging system, we contend, is essential for reducing waste-related environmental pollution.

Part of the work in the chapter is based on reports of the existing practices of managing and financing solid waste services in Indian cities. In addition, we make use of the budgets and annual reports of a few municipal bodies with a view to further understand the financing aspects of solid waste services. Data on solid waste collection efficiency was not readily available. We gathered data during our field visits regarding the solid waste generated and collected, and their expenditures (both capital and O&M) over time. Based on these data, we computed solid waste efficiency estimates for all cities in our study and compared them with their expenditures on the service. As this chapter will subsequently show, data on these aspects are extremely sparse which has restricted a proper examination of issues such as the cost of land fills, response of households to alternative systems of waste disposal, and the economic factors affecting production of refuse by households. The sparseness of data has vastly limited the scope of work regarding this important service, particularly in respect of estimating even the financial costs involved in solid waste collection, transportation, and disposal, which we attempt to partially address in this chapter.

SOLID WASTE IN INDIAN CITIES

Indian cities currently produce wastes in the aggregate, 100,000–110,000 metric tonnes, or a per capita average of 0.40–0.42 kg a day. These estimates are, at best, approximations in that these are based, as is the practice, on the trucking or hauling capacity of waste generated in different cities and towns. The National Commission on Urbanization (1988), on the basis of a sample of forty cities of over 100,000 population found the mean per capita waste per day to be 0.27 kg (with a standard deviation of 0.11 kg above or below this mean), and the same mean for cities in the population range of 50,000 (with a standard deviation of 0.08 kg above or below this mean). Another survey conducted by the Operations Research Group (ORG, 1989) indicates an average per capita solid waste of 0.35–0.40 kg; however, based on the trade and commercial activities in the surveyed towns and cities, actual per capita waste quantity is estimated by the same study to be higher than shown here (Table 6.1).

TABLE 6.1
Number of Cities by Per Capita Waste Generation

Kg Per Capita	Number of Cities		
	NCU Estimate	ORG Estimate	CPCB Estimate
< 0.20	9	4	4
0.20–0.30	21	6	13
0.30–0.40	8	11	16
0.40–0.50	7	8	12
0.50–0.75	–	3	13
0.75–1.00	–	2	1
> 1.00	–	1	0
Total	45	35	59

Sources: Report of the National Commission on Urbanization (NCU) (1988); Operations Research Group (1989); Central Pollution Control Board (CPCB) (2004–5), available at http://www.cpcb.nic.in.

The study also found significant variations in the amount of waste generated among cities, the low and high being 0.12 kg and 1.26 kg per capita, with the difference being explained by the nature of the economic base of the cities. More recent estimates from the Central Pollution Control Board suggest that the per capita waste generation varies from 0.17 kg to 0.76 kg per capita. Given the fact that city capacities (to collect and dispose waste) are often lower than the quantities of waste generated (the actual waste would be at least 30–40 per cent higher than these figures), and also the fact that rag-picking in India is an actively growing industry, these figures from all the cities should be viewed as being conservative.

THE INSTITUTIONAL, REGULATORY, AND LEGAL FRAMEWORK

Solid waste collection, treatment, and disposal in India are a *statutory* responsibility of municipal governments; the other two levels of governments, namely, the central and state governments, have a limited role in this task. In recent years, however, as a result of the increasing recognition that wastes are a major hazard combined with the fact that wastes have important economic value, the Government of India through the Ministry of Environment and Forests (MoEF) constituted a National Waste Management Council in 1990. The Council has the following mandate:

1. Promotion of collection, collation, and publication of information regarding the availability of waste technologies and markets for recoverable materials
2. Analysis of information for overcoming constraints to use available technologies for both waste utilization and waste minimization and identification of areas in which new technologies need to be developed
3. Offering advice to the government, industry, and such other sectors on different aspects of waste management and on incentives/disincentives that may be needed to facilitate waste utilization
4. Recommendation to the government research and development schemes for developing new technologies

5. Advising government on fiscal and regulatory measures to promote waste utilization
6. Promoting awareness among the public about different aspects of solid waste

Given the lack of much information or dissemination about this council and its mandate, it is difficult to assess the effectiveness of this council and the role that it will play in this sphere.

The role of the state governments is limited to overseeing the functioning of the municipal governments' mandate to manage solid waste collection and disposal. The state governments are also responsible for financing expenditure of a capital nature, as for example, purchase of equipments, machinery, and trucks. Each state's municipal laws detail out the local governments' obligatory and discretionary functions. The provision of solid waste services is an obligatory function of municipal governments for the simple reason that it is a 'public good', it is 'non-exclusive', and it is 'non-rivalled'. This service is non-exclusive, meaning that once it is provided to a city or a community, it benefits the overall public welfare. It is also non-rivalled, meaning that any resident can enjoy the benefit of the service without diminishing the benefit to anyone else. It is not feasible to exclude from service those who do not pay, because public cleanliness and safe disposal of waste water are essential to public health and environmental protection. These laws vary from state to state. The Gujarat Municipalities Act, for instance, provides that the municipal councils shall make provision for cleaning of public streets and places. The Madhya Pradesh Act vests this responsibility partly on households by requiring them to deposit the refuse and other offensive matter in public dustbins, leaving the municipal governments responsible for collection of waste from dustbins and for transportation and disposal.

The regulatory framework in India for waste collection is dispersed. While environmental standards have been set for water and air quality in specific and general environmental laws, there exists no separate legislation for solid waste management. At present, pollution owing to disposal of solid waste falls within the purview of the 1974 and 1977 Water Acts, the 1981 Air Act, and the 1986 Environment Protection Act. Hazardous wastes are regulated under the 'Hazardous Waste (Management and Handling) Rules, 1989', and the manufacture, storage, and import of hazardous chemicals rules, which are in different stages of implementation and which make it mandatory for organizations handling hazardous waste to take steps to ensure that all specified wastes are properly handled and disposed of. These rules also regulate the storage of hazardous substances, hazardous accidents control, and pipelines for pumping hazardous substances.

CONTEMPORARY CONCERNS

Much of the attention in India by the central, state, and local governments to environmental problems arising from solid waste has focused on the management of the increasing quantities of waste, application of technologies to solid waste disposal and recycling, and introduction of regulatory instruments. A study of the Central Pollution Control Board (1995) identified, for instance, the following priority areas for solid waste:

1. Utilization of solid waste for resource recovery
2. Selection of proper sites for waste disposal on the basis of environmental impact assessment
3. Application of appropriate technology for solid waste through (a) proper design of landfills and (b) incineration of garbage for power generation, wherever feasible
4. Greater use of solid waste for anaerobic digestion/biogas generation, composting, etc.
5. Use of solid waste for fuel pelletization
6. Recycling of paper, plastic, glass, battery waste, etc.
7. Provision of facilities for disposal of hospital waste

In addition, industrial and hazardous wastes disposed of by industries pose a big problem. According to the National Productivity Council, New Delhi, there are more than three million small- and medium-scale enterprises (SMEs), which are spread throughout the country in the form of clusters/industrial estates. SMEs in India cannot afford to adopt and maintain adequate hazardous waste treatment and disposal technologies. The lack of common facilities has been a major factor in mushrooming of illegal dump sites since most of the units in the small and medium sector do not have adequate space within their premises to arrange for storage over several years. Therefore it is urgently required to make available common hazardous waste treatment and disposal facility in the areas in all the states where SMEs are operating. Construction waste is another neglected area. While dumping of construction waste on the roadside continues 'in spite of having designated dumpsites', there are no readily available estimates of construction waste generated in the country.

No attention has also so far been placed on 'charging' mechanisms for solid waste services, and assessing the possible impact that appropriate charging could have on the pattern of household consumption, the quantum of waste, and consequently on urban environment. Also, no attention has been given to proper identification of the direct and indirect costs involved in solid waste management or to mechanisms for internalizing those costs. The solid waste services continue to be financed out of general taxation, mainly out of the receipts from property taxes.

COSTS AND CHARGING MECHANISMS

Solid waste services in India are financed out of the general tax revenues raised by municipal governments. The general tax revenues of municipal governments, it needs to be noted, consist of revenue yields from property taxes, octroi (a tax on the entry of goods) where it is levied, and taxes on advertisements, non-motorized vehicles, animals, and selectively on entertainment. In the intergovernmental allocation of tax powers, the more elastic and buoyant taxes are assigned to the central and state governments, leaving with municipal governments taxes that would generally be characterized by low level of elasticity and buoyancy. Thus, their yields are rarely able to keep pace with the rising citywide expenditure on basic services.

Taxes on land and property are commonly taken by municipal governments as a source of revenue. A distinguishing feature of these taxes is that the base of these taxes, which happens to be the rental value, is widely used for other service taxes as well. Thus, it is common to observe in most Indian cities and towns, a conservancy tax, latrine tax, drainage tax, sanitation tax, sewerage tax, and fire tax, are levied in the form of a surcharge on the same base as is used for property taxes. In Bombay, for instance, apart from a general property tax, there is water tax, water benefit tax, sewerage tax, sewerage benefit tax, education cess, street tax, tree tax, employment guarantee tax, and building repair tax, all levied on the rental value of properties. For the households, industry, and business, comprehensive property taxes are the main taxes that serve to provide them with essential services.

There exists no specific charge or a fee for solid waste services, implying that there is no relation between waste generated and what the waste generators might pay. This way, the marginal cost of waste generation is taken to be zero. Thus, apart from a general understanding that revenues generated from the general category of taxes on conservancy, drainage, and sanitation will be used for the provision of solid waste services, nothing else is known about their financing. Consequently, several critically important financing aspects, such as, the behaviour of households to alternative forms of charging, the effect of the volume or weight-based pricing on the pattern of household consumption, or of tax policies on waste generation and recycling remain grey areas in the Indian context. Other aspects about which little is known relate to the extent of subsidy in the provision of these services and its effect on the overall municipal finances.

Financing Solid Waste Services

General Taxation

As pointed out earlier, there is no direct charging system for solid waste services in Indian cities and towns. These services are charged, or indeed financed, out of general taxation which, in the case of the sample covered under this study, consists of property taxes and octroi taxes where these taxes are levied. Together with property taxes are the other minor municipal taxes such as advertisement taxes and taxes on non-motorized vehicles which have little significance from the standpoint of revenue generation. Where these sources are not able to meet out the expenditure, grants made by the state governments are used.

A number of observations on the cost and financing mechanisms may be made at this stage.

1. The cost data on solid waste relate primarily to establishment, repairs and maintenance, materials, and miscellaneous components. Landfill or the dumping site costs are not included in the cost data nor are the other indirect costs particularly as these relate to depletion costs associated with landfill. Thus, the costs are grossly understated.

2. The cost per tonne or on a per capita basis would also be higher if the municipal governments were collecting 80–90 per cent of waste, as against the current average of 60–5 per cent of the total waste. To this extent, the cost data need to be adjusted.

3. The cost data on solid waste services show wide variations between cities, the explanation of which is to be found in a number of factors, such as the methods employed in waste collection, transportation, and disposal; the size of the city; and the physical characteristics of cities. The data scarcity has not permitted any analysis of the economies of scale across the services of collection, transportation, and disposal.

4. The solid waste services in Indian cities and towns are financed out of the general tax revenues. There is no specific charge or fee for the services. Composting as a method of disposal is carried out on a very small scale, notwithstanding the fact that the waste composition is suited for composting. Income from composting is insignificant. Also, in a number of cities, compost is a commodity that is used by the concerned departments of municipal bodies without any accounting on the income side. For most cities, the growth rate of the general tax revenues lies far behind the growth rate of expenditure. Property tax which is an important source of tax revenue has shown signs of stagnation and is constrained by large-scale exemption of properties from tax purview and rent control acts. The rental values are hardly updated to reflect the market conditions. As a result, revenues from such taxes do not yield enough to meet the cost of such services as solid waste, street lighting, road maintenance, and the like.

5. On account of the existing practice of financing solid waste services out of the general tax revenue, there is no incentive or disincentive for households, industry, and business to change the pattern of their consumption. It carries the strong assumption

that the taxes paid by them are adequate for meeting the cost of the services.

Charging for Solid Waste

It is necessary to reiterate here that solid waste services in India have traditionally been viewed as 'public goods'. This view has been accompanied by a somewhat simplistic argument that public goods should be paid for by public funds and also delivered by public agencies. In recent years, however, there has occurred an adjustment to this view, and as pointed out earlier, this sector has been opened up, *albeit* in only a few places, to private sector participation. It recognizes the proposition that there are certain aspects of solid waste services that have the characteristics of 'private goods'. It is this point of departure that is used here as the basis for outlining the financing options for solid waste services. The financing options as outlined here fall under two possible institutional arrangements: (*a*) where solid waste collection, transportation, and disposal will continue to be a 'public responsibility', and (*b*) where these services may be provided, either in full or in part, by the private sector.

Under the assumption that it remains a public responsibility, three options appear feasible keeping in view the fact that the objectives are to gain environmental sustainability:

1. To continue with the present system of financing the services, that is, out of the general tax revenues raised by the municipal governments. This option, if persisted, will further diminish the availability of solid waste services in Indian cities and most likely, exacerbate environmental conditions arising from solid waste.

2. To continue financing the solid waste services out of the general tax revenues, but introduce some basic reform measures, particularly in property taxation, so as to generate additional resources. Property tax reform is currently an important agenda in several states of the country. In the state of Andhra Pradesh and in Patna city, the basis of determining the rental value of properties has been changed from that of 'rents' to 'square meter rates differentiated by the locational characteristics of different areas within cities', which has led to a substantial increase in

revenue receipts from property taxes. Given the fact that the 'rate basis' is simple and transparent, it offers a large potential for revenue generation from property taxes, and consequently for larger availability of funds for solid waste services. Financing solid waste services out of general taxation carries the distinct advantage of being 'equitable', in that property tax payments reflect the ability to pay.

3. Replace the indirect charging system by a direct charging system, either with a 'flat fee' or a fee determined on the basis of volume/weight of waste. Direct charging has the obvious and unique advantage of being a 'charge' as distinct from a 'tax', and can therefore be used directly for achieving the objective of environmental sustainability. At the same time, charging according to volume/weight is administratively costly, prone to leakages, and difficult to administer. A 'flat fee' as a direct charging mechanism is iniquitous, particularly in Indian cities where intra-city income disparities are extremely high, and where a large proportion of households—often as large as 30–40 per cent—live in slums and squatter settlements.

Under the second assumption which in a sense, questions the efficiency gains of a purely municipal monopoly, the option will be to contract/sub-contract solid waste services or run the services in partnership with them, under the following different arrangements:

1. To permit the private sector to operate and manage the solid waste to the extent that the private sector sets the 'charge' and payment mechanism, and bears the attendant costs including those of the landfill and dumping sites.
2. To provide subsidies to the private sector in so far as these are necessary for allotting them the dumping sites and making capital investments.

These options have so far not been examined in the Indian context and it is far from clear as to how the municipal governments would deal with issues such as the refusal by households to pay for the solid waste services or to enter into agreements with the private sector. How would the municipal governments regulate the charges and limit price-setting and collusion? These issues constitute a large research agenda in the Indian context.

There is a new dimension in the matter of service financing with the setting up of Finance Commissions in each state of the country. The State Finance Commissions, set up in pursuance of the 73rd and 74th Amendments to the Constitution of India are required to decide on: (*a*) the taxes, duties, tolls, and fees which may be assigned to, or appropriated by, the municipalities; (*b*) the distribution between the state and the municipalities of the net proceeds of the taxes, duties, tolls, and fees leviable by the state; (*c*) the grants-in-aid to the municipalities from the Consolidated Fund of the State; and (*d*) other measures that may be needed to improve the financial position of the municipalities. The issue of financing of solid waste services is vitally linked with the work of the State Finance Commissions.

Table 6.2 presents some solid waste cost–income data from selected large cities in the country.

There is a roughly one-to-one relationship between the size of cities, the solid waste generated, and the per capita expenditures on solid waste, at least for the data based on 1998–9 reports and budgets.

Findings from Primary Data

For the following six cities—Bangalore, Chandigarh, Jaipur, Lucknow, Pune, and Surat—we examined city-level (per capita) expenditures on solid waste and compared this with their solid waste collection efficiency over time, based on the assumption that a city's financial position determines its solid waste collection efficiency. Solid waste collection efficiency represents the solid waste that is collected and disposed, as a proportion of what is generated.

Various committees have laid down the minimum physical standard of services to be 100 per cent collection and disposal of solid wastes. For purposes of estimating costs, we examined expenditures classified by different categories of cities so that we can determine what is needed for 100 per cent solid waste collection efficiency in the Indian cities. This is, of course, assuming that spending levels determine solid waste collection and disposal, to some degree.

TABLE 6.2
Solid Waste Cost–Income Data

Key Indicators	Bombay	Delhi	Madras	Calcutta	Hyderabad	Bhopal
Population (million)	9.91	7.17	3.85	4.39	2.91	1.06
Solid waste (tonnes/day)	6,000	4,500	3,500	2,600	1,800	1,300
Per capita expenditure on solid waste (Rs)	79.15	85.90	60.60	46.56	37.02	38.17
Per tonne expenditure on solid waste (Rs)	429.77	367.00	185.39	158.07	105.58	222.47
Expenditure on solid waste as a % of total corporation expenditure (%)	13.46	20.16	21.99	–	10.63	24.54
Per capita revenue generation from solid waste (Rs)	2.33	0.78	0.05	1.48	27.45	0.63
Income from solid waste as a % of total corporation income (%)	0.38	0.18	0.02	0.50	–	0.44
Per tonne income from solid waste (Rs)	12.66	3.35	0.16	4.97	78.28	3.70
Expenditure on solid waste as a % of revenue from property taxes (%)	111.41	48.49	60.10	31.29	124.52	238.86

Sources: Various city corporations' budgets and authors' computations.

The solid waste efficiency in cities with million-plus population, as reported by the India Infrastructure Report (IIR) (1996), is 83 per cent. Tables 6.3–6.5 summarize the solid waste collection efficiency of various cities we study, classified by category. Clearly, the *benchmark* cities (Chandigarh and Surat) demonstrate higher solid waste collection efficiency than their *non-benchmark* counterparts in all the years of our study. The average efficiency for benchmark cities is 96 per cent, whereas for the other cities, it is only 72 per cent (Table 6.3). In general, we find that most cities spend more on O&M than on creating capital assets as far as solid waste is concerned. Clearly, the benchmark cities spend [average total (capital and O&M) per capita expenditures] more on solid waste than the other cities. Given this, the differences in solid waste collection efficiency might well be explained by finances.

TABLE 6.3
Solid Waste Collection Efficiency and Expenditures in
Benchmark and Non-benchmark Cities

Year	Benchmark Cities		Non-benchmark Cities	
	Average Capital and O&M Per Capita Expenditure (in Rs, 1993–4 = 100) (Chandigarh, Surat)	Solid Waste Collection Efficiency	Average Capital and O&M Per Capita Expenditure (in Rs, 1993–4 = 100) (Pune, Bangalore, Jaipur)	Solid Waste Collection Efficiency
1993	108.98	NA	NA	0.60
1994	91.90	NA	3.69	0.60
1995	90.51	0.98	3.69	0.65
1996	98.83	0.98	33.25	0.65
1997	46.18	0.98	29.56	0.70
1998	46.64	0.98	23.09	0.70
1999	45.72	0.98	24.94	0.70
2000	46.18	0.93	27.71	0.70
2001	46.18	0.95	52.18	0.70
2002	45.72	0.93	30.48	0.93
2003	42.49	0.97	46.64	0.93
2004	NA	0.97	NA	0.91
Average	*64.48*	*0.96*	*27.52*	*0.72*

Sources: Chandigarh Municipal Corporation; Surat Municipal Corporation; Pune Municipal Corporation; Bangalore Mahanagara Palike; Jaipur Municipal Corporation; and authors' computations.

Next, we examine differences in solid waste efficiency and per
capita expenditures between *fast-growing* and *slow-growing* cities
in terms of population growth (Table 6.4). We find that the fast-
growing cities (Surat, Jaipur and Pune) to be more efficient in their
collection of solid waste (98 per cent vis-à-vis 73 per cent for the
slow-growing cities [Chandigarh and Bangalore], over time). The
surprising finding is that the slow-growing cities, on average, spend
more per capita (Rs 78.88) on solid waste than the fast-growing ones
(that spend only Rs 24.57 on average per capita). We noted that the
slow-growing cities (primarily Chandigarh) spend more on O&M
than on capital expenditures and exhibit a higher level of collection
efficiency. A slow-growing city, Bangalore, by contrast, spent more

TABLE 6.4
Solid Waste Collection Efficiency and Expenditures in Cities
by Population Growth during 1990s

Year	Fast-growing Cities		Slow-growing Cities	
	Average Capital and O&M Per Capita Expenditure (in Rs, 1993–4 = 100) (Surat, Jaipur, Pune)	Solid Waste Collection Efficiency	Average Capital and O&M Per Capita Expenditure (in Rs, 1993–4 = 100) (Chandigarh, Bangalore)	Solid Waste Collection Efficiency
1992	NA	NA	NA	0.60
1993	NA	NA	108.98	0.60
1994	3.69	NA	91.90	0.60
1995	3.69	0.98	90.51	0.65
1996	33.25	0.98	98.83	0.65
1997	23.09	0.98	83.12	0.70
1998	17.55	0.98	87.28	0.70
1999	19.86	0.98	82.20	0.70
2000	23.09	0.98	78.04	0.79
2001	44.79	0.98	57.26	0.81
2002	29.56	0.99	47.10	0.87
2003	47.10	0.99	42.49	0.90
2004	NA	0.95	NA	0.90
Average	*24.57*	*0.98*	*78.88*	*0.73*

Sources: Chandigarh Municipal Corporation; Surat Municipal Corporation;
Pune Municipal Corporation; Bangalore Mahanagara Palike; Jaipur Municipal
Corporation; and authors' computations.

on capital expenditure, but was less efficient than Chandigarh. This implies that higher capital expenditures do not necessarily translate into increased service levels. Increased expenditures might just mean buying new trucks that are used to transport garbage, include the cost of their fuel, and salaries of the drivers, and not necessarily cleaning the existing trucks more. This explains why the seemingly higher expenditures of the slow-growing cities have not meant improved solid waste collection efficiency in those cities.

In contrast, the fast-growing cities (with higher solid waste efficiency) (such as Pune) also spend more on O&M expenditure, but they seemed to have *managed* their solid waste in a much better way. For evidence regarding this, refer to the (Surat) case study in solid waste and civic management later in this section.

When we examine solid waste in the octroi and non-octroi cities (Table 6.5), a finding of interest is that the non-octroi cities spend more on average per capita (Rs 51.81) than octroi cities, but their solid waste efficiency is only around 73 per cent. The octroi cities, on the other hand, spent much lower per capita than the non-octroi cities (Rs 36.71), but are able to ensure higher levels of solid waste efficiency (at 98 per cent). This is partly due to the fact that an octroi-levying city (Surat) has also been adjudged the 'cleanest city' in the country, and dominates the finding regarding solid waste collection efficiency in octroi cities. There, as we document later, overall, solid waste management, rather than its finances alone, is the secret behind its success.

Overall, we find that cities spend quite little on capital expenditures as they pertain to solid waste, in absolute terms. Further, even with sketchy data, we make an attempt to determine how much more expenditure is required in the cities that would ensure 100 per cent solid waste collection efficiency.

As far as a desired level of service is concerned with respect to solid waste, various committees have recommended 100 per cent collection of the generated waste, with its proper disposal. For instance, see the Report of the Third Working Group on Norms and Standards for Provision of Basic Infrastructure and Services, prepared for State Finance Commissions, 1995. To implement this 100 per cent norm, India's urban local bodies (ULBs) are guided by the directives in the Municipal Solid Waste (Management and

TABLE 6.5
Solid Waste Collection Efficiency and Expenditures in
Octroi and Non-octroi Cities

	Octroi Cities		Non-octroi Cities	
Year	Average Capital and O&M Per Capita Expenditure (in Rs, 1993–4 = 100) (Surat, Pune)	Solid Waste Collection Efficiency	Average Capital and O&M Per Capita Expenditure (in Rs, 1993–4 = 100) (Chandigarh, Bangalore, Jaipur)	Solid Waste Collection Efficiency
1992	NA	NA	NA	0.60
1993	NA	NA	108.98	0.60
1994	NA	NA	48.03	0.60
1995	NA	0.98	47.10	0.65
1996	65.11	0.98	50.34	0.65
1997	34.17	0.98	41.56	0.70
1998	25.86	0.98	43.87	0.70
1999	29.09	0.98	41.56	0.70
2000	34.64	0.98	39.25	0.79
2001	31.86	0.98	61.42	0.81
2002	36.94	0.99	36.48	0.87
2003	36.02	0.99	51.26	0.90
2004	NA	0.99	NA	0.89
Average	*36.71*	*0.98*	*51.81*	*0.73*

Sources: Chandigarh Municipal Corporation; Surat Municipal Corporation; Pune Municipal Corporation; Bangalore Mahanagara Palike; Jaipur Municipal Corporation; and authors' computations.

Handling) Rules 2000, issued by the MoEF, Government of India. These directives are as follows (see Asnani, 2006):

1. Prohibition of littering on the streets by ensuring storage of waste at source in two bins (one for biodegradable waste and another for recyclable material)
2. Primary collection of biodegradable and non-biodegradable waste from the doorstep at pre-informed timings on a day-to-day basis
3. Street sweeping covering all residential and commercial areas on all days
4. Replacement of open waste storage containers with closed ones

5. Transportation of waste in covered vehicles on a day-to-day basis
6. Treatment of biodegradable waste
7. Minimization the waste going to the landfill

In addition to the above, some existing studies also indicate the amount of financial resources required for effective solid waste management in cities of various sizes, to attain the status of a 'clean city'. The costs estimated by Asnani (2006) for vehicles, tools, equipment, and composting for cities of various sizes are summarized in Table 6.6.

TABLE 6.6
Estimates of the Cost of Solid Waste Management by City Size

City population (in Million)	Cost of Vehicles, Equipment (in Rs Lakh)	Cost of Composting (in Rs Lakh)	Total (in Rs Lakh)	Total (in $ at $1 = Rs 46.18)
<0.1	50.97	20	70.97	$ 153,681.25
0.1 to < 0.5	295	150	445	$ 963,620.61
0.5 to <1.0	511	500	1011	$ 2,189,259.42
>2.0	948	1000	1948	$ 4,218,276.31

Source: Asnani (2006).

All cities for which expenditures are reported in this chapter (except Chandigarh) are in the greater than 2 million population category. Based on Asnani (2006)'s estimates, the total cost of solid waste management (SWM) in a million-plus city should be Rs 194.8 million. At their respective populations we projected for 2005 for these five cities, the per capita total cost of SWM in Bangalore, Jaipur, Pune, and Surat, turn out to be Rs 191.65, Rs 69.73, Rs 63.27, and Rs 66.04, respectively. Compared with these cities' actual spending of Rs 25.40, Rs 16.62, Rs 54.49, and Rs 12.47, respectively, on SWM, spending in all cities (except Pune) is highly inadequate.

On the basis of the estimates in Table 6.6, for Chandigarh (which is in the population category 0.5–1 million) the total cost of SWM should be approximately Rs 101,100,000. This translates to a per capita cost of Rs 104.04 for 2005, using the population projection we arrive at for Chandigarh (971,724). We find Chandigarh's annual average spending during 1993–4 to 2003–4, like other cities, has been less than the required Rs 104, at Rs 85.43.

A report by the All India Institute of Local Self-Government (2004) estimates the capital costs of collection and transportation for Pune. Assuming that these estimates are for the most recent year, the minimum total cost (of collection, transportation, and processing) for Pune appears to be around Rs 210,839,115 (73,100,000 [lowest cost model, Table 6.7] + 137,739,115 [Table 6.8]). In per capita terms, this turns out to be Rs 68.48. Note the similarity of this estimate with what is arrived at, based on the IIR (2006) above (which is Rs 63.27). Comparison of this required expenditure with Pune's average annual per capita expenditure on solid waste (which is Rs 54.49) shows that the city needs to increase its spending by roughly Rs 13.85 per capita (at its current population); this turns out to be a total of Rs 42,656,756.

SOLID WASTE MANAGEMENT IN SURAT

As in the case of the balance of payments which triggered economic reforms in India, in the case of Surat, it was a crisis in the form of the plague that acted as the catalyst of urban and civic management in the city. A case study of the Urban Management Program of the UN Habitat by Swamy et al. (2000) summarizes Surat's experience

TABLE 6.7
Total Cost of Collection and Transportation for Pune

Model Assumption	Capital cost (in Rs)	Per tonne cost (in Rs)
Model 1: Combination of tricycle and tractor trailer	146,405,000	599.43
Model 2: Combination of tricycle and tractor container carrier	131,238,333	584.58
Model 3: Auto rickshaw	157,500,000	960.87
Model 4: Combination of auto rickshaw and refuse compactor	187,477,650	411.53
Model 5: Tricycle	73,100,000	721.46
Model 6: Combination of auto rickshaw and tractor container carrier	88,959,533	325.77

Source: 'Action Plan for Implementation of MSW Rules 2000 in Maharashtra', 2004, All India Institute of Local Self-Government.

TABLE 6.8
Consolidated Cost of Processing and Sanitary Landfilling Activity for Pune
(in Rs)

Waste	Capital Cost	Annualized Capital Cost	Operation and Maintenance	Manpower Cost	Total Annual Cost	Per Tonne Cost Waste Processing Cost
1000 tonnes	137,739,115	27,426,247	36,564,793	9,269,249	73,760,289	171.39

Source: 'Action Plan for Implementation of MSW Rules 2000 in Maharashtra', 2004, All India Institute of Local Self-Government.

and management of the city, transforming it from the plague to one of the cleanest cities of the country. Soon after the outbreak of the plague in 1994, a massive cleanup operation was launched by the Surat Municipal Corporation in early 1995, followed by administrative reforms. These reforms consisted of sub-dividing the pre-existing six zones in the city into fifty-two sub-zones making sanitary inspectors responsible for each of them. Further, a system of strict enforcement and monitoring ensured that the checks were in place. For instance, a system of fines for littering public places was instituted. Finally, contracting was introduced to improve the waste collection efficiency and street cleaning.

On average, based on the data we obtained from the Surat Municipal Corporation, during the period 1997–2004, Surat spent a total (including both capital as well as revenue expenditures) of only about Rs 12.61 on solid waste per capita (in constant terms, with 1993–4 = 100). On the other hand, other cities we studied (excluding Surat) spent an average of Rs 45.26 on solid waste over 1993–4 to 2003–4 (total capital and O&M, in constant terms, with 1993–4 = 100). So we find that the size of the actual spending on solid waste (per capita terms) even in benchmark cities like Surat is several times less than what is actually required.

Based on this, we conclude that the estimates presented above are plausible in the context of the tasks required as part of solid waste management. However, in addition to the financial resources a city has to spend in order to get rid of all garbage on its roads, it is important to practice initiatives in financial innovation and urban reform, as much as spending adequately, to attain the status of 'clean cities'.

NOTE

1. The findings reported in the various tables in this chapter, as with those in Chapter 4, are all based on our primary data gathered from the cities and budget documents. Where secondary sources such as the Census or others have been used, they are indicated.

CHAPTER 7

Other Urban Services
Patterns in Expenditure

In this chapter, we study the provision of sewerage, street lights, and municipal roads. We study the physical levels of these services, and the actual expenditures incurred by cities on these services wherever the data were available. Then we compare the actual expenditures incurred by the cities, to estimates generally considered to be norms for providing these services. As in the case of other services, we study these patterns of expenditures and physical level of services by various categories of cities. We start the next section with sewerage. While sewerage services are necessary to be studied, we agree that its treatment in this chapter is rather limited due to data limitations.

SEWERAGE

A sewerage system implies the network of mains and branches of underground pipes for carrying waste water (sewerage) to the point of disposal. Sewers that carry only household and industrial wastage are called separate sewers; those that carry storm water from roofs, streets, and other surfaces are known as storm water drains, while those carrying both sewage and storm water are called combined sewers. To put this in perspective, Chandigarh has a system of underground covered drains. Towns which are not provided with such underground sewerage systems normally have open surface drains, box drains, or drains of other patterns.

Table 7.1 summarizes data from the Census of India 2001 regarding the existence of drainage facility across rural and urban areas of the country. Only one-third of India's urban areas have a closed drainage system (similar to that of Chandigarh), less than half have access to an open drainage system, and nearly one-fourth of urban households do not have access to a drainage system at all. The situation is even worse in the rural areas of the country.

TABLE 7.1
Type of Drainage Connectivity for Waste Water
Outlet in India's Urban and Rural Areas

Drainage Type	Total Households	%	Rural Households	%	Urban Households	%
Closed drainage	23,925,761	12.5	5,402,679	3.9	18,523,082	34.5
Open drainage	65,142,354	33.9	41,857,772	30.3	23,284,582	43.4
No drainage	102,895,820	53.6	91,011,108	65.8	11,884,712	22.1
Total	*191,963,935*	*100*	*138,271,559*	*100*	*53,692,376*	*100*

Source: Census of India 2001.

In the case of cities covered in this chapter, in Bangalore, Lucknow, and Jaipur, both underground sewers and open surface drains co-existed according to the 1991 Census of India (see Table 7.2). Pune and Chandigarh had only underground sewer systems (all in their municipal corporation limits), no open surface drains, based on 1991 data. As of 1991, Surat was the only one using cess

TABLE 7.2
Sewerage Systems in Cities, 1991*

Name of the Town	Two Most Prevalent Systems of Sewerage						
	Sewer	Open Surface Drains	Box Surface Drains	Sylk Drains	Cess Pool Method	Pit System	Others
Bangalore	√	√	–	–	–	–	–
Chandigarh	√	–	–	–	–	–	–
Jaipur	√	√	–	–	–	–	–
Lucknow	√	√	–	–	–	–	–
Pune	√	–	–	–	–	–	–
Surat	√	–	–	–	√	–	–

Source: Census of India 1991, Town Directory.
Note: * By 2001, all cities had a sewer network in place, along with other systems (such as open surface and block surface drains and soak pits in the case of Bangalore, open surface drains in the case of Lucknow, and open surface drain and soak pits in the case of Jaipur).

pools, apart from underground sewers. As per Census 2001, all these cities have underground sewer networks.

In Surat, as of 2005, out of the total city area of 112.27 sq. km, 90.54 per cent area and 94.68 per cent of the present population had been covered with sewerage systems (http://www.suratmunicipal. org). Surat Municipal Corporation has prepared a master plan for comprehensive sewerage system (planning for more than 500 km of sewers and six sewage treatment works) to serve not only the domestic and commercial but also the industrial developments for the year 2021.

Tables 7.3–7.5 show, wherever they were available, expenditure on sewerage by category, collected and summarized from our primary data. Surprisingly, there are no significant differences in per capita expenditures on sewerage across benchmark and non-benchmark cities (Table 7.3) or BIMARU and non-BIMARU cities, over time

TABLE 7.3
Per Capita Expenditure on Sewerage across
Benchmark and Non-benchmark Cities

Year	Average Capital and O&M Per Capita Expenditure (in Rs, 1993–4 = 100) in Benchmark Cities (Chandigarh and Surat)	Average Capital and O&M Per Capita Expenditure (in Rs, 1993–4 = 100) in Non-benchmark Cities (Pune, Lucknow, and Bangalore)
1991	35.10	36.02
1992	26.32	23.55
1993	28.17	19.40
1994	41.10	124.22
1995	62.34	134.38
1996	55.42	37.41
1997	48.03	78.04
1998	71.58	42.02
1999	88.20	39.71
2000	101.13	24.94
2001	92.36	47.10
2002	65.58	59.57
2003	38.79	93.75
Average	*58.01*	*58.47*

Sources: Chandigarh Municipal Corporation; Surat Municipal Corporation; Pune Municipal Corporation; Bangalore Water Supply and Sewerage Board; Lucknow Jal Sansthan; and authors' computations.

(Table 7.4). Nevertheless, the comparisons between benchmark and non-benchmark cities are relevant because Chandigarh (which has been designated as a benchmark city) has a system of closed, underground drainage network. Expenditures on this network need to be compared with those in other cities. Distinctions are necessary to be made between BIMARU and non-BIMARU set of cities since the BIMARU cities are traditionally known to have low spending and low budgetary deficits, given their lack of adequate spending on even essential services.

The only significant differences in terms of per capita spending on sewerage are across octroi and non-octroi cities (Table 7.5). We find, consistent with our expectation, that the octroi cities (Surat and Pune) spend significantly more per capita on sewerage than their non-octroi counterparts. With its spending, Surat has been

TABLE 7.4
Per Capita Expenditure on Sewerage across
BIMARU and Non-BIMARU Cities

Year	Average Capital and O&M Per Capita Expenditure (in Rs, 1993–4 = 100) in BIMARU Cities (Lucknow)	Average Capital and O&M Per Capita Expenditure (in Rs, 1993–4 = 100) in non-BIMARU cities (Surat, Chandigarh, Pune, and Bangalore)
1991	NA	35.56
1992	NA	24.48
1993	NA	22.63
1994	NA	96.52
1995	NA	110.37
1996	NA	43.41
1997	NA	63.27
1998	NA	56.80
1999	NA	72.04
2000	19.86	81.74
2001	48.03	81.28
2002	78.04	61.42
2003	108.98	55.42
Average	*63.73*	*61.92*

Sources: Chandigarh Municipal Corporation; Surat Municipal Corporation; Pune Municipal Corporation; Bangalore Water Supply and Sewerage Board; Lucknow Jal Sansthan; and authors' computations.

able to cover most of the city with a sewerage network. Based on our computations, we find that with its expenditure on sewerage, Pune has also been able to cover roughly 72 per cent of its land area with sewerage connections (as of 2003–4), more recently over 90 per cent of the population being estimated to be covered. Unfortunately, except for Chandigarh, we did not have information on other non-octroi cities' coverage of their sewerage networks. With its average spending of only Rs 9.70 per capita during 2000–3, Chandigarh has been able to ensure a sewerage connection for every eight people (Table 7.6). There is no question that its union territory status has contributed in no mean degree to its expenditure (Chandigarh became a municipal corporation only in 1994),[1] but this shows that finances of cities matter for provision of services.

Figure 7.1 shows the trend in total (capital and O&M) expenditures of the cities (for which the data were available) over time. Even

TABLE 7.5
Per Capita Expenditure on Sewerage across
Octroi and Non-octroi Cities

Year	Average Capital and O&M Per Capita Expenditure (in Rs, 1993–4 = 100) in Octroi Cities (Surat and Pune)	Average Capital and O&M Per Capita Expenditure (in Rs, 1993–4 = 100) in Non-octroi cities (Lucknow, Chandigarh, and Bangalore)
1991	35.56	NA
1992	30.94	11.55
1993	30.02	6.93
1994	128.38	32.33
1995	159.78	11.08
1996	58.65	12.47
1997	115.45	10.62
1998	96.98	16.16
1999	97.90	20.32
2000	119.61	12.93
2001	118.68	26.78
2002	83.59	48.03
2003	76.66	60.96
Average	*88.63*	*22.51*

Sources: Chandigarh Municipal Corporation; Surat Municipal Corporation; Pune Municipal Corporation; Bangalore Water Supply and Sewerage Board; Lucknow Jal Sansthan; and authors' computations.

TABLE 7.6
Population Coverage of Sewerage Network, Chandigarh

Year	Per Capita Expenditure (in Constant Terms (1993–4 = 100))	Population (Number) Covered by each Connection
2000–1	6.00	7.64
2001–2	6.00	7.94
2002–3	17.55	8.25
Average	*9.85*	*7.94*

Source: Chandigarh Municipal Corporation.

in absolute terms, Surat and Pune are the highest spenders, both of which are octroi-levying cities. And, both these cities appear to have a fairly well-covered sewerage network as observed above. So it does seem that the solution to many the problems faced by Indian cities regarding sewerage is lack of adequate spending. Even a high-water spender such as Bangalore has not invested much in the city's sewer networks. In the interests of comparing the actual expenditure of cities in the study with some requirements and benchmarks, we drew upon a few studies in the IIR (2006).

Zérah (2006) summarizes the requirements of incremental investment in sewerage as being between Rs 91.2 billion corresponding to a low urban population projection and Rs 165 billion for a high urban population projection scenario, over 2001–11, at 1995 prices. This assumes for large cities, full coverage by sewage with treatment; for medium towns, public sewers with partial coverage by septic tanks; and for small towns, low cost sanitation methods. These estimates have been summarized by Zérah (2006), based on a 1997 study by the National Institute of Urban Affairs (NIUA). Using the urban population projection of 404.17 million for 2011 for urban India (National Institute of Urban Affairs, 2000, http://www.niua.org/newniuaorg/handbookindex.htm), this incremental investment need (for the low urban population projection) translates to a per capita requirement of nearly Rs 225.82 (Rs 407.77 per capita for the high urban population projection) for the urban population's sewerage needs during the entire period 2001–11. Actual spending on sewerage infrastructure by the four cities that had information (Surat, Pune, Bangalore, and Lucknow) are quite low. On average, annually during the period 1991–2004, these cities

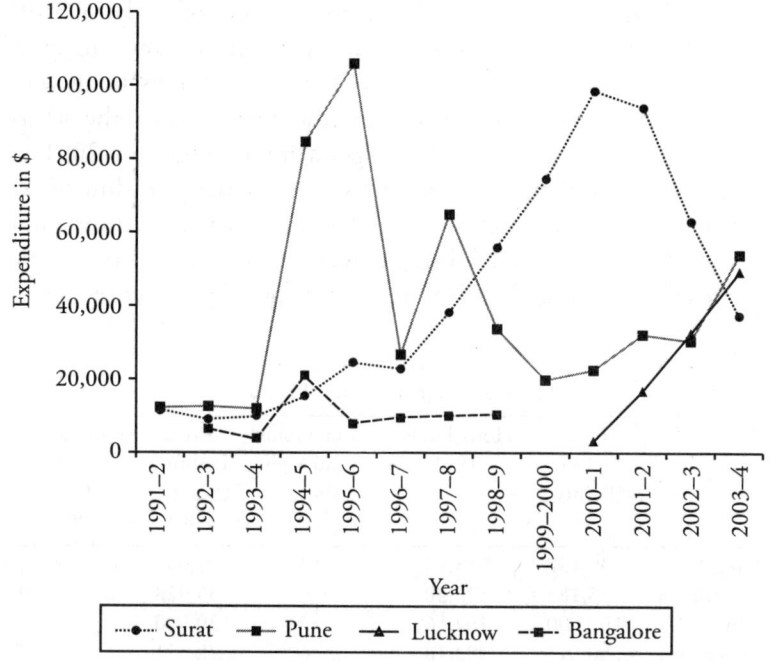

FIGURE 7.1: Capital and O&M Expenditures on Sewerage by City

Sources: Surat Muncipal Corporation; Pune Municipal Corporation; Lucknow Jal Sansthan; Bangalore Water Supply and Sewerage Board; and authors' computations.

spent about Rs 53.57 per capita (as annual average) on sewerage in constant 1995 terms. Surat was the highest spender with spending of Rs 90.05 per capita on sewerage, trailed by Pune at Rs 87.28 per capita. The high water spender Bangalore is a distant fourth in terms of spending on sewerage at only Rs 14.29 per capita. However, the physical coverage of the sewerage to the city's residents is much inadequate in all the cities, based on visual inspection during field visits, since quantitative estimates are not available. So we find the estimates given by Zérah (2006) are conservative, and there is no question that as far as sewerage is concerned, municipal finances are the core of the problem.

STREET LIGHTS

The Census of India's 1991 and 2001 town directories contain information regarding the number of road lighting points by city.

Table 7.7 summarizes these data for the six cities of study for 1991 and 2001. Table 7.7 shows that Jaipur, Chandigarh, and Lucknow provided the best coverage in terms of coverage of households with their road lighting points, whereas Pune and Surat trailed the others in 1991. The same pattern holds good interestingly for 2001 as well, except that Bangalore joins the league of cities providing better coverage with street lights. Note that the town directories summarize data on the road lighting points, that is, number of electric connections existing for street lights, not street lights per se.

TABLE 7.7
Road Lighting Points by City, 1991 and 2001

Town	Road Lighting (Points), 1991	Households, 1991	Households/ Road Light Point, 1991	Road Lighting (Points), 2001	Households/ Road Light Point, 2001
Bangalore	39,487	515,138	13	191,009	5
Chandigarh	23,184	128,306	6	35,928	5
Jaipur	107,000	262,560	2	130,000	3
Lucknow	50,513	283,188	6	72,351	5
Pune	18,125	316,347	17	59,001	9
Surat	10,389	279,907	27	31,022	18
Average	*41,450*	*297,574*	*12*	*86,552*	*8*

Source: Census of India 1991 and 2001 Town Directories.

While even the IIR 2006 is characterized by the conspicuous absence of any discussion on street lights, we make an attempt in this study to examine the efficacy of expenditures on street lights in the chosen cities.

In order to develop a measure for street lights based on the primary data we collect, we attempted to capture the number of households (or housing units) covered by *new* street lights installed every year or the *total* number of street lights existing in a city in a given year.[2] For purposes of developing this measure of the service, we obtained data on population and households. Population and household data were readily available from the Census of India for 1991 and 2001. Since household data, as with population data, were unavailable for the non-census, intervening years, to get this for all years, we took the ratio of households to population for 1991 and 2001, using the respective year's census data. This provided information on the approximate number of persons per household for 1991 and 2001. We assumed that a similar trend regarding household size continued during 1992–2000. Making this assumption, we adjusted the projected population (described in an earlier section) for all intervening years, by the 1991 household–population ratio. This way, we arrived at estimates of the number of households for every non-census year. For post-2001 years, we made a similar assumption about household size remaining constant since 2001, and estimated the number of households for all years during 2001–5.

Next, for purposes of understanding how many households are covered by a street light, we divided the number of households per year by the total number of street lights every year for cities in the study. So we study the total number of households covered by total number of street lights existing in the city (with the exception of Pune and Bangalore, where only data on the number of *new* street lights constructed every year were available).

Tables 7.8–7.10 summarize the per capita expenditures (capital and O&M) and service levels as defined above for cities classified by various types, based on the data we obtained from the cities. As with the other services, Table 7.8 shows that while average per capita expenditures on street lights are higher in the benchmark cities (Rs 21.70) than in the non-benchmark ones (Rs 12.93), the household coverage of street lights is remarkably better in the non-benchmark cities than in the benchmark cities. For instance, in the benchmark cities (Chandigarh and Surat), there is a street light for every twelve households, but in the other cities, there is one street light for every four households. Table 7.9 is quite revealing because it shows that higher per capita expenditures do not always translate into better service levels. To corroborate this further, we find that in one of our benchmark cities, Surat, over half of its expenditure over the years is on O&M expenditures, hence household coverage by street lights is smaller compared with the other cities. Further, in both the benchmark cities, despite their higher expenditures (higher capital expenditures in the case of Chandigarh), installation of street lights has not kept pace with the growth in the number of households, whereas our non-benchmark cities such as Lucknow

TABLE 7.8

Per Capita Expenditure on Street Lights and Service Levels across
Benchmark and Non-benchmark Cities

Year	Benchmark Cities (C, S)		Non-benchmark Cities (L, J)	
	Average Capital and O&M Per Capita Expenditure (in Rs, 1993–4 = 100)	Households/ Street Light	Average Capital and O&M Per Capita Expenditure (in Rs, 1993–4 = 100)	Households/ Street Light
1996	30.48	15.21	11.08	NA
1997	26.78	14.51	12.47	NA
1998	25.86	14.18	12.93	NA
1999	30.02	12.38	13.85	NA
2000	26.78	11.84	6.47	5
2001	16.62	12.77	11.55	5.02
2002	16.16	11.58	30.48	4.93
2003	20.78	10.76	16.62	4.5
2004	0	11.19	18.47	4.53
Average	*21.50*	*12.71*	*14.88*	*4.8*

Sources: Chandigarh Municipal Corporation; Surat Municipal Corporation; Lucknow Municipal Corporation; Jaipur Municipal Corporation; and authors' computations.

and Jaipur have done a much better job there. Since street lights are considered a proxy for safety, expenditures on this service throw light on the extent of crime in these cities as well.

When we examine expenditure on street lights by other categories of cities, the octroi and fast-growing cities are the highest spenders (although still very low in per capita terms) on street lights (Tables 7.9 and 7.10). On average, octroi cities spend about Rs 29.25 and the fast-growing cities spend about Rs 24.22, compared with Rs 13.58 in the non-octroi cities and Rs 6.47 in the slow-growing cities, respectively. These are per capita expenditures, so it is clear how much the cities are spending on this service. In terms of coverage, the non-octroi cities are better because they are able to ensure a street light for every five households whereas the octroi cities (only data on Surat were comparable with that of other non-octroi cities) provide one only for every fourteen households. Surprisingly again, the slow-growing cities, with their lower average spending, provide a street light for every five households whereas the high spending fast-growing ones are able to afford a light only for every thirteen households (Table 7.10).

Thus in the case of street lights, we fail to find a one-to-one relationship between spending and level of the service. It does appear that better spending cities are unable to ensure greater coverage of households with lights, and end up spending only on O&M of existing ones. Even when they spend on capital projects, they are unable to keep pace with population growth.

A study by PricewaterhouseCoopers (2001) updates the expenditure norms of the Zakaria Committee report for Chhattisgarh for various urban services. It estimates the per capita norm for street lights in towns with greater than 2,000,000 population to be Rs 59.26 per annum (at 2000–1 prices). While this study is only for

TABLE 7.9
Per Capita Expenditure on Street Lights and Service
Levels across Octroi and Non-octroi Cities

Year	Octroi Cities (Surat)		Non-octroi Cities (C, L, J)	
	Average Capital and O&M Per Capita Expenditure (in Rs, 1993–4 = 100)	Households/ Street Light	Average Capital and O&M Per Capita Expenditure (in Rs, 1993–4 = 100)	Households/ Street Light
1991	NA	18.18	NA	NA
1992	NA	17.56	NA	NA
1993	NA	17.43	NA	NA
1994	NA	17.71	NA	NA
1995	NA	17.34	18.01	NA
1996	30.48	15.21	11.08	NA
1997	26.78	14.51	12.47	NA
1998	25.86	14.18	12.93	NA
1999	50.80	12.38	13.85	NA
2000	47.10	11.84	7.39	5
2001	24.94	12.77	9.70	5.02
2002	26.32	11.58	23.09	4.93
2003	30.94	10.76	12.93	4.5
2004	0	10.66	14.32	6.93
Average	*29.25*	*14.44*	*13.58*	*5.28*

Sources: Chandigarh Municipal Corporation; Surat Municipal Corporation; Lucknow Municipal Corporation; Jaipur Municipal Corporation; and authors' computations.

TABLE 7.10

Per Capita Expenditure on Street Lights and Service
Levels across Cities by Population Growth

Year	Fast-growing Cities (Surat, Jaipur)		Slow-growing Cities (C, L)	
	Average Capital and O&M Per Capita Expenditure (in Rs, 1993–4 = 100)	Households/ Street Light	Average Capital and O&M Per Capita Expenditure (in Rs, 1993–4 = 100)	Households/ Street Light
1991	NA	18.18	NA	NA
1992	NA	17.56	NA	NA
1993	NA	17.43	NA	NA
1994	20.32	17.71	NA	NA
1995	10.16	17.34	NA	NA
1996	11.08	15.21	3.69	NA
1997	25.86	14.51	4.16	NA
1998	24.01	14.18	3.69	NA
1999	21.70	12.38	10.62	NA
2000	29.09	11.84	7.39	5
2001	32.79	8.79	5.54	5.22
2002	40.18	8.09	6.47	5.25
2003	26.32	7.72	6.47	4.33
2004	24.94	7.77	10.16	7.95
Average	*24.22*	*13.48*	*6.47*	*5.55*

Sources: Chandigarh Municipal Corporation; Surat Municipal Corporation; Lucknow Municipal Corporation; Jaipur Municipal Corporation; and authors' computations.

cities in the state of Chhattisgarh, and we do not have any from the state chosen in this study, we use this study's estimates in the absence of better benchmarks. In contrast to this benchmark estimate of Rs 59.26 as the per capita annual required spending on street lights, we find cities in our study, on average, spent an average of only Rs 16.62 per capita (annual average) during 1994–2003, in constant 1993–4 prices. This is three and a half times lower than even the conservative estimates summarized by the Pricewater-houseCoopers study.

The IIR (1996) points out the standard (physical) norm for street lights in terms of distance between two lamp posts as being 30 m. In our study, we were able to get information on physical norms only for Chandigarh. Here international norms are used for street lighting. The average distance between poles used for different types of roads is 27.67 m, exceeding the standard norms summarized by the IIR (1996). The per capita total (annual) expenditure to exceed the standard norms has been only Rs 7.85 in Chandigarh Municipal Corporation during 1999–2004, much lower than the average of all cities. While the physical norm based on distances between the lamp posts has been exceeded in Chandigarh, the city's performance is unsatisfactory based on the measure we have developed—household coverage with street lights. With its expenditure, Chandigarh has been able to cover every eleven households with a street light, but has been unable to keep pace with a growing population. As summarized above, other cities such as Lucknow and Jaipur have ensured much better coverage of households with street lights with their per capita expenditure of Rs 5.54 and Rs 22.17, respectively.

This is a source of concern since the cities that cannot afford to spend cannot provide safety to their public. Hence they also cannot compete to attract residents or firms.

SANITATION

Next we turn our attention to public sanitation. While solid waste refers to street cleaning, public sanitation refers to toilet facilities. Table 7.11 summarizes sanitation data for all South Asian countries, including India, based on data reported by Water and Sanitation Program (South Asia). It shows that sanitation coverage in India leaves much to be desired when compared with countries such as Sri Lanka, Pakistan, Maldives, and even Bangladesh.

Table 7.12 summarizes data from the Census of India 2001 on the type of sanitation facility rural and urban households have access to. While majority (70 per cent) of urban households have access to a bathroom facility within the house, less than half of the urban households have water closets. One-fourth of urban households do not have access to latrine within the house.

Motivated by the census data, we examined cities' expenditure on sanitation. With a view to studying how to make cities open-defecation free, we would have liked to study construction of new sanitation facilities by year for every city. However the physical measure of sanitation we had, the number of new public toilets constructed every year, was not reliable.[3] A caveat is also that private

TABLE 7.11
Access to Sanitation in South Asian Countries

Country	Year	Population Total	Population % Urban	Sanitation Coverage (%) Total	Sanitation Coverage (%) Urban
Afghanistan	1990	13,799,000	18	NA	NA
	2002	22,930,000	23	8	16
Bangladesh	1990	109,402,000	20	23	71
	2002	143,809,000	24	48	75
Bhutan	1990	1,696,000	5	NA	NA
	2002	2,190,000	8	70	65
India	1990	846,418,000	26	12	43
	2002	1,049,549,000	28	30	58
Iran (Islamic	1990	56,703,000	56	83	86
Republic of)	2002	68,070,000	66	84	86
Maldives	1990	216,000	26	NA	100
	2002	309,000	28	58	100
Nepal	1990	18,625,000	9	12	62
	2002	24,609,000	15	27	68
Pakistan	1990	110,901,000	31	38	81
	2002	149,911,000	34	54	92
Sri Lanka	1990	16,830,000	21	70	89
	2002	18,910,000	21	91	98

Source: WHO-UNICEF, Joint Monitoring Programme, retrieved from the Water and Sanitation Program's website http://www.wsp.org/, last accessed 22 May 2006.

TABLE 7.12
Sanitation and Type in Rural and Urban India

Sanitation Access and Type	Total Households	%	Rural Households	%	Urban Households	%
Number of households having bathroom facility within the house	69,371,158	36.1	31,569,044	22.8	37,802,114	70.4
Type of latrine within house						
Pit latrine	22,076,486	11.5	14,236,297	10.3	7,840,189	14.6
Water closet	34,598,446	18	9,837,054	7.1	24,761,392	46.1
Other latrine	13,210,867	6.9	6,231,008	4.5	6,979,859	13
No latrine	122,078,136	63.6	107,967,200	78.1	14,110,936	26.3
Total	*191,963,935*	*100*	*138,271,559*	*100*	*53,692,376*	*100*

Source: Census of India 2001.

toilet facilities are not taken into account here. So we were able to compare only cities' expenditures on sanitation.

Tables 7.13–7.15 summarize the per capita expenditures on new public toilets constructed by year and by type of city. When we compare the benchmark with the non-benchmark cities (Table 7.13), the average per capita expenditure on new public toilets is much higher (Rs 103.15) in the benchmark cities when compared to our non-benchmark cities (Rs 18.29). This is according to our expectation, since Surat, with its major focus on and innovations regarding sanitation following the plague, has been included as a benchmark city. We do also confess that its not just spending, but management that is important in provision of the service.

As Table 7.14 summarizes, the non-BIMARU cities spend higher (Rs 88.53 per capita) than their BIMARU counterparts (Rs 0.88) on sanitation, consistent with our expectation. The amount of spending on such a basic service by BIMARU cities is abysmally

TABLE 7.13
Per Capita Expenditure on Public Toilets,
Benchmark and Non-benchmark Cities

Year	Average Per Capita Capital and O&M Expenditure (in Rs, 1993–4 = 100), Benchmark Cities	Average Per Capita Capital and O&M Expenditure (in Rs, 1993–4 = 100) Non-benchmark Cities
1994	102.06	NA
1995	111.76	NA
1996	70.66	NA
1997	66.50	NA
1998	139.46	NA
1999	132.07	NA
2000	131.15	19.86
2001	126.53	14.78
2002	128.84	30.94
2003	125.61	25.86
2004	0	0
Average	*103.15*	*18.29*

Sources: Chandigarh Municipal Corporation; Surat Municipal Corporation; Lucknow Municipal Corporation; Jaipur Municipal Corporation; Bangalore Mahanagara Palike; Pune Municipal Corporation; and authors' computations.

TABLE 7.14
Per Capita Expenditure on Public Toilets,
BIMARU and Non-BIMARU Cities

Year	Average Per Capita Capital and O&M Expenditure (in Rs, 1993–4 = 100), BIMARU Cities	Average Per Capita Capital and O&M Expenditure (in Rs, 1993–4 = 100) Non-BIMARU Cities
1994	2.77	102.06
1995	0.92	111.76
1996	1.39	70.66
1997	0.46	66.50
1998	0.46	139.46
1999	0.46	132.07
2000	0.46	79.89
2001	0.92	54.49
2002	0.46	67.88
2003	0.46	60.50
2004	NA	NA
Average	*0.88*	*88.53*

Sources: Chandigarh Municipal Corporation; Surat Municipal Corporation; Lucknow Municipal Corporation; Jaipur Municipal Corporation; Bangalore Mahanagara Palike; Pune Municipal Corporation; and authors' computations.

low. It should be noted that even at the state level, BIMARU states are often known to be states with low budgetary deficit. This is not because their revenues are high, but because they do not spend enough on basic services, hence their deficits are also low. The local level picture is quite consistent with that of the state.

The non-octroi cities spend higher in per capita terms (Rs 110.19) than the octroi cities (Rs 11.20) which is surprising (Table 7.15). One would expect the low level of spending in octroi cities to also translate into a very poor level of service there relative to the non-octroi cities. Unfortunately we did not have data on physical services to confirm this.

It is possible that access to both *private and public* toilets is a much better measure of what we are trying to represent here. That is, what causes a city to be open-defecation free? However, apart from the Census, there is no micro-level data on sanitation facilities. The Census town directory of 1991 and 2001 summarize

TABLE 7.15
Per Capita Expenditure on Public Toilets, Octroi and Non-octroi Cities

Year	Average Per Capita Capital and O&M Expenditure (in Rs, 1993–4 = 100), Octroi Cities	Average Per Capita Capital and O&M Expenditure (in Rs, 1993–4 = 100) Non-octroi Cities
1994	NA	103.91
1995	NA	109.91
1996	5.54	132.07
1997	6.93	119.14
1998	3.69	137.62
1999	1.85	131.61
2000	28.63	129.30
2001	22.17	65.11
2002	12.93	89.59
2003	7.85	83.59
2004	NA	NA
Average	*11.20*	*110.19*

Sources: Chandigarh Municipal Corporation; Surat Municipal Corporation; Lucknow Municipal Corporation; Jaipur Municipal Corporation; Bangalore Mahanagara Palike; Pune Municipal Corporation; and authors' computations.

data on both public and private toilets for cities. Table 7.16 and Table 7.17, respectively, display this for the selected cities of the study for 1991 and 2001. On the basis of this, it does appear that sanitation access and coverage are much better in Pune, Surat, and Bangalore (along with Jaipur in 2001) than in the other cities. By far, the worst provider of sanitation is Lucknow in both 1991 and 2001, which is broadly consistent with what we observed during our field visits.

Table 7.18 tabulates and summarizes from the Census of India (which may be derived from Table 7.16 as well). In 1991, the octroi, fast-growing, benchmark and non-BIMARU cities, respectively, have a toilet for every ten, fourteen, and twelve (each in the benchmark and non-BIMARU cities) persons, and perform better than their counterparts in terms of their coverage of population. In 2001, we found that the octroi cities, fast-growing, and non-BIMARU cities offer the best sanitation facilities (at seven persons per toilet). We find that the total number of toilets (public and

TABLE 7.16
Summary of Sanitation Facilities for Selected Cities, 1991

Town	Pop., 1991	Water Borne	Service	Others	All Latrines	Pop./ Latrine
Bangalore	3,302,296	223,227	–	–	223,227	15
Chandigarh	510,565	NA	NA	NA	NA	NA
Jaipur	1,458,483	60,000	9,000	275	69,275	21
Lucknow	1,619,115	25,502	32,300	–	57,802	28
Pune	1,566,651	200,000	2,500	4000	206,500	8
Surat	1,505,872	122,832	–	–	122,832	12
Average	*1,660,497*	*126,312*	*14,600*	*2138*	*113,273*	*17*

Source: Census of India 1991 Town Directory.

TABLE 7.17
Summary of Sanitation Facilities for Selected Cities, 2001

Town	Water	Service Borne	Others	All Latrines	Pop./ Latrine
Bangalore	680,282	NA	8,900	689,182	6
Chandigarh	NA	NA	NA	0	NA
Jaipur	260,995	0	62,100	323,095	7
Lucknow	155,020	29,120	NA	184,140	12
Pune	352,635	0	4,200	356,835	7
Surat	345,500	NA	NA	345,500	8
Average	*299,072*	*7,280*	*15,040*	*316,459*	*8*

Source: Census of India 2001 Town Directory.

TABLE 7.18
Public and Private Toilets per Person by
Type of City, 1991 and 2001

Type of City	Average Persons/ Toilet, 1991	Average Persons/ Toilet, 2001
Benchmark cities	12	8
Non-benchmark cities	18	8
Cities with octroi	10	7
Non-octroi cities	21	8
Fast-growing cities	14	7
Slow-growing cities	21	9
BIMARU cities	25	10
Non-BIMARU cities	12	7

Source: Tabulated from the Census of India 1991 and 2001 Town Directories.

private) is a good measure of what takes a city to be open-defecation free (which is what the Census town directories measure). Hence, based on data on the total (public and private) number of toilets and the cities' spending record, it does seem that lack of adequate spending might be the core of the issue here.[4]

Zérah (2006) summarizes data on the per capita expenditure on sanitation from the Mumbai Metropolitan Regional Development Authority (MMRDA). These data show that the Mumbai Municipal Corporation spends Rs 54 per capita on sanitation, higher than the average of all cities and time periods taken into account here in this study (roughly Rs 36.94). As this study by Zérah (2006) summarizes, the average spending on sanitation by all municipal corporations and councils in the Mumbai urban agglomeration was much less than that incurred by cities of this study, at Rs 11.05 as of 1999.

The III Working Group for the State Finance Commission on developing norms for various services summarizes past studies with regard to these services. For sanitation/sewerage, an ORG (1989) study calculates the cost of providing sanitation/sewerage at Rs 587 per capita in metro centres (those with population of greater than a million).[5]

In cities with population between 100,000 and 1 million (Chandigarh's size), this study estimates this cost to be Rs 604. Further, the IIR (1996) summarizes that to provide 100 per cent sanitation coverage by the end of the Eighth Plan (i.e., until 1997) itself required an investment of Rs 202.60 billion at 1995 current prices. In per capita terms, using the NIUA's population projection of 255 million for 1996, this investment requirement translates to Rs 785.

Comparing these investment requirements with the actual spending on sanitation by these cities (Rs 36.94 per capita, summarized above), is only 6 per cent of the recommended standard by the III Working Group (ORG study) and only 5 per cent of the 1995 report's recommendation. Even the 1996 expert group report points out that the Eighth Plan provided for a meagre Rs 57.57 billion for urban water supply and sanitation combined together. So we find lack of adequate spending is the problem.

ROADS

As promised, next, we move our attention to roads. While there are various kinds of roads, we consider and study only municipal roads. The IIR 2006 makes an attempt to project travel demand for different categories of cities. Agarwal (2006) in the IIR 2006 summarizes travel demand projected by Rail India Technical and Economic Services (RITES). This study points out that although the population in class A cities (with population between 100,000 and 250,000) is estimated to grow 2.5 times during 1991–2021, the corresponding intra-city travel demand would grow by 3.5 times during this period. Savage and Dasgupta (2006) summarize that in Bangalore the current vehicular number is 2 million, but is projected to go upto 3.7 million in 2021.

If this phenomenal increase in vehicular traffic were to continue, one solution is to build adequate length of good quality roads.[6] Wherever data on expenditures on municipal roads were available, we summarize them by relevant categories of cities used earlier. Tables 7.19 and 7.20 summarize the data we collect and compute on per capita expenditures on municipal roads for benchmark/non-benchmark cities and octroi/non-octroi cities, respectively. While the census data (Table 7.22 on road density for cities) show that Chandigarh in 1991 and Lucknow in 2001 had the most dense network of roads (with 2.77 km and 2.31 km of roads for every 1,000 population, respectively), Table 7.19 (on expenditure by our benchmark and non-benchmark cities) based on our primary data shows that these cities (that includes Chandigarh) have spent less per capita on municipal roads than cities such as Pune and Bangalore, since 1991.

According to 2001 Census data, Chandigarh was the city that had the highest proportion (100 per cent) of surfaced roads to the total (Table 7.21), followed by Surat. While in per capita terms the octroi cities in our study spent slightly more on municipal roads per capita than the non-octroi cities (Bangalore and Chandigarh) since 1991, the difference is not significant.

Figure 7.2 shows the total (capital and O&M) actual expenditure incurred by cities over time, based on the data available. We observe that in absolute terms, Bangalore is the highest spender with peak

TABLE 7.19
Per Capita Expenditure on Municipal Roads across
Benchmark and Non-benchmark Cities

Year	Average Capital and O&M Per Capita Expenditure (in Rs, 1993–4 = 100) in Benchmark Cities (Surat and Chandigarh)	Average Capital and O&M Per Capita Expenditure (in Rs, 1993–4 = 100) in Non-benchmark Cities (Pune and Bangalore)
1991	NA	30.48
1992	NA	34.17
1993	NA	41.56
1994	NA	28.63
1995	NA	56.34
1996	NA	48.49
1997	NA	47.57
1998	NA	58.19
1999	78.51	88.20
2000	54.03	121.45
2001	59.57	145.47
2002	68.35	129.30
2003	65.58	146.39
Average	*65.21*	*75.10*

Sources: Chandigarh Municipal Corporation; Surat Municipal Corporation; Pune Municipal Corporation; Bangalore Mahanagara Palike; and authors' computations.

in 2001–2. Pune exhibits a secular trend of increasing expenditures on roads.

We also made an attempt to assess the extent of damage to roads imposed by an increasing population and increasing number of vehicles on the roads, and what is needed to offset the costs. In the cities we visited, we attempted to find if there was a discrepancy between the life of municipal roads that they were ideally constructed for and the actual period for which they lasted. We did this in order to examine if there were demands imposed by an increasing population and traffic density on the city's road infrastructure. We did find in the case of many cities that there was discrepancy between the optimal and the actual life of municipal roads, as for example, in Lucknow. While such discrepancies existed in the life of municipal roads in the case of all cities where we visited, the discrepancy was attributed by officials to corruption. The use of

TABLE 7.20
Per Capita Expenditure on Municipal Roads across
Octroi and Non-octroi Cities

Year	Average Capital and O&M Per Capita Expenditure (in Rs, 1993–4 = 100) in Octroi Cities (Pune and Surat)	Average Capital and O&M Per Capita Expenditure (in Rs, 1993–4 = 100) in Non-octroi Cities (Bangalore and Chandigarh)
1991	30.48	NA
1992	34.17	NA
1993	41.56	NA
1994	28.63	NA
1995	56.34	NA
1996	77.58	18.93
1997	68.35	26.32
1998	83.12	32.79
1999	92.36	81.28
2000	84.51	91.44
2001	85.89	119.14
2002	102.52	94.67
2003	119.61	92.36
Average	*69.63*	*69.62*

Sources: Chandigarh Municipal Corporation; Surat Municipal Corporation; Pune Municipal Corporation; Bangalore Mahanagara Palike; and authors' computations.

TABLE 7.21
Proportion of Surfaced Roads in Selected Cities, 2001

City	Per Cent of Surfaced Roads to Total
Bangalore	89.98
Chandigarh	100.00
Jaipur	76.57
Lucknow	92.18
Pune	88.37
Surat	94.63
Average	*90.29*

Source: Census of India 2001 Town Directory.

sub-standard material by contractors ensured that the roads would get washed away, or become speckled with potholes and muddles, in the event of a downpour, much earlier than anticipated. This indeed is the factor that confounds the effect of migration on the quality of the service.[7]

TABLE 7.22
Road Density for Cities, 1991 and 2001

Name of the Town	Total Road Length (in km), 1991	Road Length/1,000 Population, 1991	Total Road Length (in km), 2001	Road Length/1,000 Population, 2001
Bangalore	1,925.00	0.58	2,125	0.49
Chandigarh	1,412.00	2.77	1,360	1.68
Jaipur	975.00	0.67	2,339	1.01
Lucknow	3,131.64	1.93	5,052	2.31
Pune	826.40	0.53	860	0.34
Surat	777.52	0.52	764	0.28
Average	1,508	1.17	2,083.34	1.02

Sources: Census of India 1991 and 2001 Town Directories.

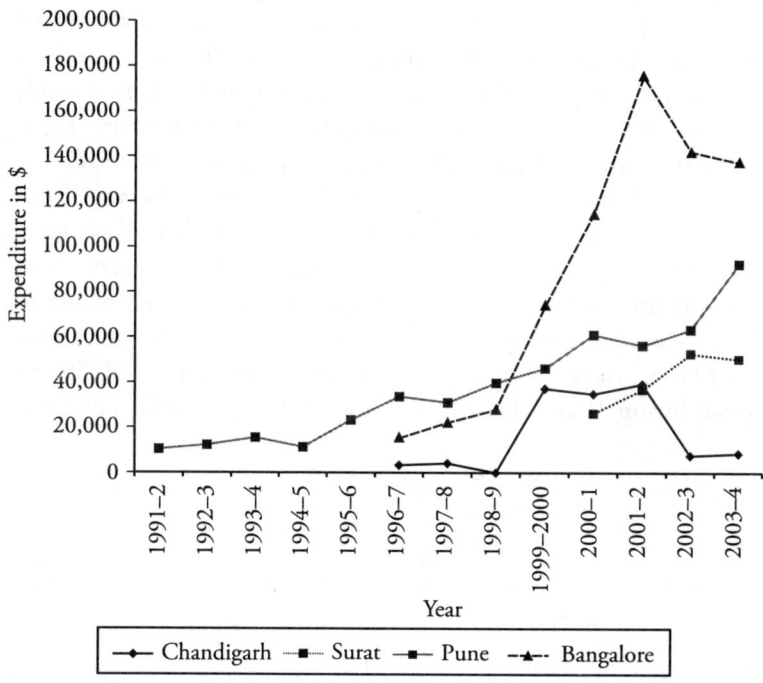

FIGURE 7.2: Total (Capital and O&M) Municipal Road Expenditures by City

Sources: Chandigarh Muncipal Corporation; Surat Muncipal Corporation; Pune Municipal Corporation; Bangalore Mahanagara Palike; and authors' computations.

In the case of Bangalore, where migration into the city is of a highly skilled nature, it is possible to believe that the city's high-technology firms have contributed significantly to the state of the roads (for instance, only 90 per cent of surfaced roads to total as of 2001, Table 7.21). There are several high-technology giants such as Infosys and WIPRO that have several thousands of employees that commute to work daily and these migrants are the biggest cause of the problem.[8] Savage and Dasgupta (2006) in fact report that Bangalore's travel time (one way work trip) increased from 24 minutes in 1991 to 40 minutes in 2001–2. In relation to the size of the problem, it does seem that the spending by Bangalore, while being high in absolute terms, has not kept pace with its population growth. However, spending is not the only problem in monitoring or improving service levels in Bangalore (Monitor, 2004).

We computed per capita investment requirements for municipal roads based on the IIR (1996) for the states in which our cities are located and compared them with the actual expenditure on roads by these cities. Table 7.23 summarizes the various estimates of (per capita) investment requirements for municipal roads. The results are startling. While the per capita investment requirements range from a low of Rs 39.25 (Zakaria Committee's estimate for Karnataka) to Rs 81.74 (Government of India Planning Commission's high end estimate for Uttar Pradesh), cities in these states according to the data available to us are spending about Rs 70.66 per capita in 1994–5 prices, with Bangalore spending in fact Rs 95.59 per capita during 1996–2003 in per capita terms on municipal roads,

TABLE 7.23
Requirements of Per Capita Investment in
Urban Roads, 1994–5 Prices

State	Planning Commission		Zakaria Committee's Estimate
	Low	High	
Gujarat	48.49	72.50	40.18
Karnataka	47.10	69.73	39.25
Maharashtra	50.80	76.20	42.49
Rajasthan	52.18	78.97	43.87
Uttar Pradesh	54.49	81.74	45.72

Sources: IIR (1995) and authors' computations.

much higher than these required estimates. But the traffic woes of Bangalore do show that the investment requirements in urban roads made by the IIR (1996) are highly conservative.

Summarizing, the findings from this chapter on other core municipal services show that while in the case of sewerage and sanitation, finances are the core of the service delivery problem in Indian cities, this is less obvious in the case of street lighting and municipal roads, where governance is part of the problem.

The next couple of chapters will focus on the promise of reforming public service delivery in Indian cities, rising above the issue of finances. We focus on the cases of Ludhiana (Punjab) and Rajkot (Gujarat) to examine issues of urban reforms. There we discuss institutional arrangements in the provision of services, the ability of governance, leadership, and willingness to raise user charges, and public participation, as factors determining service delivery. Chapter 8 focuses on the case of Ludhiana, Punjab, and Chapter 9 describes the case of Rajkot, Gujarat, in reforming public service delivery.

NOTES

1. All data we have presented for Chandigarh's public services are for the post-1996 period, after it became a municipal corporation.

2. In the case of Chandigarh, Surat, Lucknow, and Jaipur, we had data on the *total* number of street lights in the city by year, whereas in the case of Pune and Bangalore, we had data only on the *incremental* number of new street lights installed in the city by year. Since we are interested in coverage with the total number of street lights, we have left out Pune and Bangalore for purposes of analyses.

3. We had data on the total number of public toilets by year in only two cities: Bangalore and Chandigarh. For the other cities, Jaipur, Pune, and Surat, we had data only on the *incremental* number of new public toilets built by the city by year. The sanitation (number of public toilets) data for Lucknow was not available. The expenditure on sanitation for Lucknow was combined with that for sewerage. Because of these problems, we decided not to compare a physical measure of sanitation with cities' expenditure on the service.

4. Recall we do not venture into private provision of services here. In the context of sanitation, this could refer to those managed and operated by Sulabh International.

5. Recall that all cities chosen for this study, with the exception of Chandigarh, are million-plus cities.

6. Another solution is of course to restrict the rising number of private vehicles and encourage mass transportation options such as the metro, or bus systems. But the scope of the study does not permit us to get into such issues.

7. One assumption might be that the use of roads by migrants (skilled or unskilled) deteriorates the quality of roads. However, if the use of material by contractors were to be of sub-standard quality, then irrespective of whether or not the roads are used by migrants, the roads would come to have potholes. In order to isolate the effects of corruption from that of migration on the quality of roads, it would have been good to distinguish the roads used by migrants from those used by non-migrants. However, this is a near impossibility. To enable us to make such a distinction, first, we need to have information on the nature of migrants—whether they are skilled or unskilled. Next, we need to have information on their spatial distribution in the city, their pattern of residence, employment and trips. Then with the help of geographic information systems, it is possible to distinguish between the migrant roads and non-migrant used roads. As is clear, the data needs of such an effort are huge, hence it is not possible to make such a distinction between migrant and non-migrant used roads.

8. This was confirmed in some discussions we had in Bangalore. We refrain from reporting the names of individuals or organizations for reasons of confidentiality.

CHAPTER 8

Urban Reforms
*A Case Study of Ludhiana**

The previous chapters have dealt with issues of marginal costs incurred by cities in the provision of water supply, the issue of the actual pricing as it relates to water supply in a few cities, costs for other services, their actual expenditure on various services, and how they compare with norms generally recommended for these services. We also made an attempt to examine the physical provision of these services. In this chapter, we examine the broader issue of reforming service delivery in Indian cities. We do this using the case study of Ludhiana in Punjab.

To address the issues that plague public service delivery and make cities engines of growth, the Government of India (GoI), in its 2005 budget, initiated the Jawaharlal Nehru National Urban Renewal Mission (JNNURM) to stimulate urban reform. The objectives of the JNNURM are the integrated development of infrastructure services in selected cities and planned development of identified cities leading to urbanization in a dispersed manner. Ludhiana (in the north Indian state of Punjab) and Rajkot (in the state of Gujarat) are among the sixty-three cities identified in the country, under the JNNURM. This and the next chapter on Rajkot, Gujarat, focus on these cities' urban services and their reform, since

* This chapter is a revised version of an article originally published as 'Reforming Delivery of Urban Services in Developing Countries: Evidence from a Case in India', *Economic and Political Weekly*, 18 August 2007, 42(33): 3404–13.

they are representative of many growing cities in developing economies and have lessons and implications for similar cities.

Objectives

Given the importance of urban public services in facilitating national economic growth in developing economies, in this chapter, we examine the following questions: Is there a need for reforming public service delivery in Ludhiana, when judged against national benchmarks? Further, to corroborate what we have been examining in the earlier chapters, we study whether there is a relationship between the city's financial performance and its delivery of urban services. Specifically we attempt to understand what the potential bottlenecks are to reform in service delivery. Finally, we try to understand what are the triggers for reform and reform actions for improving service delivery, if any.

The answers to these questions are critical for many governmental policies as they relate to urban institutions and finances. In India, the 74th Constitutional Amendment Act (1992) recognized urban local bodies (ULBs) as the third tier of government. Despite this, after more than thirteen years of this landmark development, a majority of Indian cities continue to provide quite low levels of urban services, as we have learned from the earlier chapters.

One reason is that city finances are in poor condition. Most of the Indian cities (except municipal corporations in Maharashtra and Gujarat) have now abolished the highly buoyant source of revenue, the octroi, which is now generally accepted to be distortionary in its effects. Further, the property tax base is at best subjective and has not yet become a resilient source of revenue. Under these circumstances, cities in India can access the capital market (as was done by the Ahmedabad Municipal Corporation more than a decade ago). For infrastructure needs, they will also be able to access funds under the JNNURM, provided they fulfil certain conditions to reform. But if better finances are not going to improve service delivery, then access to capital markets or the JNNURM might not make a difference to service delivery in Indian cities. While finances are critical underlying the delivery of any service, it is important to understand whether finances are both a necessary and sufficient condition for sustainable service delivery.

This chapter is the outcome of research regarding service delivery, finances, and urban management in Ludhiana, which can be used as a benchmark for assessing other cities' public service delivery and for understanding what could trigger the reforms there. Several measures we examine including service delivery and current finances suggest a need for financial as well as institutional reforms in Ludhiana. The major bottlenecks to reform in Ludhiana (as well as that in Rajkot, discussed in the forthcoming chapter) are seen to be institutional, and pertain to existing arrangements for water, sewerage, and land use. Major triggers that could make the reform happen in Ludhiana pertain to changes in institutional arrangements for service delivery (privatization in service delivery and public participation), and finances (less of a trigger). We find the reform agenda in Ludhiana as well as in Rajkot should centre on getting the institutional arrangements clear for the provision of water, sewerage services, and land use. Further, management of finances is crucial once octroi is formally abolished in Ludhiana.

This chapter is organized as follows. The section that follows quickly describes our hypotheses regarding various relationships in Ludhiana's context. Then the details of the case study follow. In the case study, first, the demography and the economic base of Ludhiana, the focus of the chapter, are described, since they have implications for consumption of various public services. Then the next section contains an analysis of whether or not there is a need for reforming service delivery in the city. Finances and their relationship with service delivery are discussed in the following section. The next section of the chapter explores any potential bottlenecks to the reform process. The penultimate section of the chapter analyses possible triggers of the reform process and any reform actions. The final section summarizes the findings, implications for other cities, and contains concluding remarks.

HYPOTHESES

Since our eventual goal here is to find ways in which public service delivery could be improved, to corroborate what we have been examining in the earlier chapters, we study whether there is a relationship between the city's financial performance and its delivery of urban services. There are certain hypotheses with respect to service delivery and finances that we might a priori test.

The first hypothesis follows from the literature we have reviewed and from work in the earlier chapters. The cities in which user charges reflect the unit (or marginal) costs of providing services are able to deliver a more adequate level of the service, when compared to cities where such costs are not covered. This hypothesis assumes that finances (both capital and revenue expenditures) are important in service delivery outcomes.

Second, irrespective of whether or not finances are important in service delivery outcomes, it is likely that other factors such as institutional arrangements are likely to impact service delivery (as both bottlenecks and triggers to reform), in the context of countries with multiple tiers of government.

An examination of these hypotheses will enable to dispel myths about service delivery and finances. If it were found that finances do not affect service delivery, further examination should enable us to focus on other aspects of service delivery. Alternatively, irrespective of whether or not finances are important in determining service delivery outcomes, the hypotheses will enable to throw light on other factors that might be equally important in service delivery. Thus this case study and the Rajkot case study in the forthcoming chapter make an attempt to offer an integrated perspective of reforms in the delivery of important urban services, in the context of growing and emerging economies.

Since there is usually a multiplicity of meanings attached to the word 'reform', it is defined here and in the next chapter as a change for the better, in the form of improvements by correction of defects and errors in local public service delivery.

Case Study of Ludhiana

In this case study of Ludhiana, first the economic base and demography of the city are described since they have direct implications for the consumption and needs of various public services.

Demography and Economic Base

Ludhiana, the largest city of Punjab, is located 300 km northwest of New Delhi. Strategically located in the middle of Punjab, it is a corridor between Punjab and the rest of the country for transport of agricultural and industrial products. The city is well known for its industrial growth and is called the Manchester of India. There is considerable industrial activity in the city consisting of cycles, machine tools including sewing machinery, auto spare parts, and hosiery units. Ludhiana produces a large number of bicycles with Hero and Avon being the most popular brands. In hosiery, the city is exporter to Russia, Europe, and other parts of the world.

This description shows that Ludhiana is an economically important city of the country whose production structure has several implications for delivery and consumption of public services such as water supply, sewerage, and solid waste.

Demography

Ludhiana is one of the three municipal corporations in Punjab with its 2001 Census population of 1,398,467. The population density of the municipal corporation (MC) has been continuously increasing from roughly 5,519 per sq. km in 1981 to 7,743 per sq. km in 1991 and a 2001 population density of 8,775 per sq. km (for an area of 159 sq. km). Along with the rapid increase in its population and in-migration, the city has also witnessed tremendous expansion in its area recently. Increases in spatial expansion, as with increases in population and density, mean that the provision of various services such as water supply, sewerage, and sanitation have to be stepped up, even for maintaining constant level of these services.

The population density of Ludhiana (district) for 2000–1, 804 persons per sq. km, was also the highest of all districts in the state of Punjab, when compared to the state average of 482.3 per sq. km. This shows the need for Ludhiana Municipal Corporation (LMC) to optimize city efficiencies with respect to the delivery of all local public services.

The annual growth rate of Ludhiana's (the city's) population over 1991–2001 was 2.9 per cent, higher than India's national average for the growth rate of urban population over this period which is 2.7 per cent. This somewhat supports the notion that we are looking at a relatively well-performing city, since population is usually attracted by what it perceives to be better economic opportunity in any given area.

Economic Base

According to the 1991 Census of India, Ludhiana's occupational structure had a strong manufacturing base. Table 8.1 summarizes Ludhiana's (district's) occupational structure from the 1991 and 2001 Census. While in 1991, nearly one-fourth of Ludhiana's labour force was concentrated in non-household based manufacturing followed by cultivation and agricultural labour (which constituted 37 per cent together), three-fourths of workers in the district were employed in 'other services' by 2001. Besides, there was a significant decrease in the proportion of cultivators and agricultural labourers in 2001, reflective of an economy that is growing in services and declining in its agricultural base.[1] These trends are consistent with the national economy that has made a jump from agriculture to services and also an area that is undergoing rapid urbanization.

TABLE 8.1
Ludhiana District's Occupational Structure

Occupation Category	Employment (in %), 1991	Employment (in %), 2001
Cultivation	20.00	12
Agricultural labour	16.5	8.4
Livestock	1.44	NA
Mining	0.00	NA
Household-based manufacturing	0.48	4.8
Non-household-based manufacturing	25.29	NA
Construction	3.80	NA
Trade and commerce	13.63	NA
Transport and communications	5.27	NA
Other services	13.41	75
Total	*100*	*100*

Source: 1991 and 2001 Census of India.

Consistent with the picture of Ludhiana's economy presented by the Census summarized in Table 8.1, we found other recent data which show a large number of small, medium, and large firms in Ludhiana (district)[2] that contribute to total employment and output. Table 8.2 shows this for the more recent years, 1996 and 2003. While the data shown in Table 8.2 are cumulative, they indicate that small firms in the district accounted for nearly all (99 per cent of) the firms established during 1996 and 2003. These small units accounted for 85 per cent of all employment created in 1996 and 78 per cent of jobs in 2003. They accounted, however, for a little greater than 40 per cent of total investment and production in 1996 and only 22 per cent of investment in 2003. We observe these trends because small units are labour-intensive rather than capital-intensive.

TABLE 8.2
Industry in Ludhiana District

Indicator	Small-scale Units*		Medium-scale and Large-scale Units	
	1996	2003	1996	2003
Number of units	26,440	42,704	88	168
Investment (million Rs)	4,919.52	11,168.64	6,958.24	39,045.92
Employment	193,220	273,593	35,000	75,185
Production (million Rs)	26,414.72	8,2213.6	34,968.48	NA

Source: District Industries Centre, Ludhiana.
Note: According to the Ministry of Small Scale Industries, Government of India, a small-scale industrial unit is an industrial undertaking in which investment in fixed assets in plant and machinery does not exceed Rs 10 million.

Tables 8.1 and 8.2 reinforce the economy of Ludhiana as being non-agricultural, being focused on manufacturing and services, dotted with a large number of firms. The city's economic base has implications for various civic services. While the hosiery industry is water-intensive (dyeing), it also is quite polluting. This has impacts on water quality, sewerage, and solid waste management, as we see later in this chapter. Further, basic knowledge of the inputs and processes of the bicycle, sewing machine, and auto spare parts industry demonstrate the need for disposal of waste rubber and scrap metal. This economic base also has some implications for land use in the city, which we discuss later in the chapter.

NEED FOR REFORM IN SERVICE DELIVERY

The need, if any, for reforming service delivery in Ludhiana was assessed on the basis of (*a*) the actual state of service delivery for important services such as water supply and sewerage, compared with the recommended standards for these services; (*b*) systemic inefficiencies such as the high levels of unaccounted for water (UFW);

and (*c*) long-term irreversible consequences of business as usual, such as contamination of groundwater.

Service Delivery

WATER SUPPLY

The main source of water supply in Ludhiana is underground water, which is drawn through shallow and deep tube wells. The institutional arrangement is that while the Punjab Water Supply and Sewerage Board (PWSSB), which is a parastatal agency, undertakes the planning, development, and construction of *major* water and sewer networks, the operation, maintenance, and execution of *minor* developmental works is provided by the municipality (LMC).

The service-level statistics for water supply in Ludhiana are summarized in Table 8.3. The city has the infrastructure capacity to provide water to the entire population, but, overall, only 80 per cent have access to piped water supply (Table 8.3). As of 1998, only 60 per cent of the city's population was covered by municipal water supply.[3] According to the Ministry of Urban Development (2008), international best practices dictate that the coverage of water supply connections have to be 100 per cent. It is clear that the LMC does not have adequate financial resources to extend the water supply network.

Overall, about 88 per cent (648,000) of the total population served (748,000) represent those with household connections, with the remaining 12 per cent being served through standposts (18,000) or through independent institutional set-up (72,000). None of the private houses have metered water connections, which has implications for water usage. As there is no volumetric consumptive tariff regime, the customers in these locales are generally not concerned about water loss. Commercial connections are a very small proportion of total connections (only 15 per cent out of a total of 162,734 connections). All these together imply that recovery of costs from water supply is low.

When the access of households to water supply in urban Punjab and urban India is compared with that for Ludhiana (Table 8.4), the city has above average access, called for by its higher population density. The data in Table 8.4 for urban Punjab, urban India, and

TABLE 8.3
Service-level Statistics for Water Supply, Ludhiana, 2003

Description of Service	Number or Percentage
Population as per 2001	1,440,000
Population in 2003	1,517,000
Total number of houses (2003)	316,042
Average number of people per household	4.8
Population having access to piped water supply	1,213,600
In percentage	80%
Population served by household connections	658,000
Population served by standposts	18,000
Population served by independent institutional set-up (engineering colleges, universities, commercial and industrial establishments)	72,000
Total population served	748,000
Total number of houses with unmetered connection	137,071 (21% of population with household connections, 658,000)
Total number of private houses with metered connection	0
Total number of house connections	137,071
Total number of commercial connections	25,663

Source: PWSSB, 2003.

LMC, from India's Census, 2001, must have been actual data from 1998 or 1999. Data from the PWSSB in Table 8.3 are local, and recent, being from 2003. So while census data show 69.5 per cent tap water supply access in LMC (Table 8.4), more recent data from PWSSB (Table 8.3) show 80 per cent access of population to piped water supply in LMC. Based on these data, we conclude that the actual coverage of the city's population with piped water supply is likely to be in the range of 65–70 per cent.

As might be further clearer from Table 8.4, Ludhiana and the state of Punjab have much better access (respectively 98.5 and 98.9 per cent) to safe drinking water, when compared with the country as a whole (90 per cent of whose population are claimed to have access to safe drinking water). The disparities between access to water within the premises are more stark. Only 61 per cent of the country has access to water within the premises, whereas 92 per cent each of the population of Punjab and Ludhiana has access to water within the premises, reflecting the high income and better water infrastructure of the state compared with the country as a whole. As opposed to water within premises, tap water is available within the premises to only 50 per cent of the country's population, whereas for Ludhiana, 66 per cent of population has access to tap water within premises, even better than 63 per cent population of the state which has access to this on their premises. Thus, on all water supply indicators, LMC scores over the state and the country.

A similar story is repeated with respect to sanitation. While only 74 per cent of urban India has access to a toilet facility, nearly 87 per cent of urban Punjab and 95 per cent of LMC have access to toilet facilities (Table 8.4). Finally when we compare access to toilet within premises, only 57 per cent of urban India has toilet within its premises, but 83 per cent of urban Punjab and LMC have toilets within their premises. This shows that as far as basic public services such as water supply and sanitation are concerned, urban Punjab and LMC are way above urban India, but still the coverage is less than adequate when compared with national standards and international benchmarks.

TABLE 8.4
Access of Households to Water Supply and Toilet Facilities in Ludhiana,
State of Punjab, and India, 2001

	Access to Safe Drinking Water	Access to Water within Premises	Access to Tap Water Supply	Access to Tap Water within Premises	Access to Toilet Facility	Access to Toilet within Household
Ludhiana M. Corp	98.52	92.43	69.50	65.81	94.88	83.27
Punjab (urban)	98.88	91.70	66.81	63.44	86.52	82.76
India (urban)	90.01	60.84	68.66	49.68	73.72	57.38

Source: Census of India 2001.

Table 8.5 presents basic statistics for water supply in Ludhiana. According to the PWSSB, while the total average daily discharge capacity in LMC is 454 mld (million litres daily), actual average daily production of water is only 284 mld, out of which only 140.5 mld is charged, leaving more than half (50.5 per cent) unaccounted. Only 137 mld is consumed through house connections (which are not metered) in the city.[4] The 137 mld supplied in eight to ten hours a day accounts for a mere 98 lpcd (litres per capita daily, Table 8.5). The lack of continuous supply is due to the fact that ground water has to be pumped up through tube wells and power is a constraint for this. Further, there could be seasonal variations in the supply, about which data were not available from the PWSSB.

TABLE 8.5
Statistics for Water Supply, Ludhiana, 2003

Description of Service	Level
Actual average daily production of water (mld)	284
Total average daily water discharge capacity (mld)	454
Daily water consumption through house connections (mld)	137
Total average daily water charged (mld)	140.5
Per cent of water unaccounted for	50.5
Daily water supply duration (hrs)	8–10

Source: PWSSB, 2003.

While being above average when compared to the state of Punjab and that for the country as a whole, the level of water supply is inadequate in LMC, when compared against desirable benchmarks. The ideal norms for water supply vary greatly across cities and are based on considerations of industrial use, public use, fire demand and losses in transmission, according to the oldest committee on urban services, the Zakaria Committee (1963). It recommends a service level target of 150 lpcd for piped water supply with sewerage (70 lpcd without sewerage), which includes roughly 20 per cent wastage of water. Benchmark values published by the Ministry of Urban Development, Government of India, specify a per capita daily water supply of 135.

The actual supply of water consumed in LMC being only 98 lpcd is highly inadequate taking into account the national ideal supply standard of 135 lpcd or 175 lpcd, considering the distribution losses, recommended by India's National Commission on Urbanization, or the 150 lpcd recommended by the Zakaria Committee for cities with piped water supply systems with sewerage.

On the basis of these discussions, it does appear that the inadequacy of water supply is related at least partially to financial constraints and skill crunches that the LMC is facing.

SEWERAGE

While the Zakaria Committee and the Ministry of Urban Development recommend that for large urban centres (such as LMC), the service level target should be full coverage by sewerage with treatment, a formal sewerage system exists in only half the city's area. Sewage treatment plants are non-existent in the city, with the collected sewage being discharged into the local stream or the nearest water body. This leads to contamination of the water supply network and also pollutes the aquifer, which serves as a source of the city's water.[5]

Table 8.6 summarizes the level of service for sewerage. It may be noted that only 55 per cent (834,350) of the city's population has access to sewerage connection, much less than the coverage for water supply. Overall, only 39 per cent (585,928) of the city's population is served through a sewer house connection (with only 121,985 connections), 56 per cent of population (849,072) is covered through soak pits and septic tanks, with an additional 5 per cent being served by independent institutional sewerage (with twenty-two institutions in the city having an independent sewerage system) or through a conservancy system (10,000 served). At present only 10 per cent of the city is covered by storm water drainage facilities. Given the Zakaria Committee's and the Ministry of Urban Development's recommendation of 100 per cent coverage of city area, the extent of sewerage and storm water drainage access in LMC are highly inadequate.

Finances

While the state of the various services in LMC emphasizes the need for reform, we test the various hypotheses raised at the beginning of the chapter, based on a study of Ludhiana's finances.

First, consider the hypothesis that better finances imply better service delivery. Based on theory, there are grounds to assume that higher capital rather than revenue expenditures should imply better service delivery. The basis of this assumption seems to be that cities that spend relatively more on establishment, and salaries, when compared with capital expenditures (developmental work), are likely to be inefficient, hence unable to provide a desired level

TABLE 8.6
Service-level Statistics for Sewerage System, Ludhiana, 2003

Description of Service	Proportion/ Number Covered
Population access to sewerage in numbers	834,350
In percentage	55%
Population served through sewer house connection in (numbers)	585,928
Actual number of sewer connections	121,985
Population served through soakage pits/ septic tanks (in numbers)	849,072
Population served by independent institutional sewerage (own systems in universities, colleges, and so forth) (in numbers)	72,000
Population served through conservancy system (in numbers)	10,000
Number of institutions having independent sewerage system	22

Source: PWSSB, 2003.

of the service. Capital expenditures are generally viewed as providing pure or impure public goods (e.g., water, street lights) whereas revenue expenditures (while indirectly facilitating the provision of public goods) most directly provide private goods such as office equipment, wages, and salaries. However, in India, in actual practice, instances of water and sewerage treatment plants that are built but do not function, are commonplace. This view therefore seems to focus on the lack of adequate O&M expenditure. Hence, based on both theory and practice, there is some basis to assume that a relationship exists between both capital and revenue expenditures and service delivery.

The bulk of LMC's total expenditure (75 per cent of it) on water supply and sewerage, indeed, constitutes revenue expenditure. This refers to establishment (office furniture, administration, equipment, and so forth) and O&M expenses that respectively constituted 27 per cent and 47 per cent of total expenditure in 2003–4. Figure 8.1 shows the trends in expenditure on water and sewerage by the LMC by category. In revenue expenditure, O&M expenses have overtaken expenditure on salaries since 2001–2. It might appear that only a small part of LMC's total expenditure on water and sewer (roughly 20–2 per cent) is being spent on developmental works and investment in assets (e.g., installation of hand pump).

However, while revenue expenditure represented the same proportion in 1997–8 as in 2003–4 (78 per cent and 74 per cent of total expenditure for those years respectively, with the exception of expenditure on electricity for operating tube wells that registered an increase since 2000–1), in 2000–1, there was a spurt in capital expenditure (to 44 per cent of total expenditure from 22 per cent in 1997–8).

Based on Figure 8.1, we examined committed expenditures (such as wages and debt repayments) as distinct from discretionary expenditure (the city's preferred choice of expenditure), since it helps to illustrate the constrained choices faced by the LMC. We find that over time, LMC's committed expenditures have constituted only about one-third of its total expenditures, leaving on average nearly two-thirds for its discretionary expenditures such as O&M, electricity, and capital expenditures. Based on this, it would appear

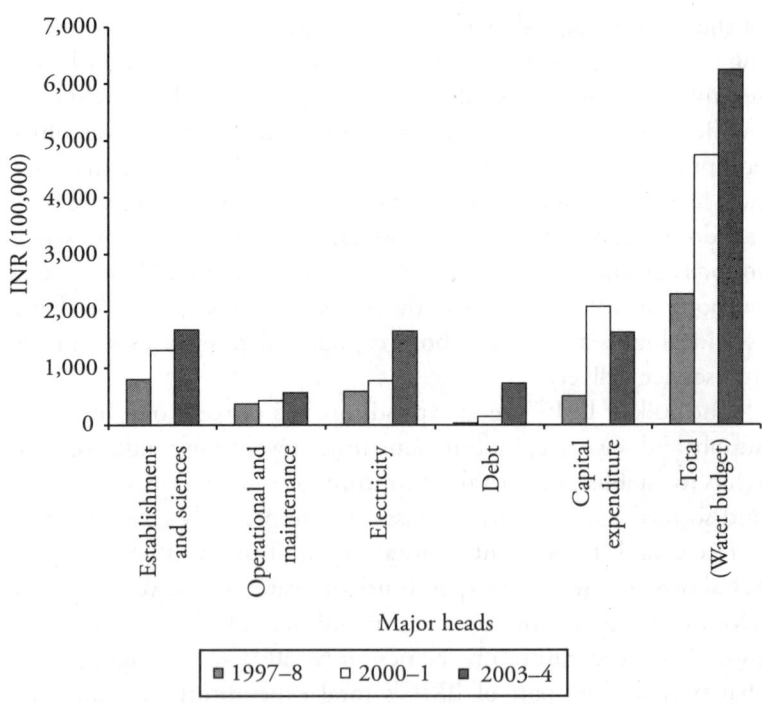

FIGURE 8.1: Expenditure on Water and Sewerage, LMC

Source: LMC.

that when compared with its commitments, LMC has considerable discretion regarding how it wants to spend its resources, is not hard-pressed for its financial commitments, and it does seem that many ULBs would have liked to spend as much on O&M as LMC.

What do these expenditures mean for service levels? Table 8.7 summarizes the trends in the service levels of various aspects of water supply over 1996–2003. It may be observed that while the actual production and discharge capacity for water supply of the LMC increased continuously throughout this period, the daily water consumption through house connections registered a decline after 2000. We also observe a decrease in the daily water supply duration from twelve hours to ten hours, a constant increase in the percentage of UFW, and decrease in the average daily water charged, since 2000–1, as summarized in Table 8.7. The only exception is during 1998–2001, when the percentage of unaccounted water decreased. This is likely due to increases in discretionary (O&M) expenditures on fixing leaking pipes on which the LMC has been able to spend (see discussion above). These findings do not lend support to the hypothesis that the general decline in the service level could be attributed to expenditures, which in fact have increased, post 2000–1. These findings are in fact consistent with what Savage and Dasgupta (2006) find with respect to Bangalore. Savage and Dasgupta's (2006) data from the Water and Sanitation Program showed significant revenue increases (accounting for inflation and population) during 1995–2003 for the various service providers in Bangalore. However even with this, they find service outcomes have declined. They point out that there is need for a city-wide set of reforms that not only entail revenue but also ensure effective expenditure management, new management approaches, and the need to focus on specific outcomes. These findings appear to hold good for Ludhiana as well.

Now, consider the other part of the hypothesis posed, pertaining to receipts (income)—that is, those cities in which user charges reflect the cost of providing the service are in a position to provide better services, judged against certain benchmarks.

Figure 8.2 shows a comparison, across time periods, of LMC's revenues (in per capita constant 1997–8 prices). The figure demon-strates some interesting aspects; while clearly own-revenue receipts

TABLE 8.7
Trends in Water Supply, LMC

Description	1996–7	1997–8	1998–9	1999–2000	2000–1	2001–2	2002–3
Actual average daily production of water (mld)	193.05	210.1	234	245	247	258	284
Total average daily water discharge capacity (mld)	360	360	390	452	484	508	454
Daily water consumption through house connections (mld)	122.39	133.2	172	184	185	131	137
Total average daily water charged (mld)	135.14	145.95	178.5	178	182	135	140.5
Percentage of water unaccounted for	30	30.50	24	25	25	47	50.50
Daily water supply duration (in hours)	12	13	12	13	12	10	10

Source: PWSSB.

form the bulk of LMC's revenues, and state transfers account for a small portion, there is a clear decline in the total per capita revenues of the LMC in 2003–4, when compared to 2000–1. State transfers to LMC have continuously fallen since 1997–8 and the LMC has been self-reliant, dependent heavily on octroi receipts, with octroi accounting for roughly two-thirds of own revenues over time.

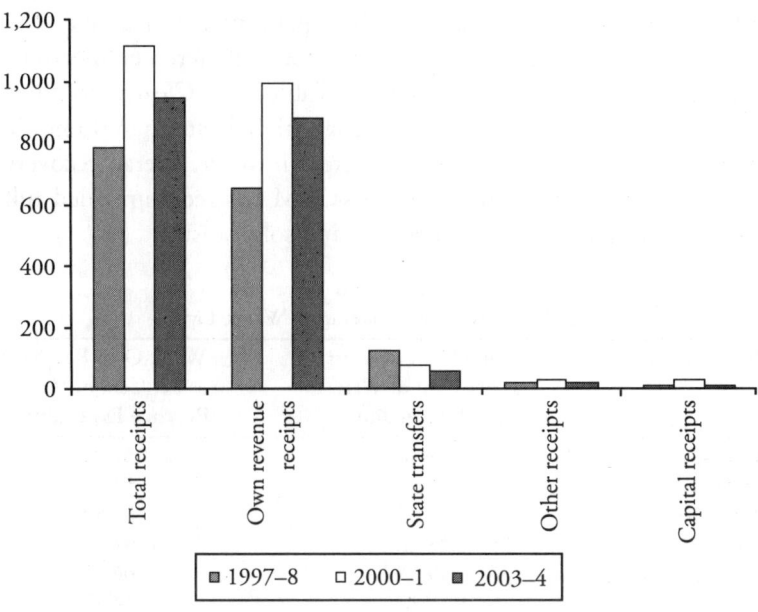

FIGURE 8.2: LMC Income Per Capita Constant Prices (INR)
Source: LMC and authors' computations.

However, own-revenue receipts in constant per capita terms have also decreased in 2003–4 relative to their level in 2000–1. This is partly due to a rising price level, and because spending has not kept pace with rising population as well. Income from capital and other receipts has been negligible. This does show LMC's finances to be precarious, when we take into account its discretionary spending.

Table 8.8 shows recovery from water user charges, the trend in water receipts as a proportion of total expenditure, and revenue expenditure on water. When total expenditure is taken into account, water receipts covered only 50 per cent in 2001–2, but have since been declining. The coverage is much better with revenue expenditure since there have been instances when water receipts (from user charges) have covered more than 90 per cent, but since 2000–1, that has also been declining. The water tariffs for unmetered water connections from 2003–4 were revised (Table 8.9) and then the revenues started increasing. This was because there was a metered connection component in the charge from 2003–4 onwards (Table 8.9) for plot size of 1 kanal (or 605 square yards) or above. The water tariffs applicable for 1999–2003 for unmetered connections (based on size of ferrule) are shown in Table 8.10. Clearly, commercial connections are always charged at a higher rate than domestic connections, as is the case everywhere. However, overall recovery remains quite low. Rightly the JNNURM has recommended full user charge recovery of water supply and solid waste.

TABLE 8.8
Trend in Share of Revenues from Water, LMC

Financial Year	Water Own Receipts as Per Cent of Water Total Expenditure	Water Own Receipts as Per Cent of Water Revenue Expenditure
1997–8	31.50	37.91
1998–9	45.58	54.27
1999–2000	19.95	37.82
2000–1	48.12	92.50
2001–2	49.14	66.07
2002–3	32.17	44.17
2003–4	40.55	48.35

Source: PWSSB and authors' calculations.

For the financial year 2002–3, the total production cost of water (in Rs per kilolitre) excluding capital expenditure was Rs 2.06 (including distribution losses), with revenue income per kilolitre being only Rs 0.92. As of 2002–3, revenue income covered roughly only 45 per cent of the total production cost of water (with or without distribution losses).

The story with regard to sewerage receipts is even worse, since as of 2003–4, while continually rising from what they have been in the past, receipts from the service covered only one-third of total expenditure and a little over half of the revenue expenditure (Table 8.11). This cost recovery is not in any case in conformity

TABLE 8.9

User Charges for Unmetered Water Connections (Domestic), 2003–4
Onwards (Rate in Rupees per Connection per Month)

Plot size	2003–4	2004–5	2005–6	2006–7	2007–8
Up to 5 marlas*	50	55	60	70	100
5–10 marlas	75	80	90	100	105
10 marlas—1 kanal**	100	110	120	130	140
1 kanal and above	Only metered connections***				

Source: Punjab Department of Local Government.
Notes: *1 Marla = 30.25 square yards; **1 Kanal = 20 Marlas; ***Metered connection charges (applicable for commercial, industrial, and institutional connections): 2003–4 (rate per kilolitre per month): Rs 2.00; 2004–5 (rate per kilolitre per month): Rs 2.60.

TABLE 8.10

User Charges for Unmetered Water Connections, 1999–2003
(Rate in Rupees per Connection per Month)

Size of Ferrule	Domestic	Commercial
3/8 "	50	100
½ "	90	180
¾ "	200	400

Source: Punjab Department of Local Government.

TABLE 8.11

Trend in Revenues from Sewerage, 1996–2003, LMC

Year	Sewerage Own Receipts as Per Cent of Sewerage Total Expenditure	Sewerage Own Receipts as Per Cent of Sewerage Revenue Expenditure
1997–8	24.53	34.25
1998–9	13.55	18.37
1999–2000	7.32	12.63
2000–1	17.34	27.83
2001–2	14.97	28.83
2002–3	40.83	54.41
2003–4	33.75	52.45

Source: PWSSB and authors' calculations.

with the Ministry of Urban Development's specified benchmark of 100 per cent cost recovery in waste water management.

LMC's sewer tariffs are shown in Table 8.12, which are again, as expected, higher for commercial than for domestic connections.

Both commercial and domestic connections are charged according to the diameter of sewer pipe, which is only one measure of their consumption/usage and does not cover all aspects of waste water management such as the precise volume to be treated and managed.

Water and sewerage being basic services, their capital expenditures cannot be covered through user charges, but for financially sustainable service delivery, at least the O&M expenditures should be covered. While our hypothesis implies that higher expenditures should lead to better service delivery, in this particular case, the decline in service levels of water supply and sewerage and a decline in expenditures seem to be moving together.

TABLE 8.12
Sewerage Charges, LMC

Diameter of Sewer Pipe	Domestic (in Rs per Connection per Month)	Commercial (in Rs per Connection per Month)
4"	50	100
6"	112.50	225
8"	200	400

Source: Punjab Department of Local Government.

Table 8.13 summarizes the service level for sewerage in LMC. It shows declining levels of population access to sewerage since 1999–2000.[6] The population serviced through house connections has been increasing since 1996–7. The actual number of sewer connections has increased from 70,000 in 1996–7 to nearly 121,985 in 2002–3. However, population served through soak pits and/or septic tanks also has been constantly increasing since then and the number of institutions having independent sewerage system has increased to twenty-two in 2002–3. All these imply that the sewerage coverage of population has not improved significantly.

A review of the LMC's financial position along with that of service delivery of water supply and sewerage indicates that there is no room for complacency. It shows that the need for service delivery reform in Ludhiana is financial as well, with the government of Punjab having abolished octroi in the state (effective from September 2006). While the city's committed expenditures are

TABLE 8.13
Sewerage Access over Time, LMC

Description	1996–7	1997–8	1998–9	1999–2000	2000–1	2001–2	2002–3
Population access to sewerage (in numbers)	731,000	775,000	1,000,000	1,050,000	720,000	740,000	834,350
Population served through sewer house connections (in numbers)	437,500	464,000	680,000	724,500	649,000	584,860	585,928
Population served through soakage pits/septic tanks (in numbers)	130,000	135,000	438,000	306,000	715,000	717,000	849,072
Actual number of sewer connections	70,000	71,000	75,000	105,000	110,000	116,972	121,985
Number of institutions having independent sewerage system	20	22	22	22	22	22	22

Source: PWSSB.

fairly low, and discretionary expenditures high as a proportion of total expenditure, they do not indicate commensurate increase in expenditure on developmental works to increase the quantum or quality of public services.

BOTTLENECKS TO REFORM

The question arises as to why the financial and service delivery performance in this city has been less than satisfactory, when judged against national benchmarks set by India's National Commission on Urbanization, Ministry of Urban Development or the Zakaria Committee, even while being above that of the country and state with respect to service levels of water supply and sanitation. What are the bottlenecks to better service delivery and reform in this and other similar cities in developing countries? It is relevant to examine the final hypothesis we have posed, regarding institutional arrangements as a factor determining service delivery and other factors which, based on our analysis, are revealed as being bottlenecks to reform.

Institutional Arrangements for Water and Sewerage Services

Despite the importance of financial resources for reforming service delivery, consider the final hypothesis that it is likely that other factors such as institutional arrangements impact service delivery. As a study by the Times Research Foundation (1997) found, there are seventeen state-level pieces of legislation and twenty-three pieces of central legislation that affect the functioning of municipal areas in Punjab. Among many other things, we identified a statutory overlap of functions for planning, preparation, and execution of 'major' water supply and sewerage schemes with the PWSSB (PWSSB Act, 1976) that also vests with the LMC (as per the Punjab Municipal Corporation Act, 1976), as it pertains to 'minor' O&M projects. This distinction between 'major' and 'minor' works does not, however, exist in the statute, making the classification of a project as 'major' or 'minor', arbitrarily causing the service to take a 'passing the buck' attitude.

Apart from the issue of statutory overlap, sometimes it is *desirable* to have local autonomy in certain functional areas. It is obvious that the LMC would be in a better position to judge which localities are served better and which ones would need infrastructure upgradation or replacement, when compared with the state government and its departments. Hence the institutional arrangements also have to be modified to reflect this.

Lack of Capacity

The LMC, however, does not have the financial resources or, more importantly, the technical expertise to execute water supply and sewerage projects independently (which is presumably why the PWSSB is currently entrusted with undertaking work of a capital nature). The technical expertise is lacking, as the proportion of the city's area covered under regular employment is continually shrinking; the city itself is expanding and retirements do keep occurring.

So what is desirable from an institutional perspective is not readily feasible due to shortage of skills and resources at the local level. Similar institutional overlaps exist with respect to land use in this city (see Sridhar et al., 2006), which has led to deterioration in the delivery of this service.

The proliferation of institutions for land use or water supply/sewerage in this city is, however, by no means, isolated. Local bodies everywhere (see Royal Town Planning Institute, Ireland [2001] for evidence from Ireland; Auzins [2004] for problems faced by the central and east European countries) have a problem with integrating policymaking and implementation. Based on the instance of water supply, there is some evidence for the hypothesis that institutional arrangements negatively impact service delivery in this city.

Inability to Increase User Charges for Services

The absence of appropriate user charges is an impediment to the effective delivery of services (see Reedy, 1986), consistent with our hypothesis and corroborated by LMC revenues from water and sewerage. A municipal corporation's finances are closely related to the various user charges and other revenue sources that determine the levels and quality of service delivery, as highlighted by the literature and discussed in earlier chapters. In India as well, the Ministry of Urban Development (MUD) and JNNURM have also been trying to support a commercial orientation as a financially sustainable approach to service delivery.

Over and above the issue of user charges not adequately covering production costs, the LMC provides public services to unauthorized slums that are not payers of property taxes. There is a need for raising water and other service charges, although in a phased manner, for both domestic and commercial users, if an attempt is made to relate water quality to the user charge. One expects a mechanism similar to Tiebout voting to work and forthcoming consumer willingness to pay (WTP).

Lack of Planning

In the case of water, the city is faced with the problem of quality. Land use has important effects on the delivery of safe and potable water supply/sanitation, given that the main source of water supply in the city is underground water. Heterogeneous land uses are spread through the city; because of this, industry in the city is spatially dispersed. If industrial use had been spatially concentrated, it would have been feasible for a single sewage treatment plant (affordable given the city's discretionary spending) to be set up for the effluents of all industrial units. However, given the spatial dispersion of industry, and the lack of a sewage treatment plant, most of the small units discharge their waste water and sewage into the open drains that enter the local stream, whose contamination has affected the ground water quality. This is causing a serious environmental sanitation hazard and the stream has become a virtual drain.

For solving this problem, the Government of India has initiated the project Sutlej Action Plan (SAP) to prevent pollution of the river and to improve its water quality. However, it is obvious that SAP is a short-term solution which treats the outcome, rather than the cause of the problem. The long-run solution is to encourage the spatial concentration of industry, through better zoning and implementation of the comprehensive plan. Zoning and comprehensive planning facilitate the regulation of land use and pollution and make them spatially concentrated. Currently, however, a laissez-faire approach has been adopted to city planning with the result that service quality is not monitored.

LACK OF PUBLIC PARTICIPATION

Where accountability or public participation exists, service delivery is likely to be successful. The question is: Do mechanisms or forum exist for grievance re-adressal and information sharing in the city? There are no non-governmental organizations (NGOs) or consumer organizations that deal with public service delivery issues in the city. Compare this with drinking water as an area where Self-employed Women's Association (SEWA) women have taken the lead in Gujarat. The outsourcing of tube well operations in LMC is an example of attempts to involve citizens in the delivery of public services. Although public services and their delivery/effectiveness are debated among the elitist groups of the city, there is no systematic discourse on the delivery of various services.

The media can do much to disseminate information and improve local government performance in public service delivery. Despite the city's above average literacy, we found that total newspaper circulation and readership in Ludhiana (of 65,700) covered only one-fourth of the city's households in 2001. Given the apparent lack of information to a substantial portion of the city's households, it is not clear what the incentives are for the policymaker cum service provider (the LMC/PWSSB) to be accountable to the public.

Currently a major problem with LMC functioning is the lack of public participation or discourse in budgeting. Certainly, better information to the public and their participation in the provision of various services is likely to act as a rapid trigger for reform. Some initiatives here could be to enable online presence of LMC budgets, its priorities and public discourse regarding the various problems associated with service delivery.

TRIGGERS FOR REFORM AND REFORM ACTIONS

Crises trigger reforms, as in the case of the balance of payments crisis of 1991 that made India take to the path of economic and political reform. There are some triggers that could make the reform of service delivery happen in LMC. These are discussed in the following sections.

Financial Resources and Abolition of Octroi

Pre-existing financial resources are a crucial factor that determines the internal readiness for reforming public service delivery in most cities. A city with a large financial base with buoyant revenue sources (such as an appropriately designed property tax) is not required to reform its service delivery, as it is presumably in a position to offer an acceptable/adequate level of services, judged against benchmarks. However a city with a small financial base is very likely to reform, in order to be eligible for accessing funds, just as the JNNURM requires.

As the LMC's finances are heavily dependent on octroi, the government of Punjab abolished octroi in the state, effective September 2006. Given the fact that octroi accounts for more than 70 per cent of LMC's own source revenues, surely the abolition will come as a trigger to persuade LMC to be financially more responsible. Some ways of making the LMC more financially responsible would be to bring into the tax net those residential properties that have remained exempt.[7] Further, discussions indicated that there are frequent under-assessments in the city of taxed (commercial or business) property that range anywhere from 2 to 20 times of their reported value.

While not possible completely, one way to compensate for octroi abolition could be to increase water charges, which could be used to finance the setting up of a sewerage treatment plant (in addition to the initiatives envisaged under the SAP). This initiative could appeal to the public because of the currently questionable water quality in the LMC area.

With abolition of octroi, the state government of Punjab will most likely come up with a compensation package for the local government. While our financial analysis indicates that transfers have not been important in the LMC context, with octroi abolition, they could very well become very important in the transition period. If this were to happen, octroi abolition might not act as a trigger to make LMC more financially accountable and might not reform service delivery.

Once the octroi abolition trigger occurs, the reform actions that need to be taken could be summarized as in the following sections.

Privatization in Service Delivery

As is clear, the LMC (or the PWSSB, respectively, being public and para-public entities) is the lead service provider of public services in most instances. The Ludhiana case demonstrates a different variant of the client-policymaker-service provider relationship highlighted by World Development Report (WDR) 2004. In Ludhiana, the policymaker is also the service provider in most instances and is directly accountable to the clients (public). Service delivery then depends on the motivation of the public sector entity in providing the service, implying not much discipline for public provision of the service since there are no incentives that pass from the policymaker to the service provider (both are one and the same).

Is privatization the panacea for a variety of problems in service delivery? Private participation in the provision of public services in Ludhiana is limited (as in most other Indian cities), as should be clear from the institutional arrangements to provide water supply. However, note that the private sector or contractors cannot move into a vacuum created by a total collapse of the public sector. The experience with the private sector world-wide and the literature reviewed in earlier chapters have shown that, wherever governance is weak, privatization of the essential water and sanitation services results in serious problems including raising costs and reducing access and quality for the less well-off (see also World Bank, 2004). This suggests that strong governance that can *regulate* as well as enable *public participation in decision-making* and *project formulation* can facilitate private sector participation, reduce cost of access, and improve quality of services rendered. So, public–private partnerships can work only if public sector governance is strong. Given strong public sector governance, privatization stimulates efficiency because it ties performance to remuneration.

Take the example of water supply. As is clear, it is quite feasible to outsource the running of tube wells which is known to be a technically simple and not a very time-consuming job. In many instances, as in the past, in the LMC, private tube-well operators have included individual shopkeepers, housewives, or senior citizens, who have offered their services in return for a small amount of remuneration. Compare this to the relatively higher salaries to government employees as tube-well operators in return for the usually poor level of services offered by them (e.g., they do attend to repairs, but usually with time delay). Thus outsourcing is certainly welcome and will act as a trigger of change and better service. In addition to the monetary savings (see below for the extent of savings that has been brought about), outsourcing can bring about the much-needed diversity in skills for service delivery. As is the case everywhere, the LMC has been unable to attract the skills needed for doing various jobs. Even if available, skills tend to be scarce because of various reasons: one is the monetary cost associated with their recruitment for the LMC. A second reason is the constant spatial expansion of the LMC which requires increasing number of employees to ensure service coverage. Because of these reasons, privatization or even mere outsourcing can act as a trigger for financial and institutional reform in LMC.

Outsourcing has been introduced by the LMC in the running of tube wells, disposal works, and desilting of sewers. Currently, a large number of tube wells (240 out of 350) have been entrusted by LMC to private operators for O&M. Tube well operators are on contract, with Rs 3,100 per month as their salary. Under the 'Neighbourhood Tube-well Operator' scheme (described above, in which housewives, shopkeepers, and senior citizens have been involved in tube-well operation and maintenance), the costs were only Rs 1,500 per month, much cheaper than that with LMC employees (which would have cost Rs 16,000 for two similar tube well operators). These attempts thus added to efficiency and cut down on LMC's salary bill. In fact, an in-house study conducted by heads of departments at LMC found that by privatizing most functions, LMC could be run in a much cheaper and effective manner with only 500 employees instead of the actual strength of 7,000 that it had.

The work of desilting interceptor sewers was given on contract by LMC during 1996–7, all steps in the right direction toward reforming these services, assuming LMC oversight.

Other reform actions in finances that could bring about reform in service delivery would be if property records were properly maintained by the city. In the past, lost records meant litigation, court cases, and significant financial losses to the city. This could be attained with e-governance initiatives, in the steps of states like Karnataka and Andhra Pradesh that have successfully computerized all their land records, making them accessible, transparent, and accountable.

Summary of Findings and Concluding Remarks

This chapter addressed the need for reforming urban service delivery; the relationship between finances and service delivery, any potential bottlenecks, and triggers for reforming service delivery in urban areas, taking the case of Ludhiana, India, as an example. The actual state of various services and finances suggest a need for reforming service delivery in Ludhiana. Besides, in the case of this city, consistent with the hypotheses, in addition to financial constraints, we find some evidence that the major bottlenecks to reforming service delivery are institutional and pertain to existing arrangements for delivery of various services such as water and sewerage.

The major lessons and triggers that could make the reform happen in the LMC and other cities in the developing world are clarifications in institutional arrangements for service delivery, encouraging privatization in service delivery and public participation, and sustainable finances, supported by user charges. Our study suggests that problems with institutional arrangements are not a local phenomenon confined merely to Ludhiana, India.

Similar experiences world-wide mean that local bodies everywhere have a problem with integrating policymaking and implementation. As this case study demonstrates, policy and action coherence is as vital for effective financial management as it is for service delivery. India's 74th Constitutional Amendment Act formally recognized local governments as the third tier of government more than sixteen years ago, but that has not affected their internal functioning. This case study demonstrates the need to identify an umbrella agency from among the numerous existing agencies, which can oversee various aspects of planning in cities for better management of finances and reforming the delivery of services, for true local autonomy, and better public participation in city planning. This observation is valid not only for cities in India, but for those in all emerging and new economies in East Asia, Latin America, and Europe, where decentralization has taken place.

The next chapter corroborates these findings by taking the case study of a fast-growing city in the western part of the country.

NOTES

1. Unfortunately, information on the sub-categories of employment for which we had information in 1991 was not available in the 2001 Census.
2. We attempted to get this data for Ludhiana Municipal Corporation (LMC) as well, only to find that the LMC limits contain only 10–15 per cent of units in the area. Hence we report the district-level rather than the city-level data here.
3. According to LMC's former Commissioner, Rs 33 crore was needed to cover the rest of the city's population with municipal water supply, but the funds were not adequate.
4. It is always possible to question the 98 lpcd of actual water consumed in the city based on the PWSSB data when the household connections are not metered. However, that questions the basis of the PWSSB actual consumption data itself. If the PWSSB consumption data are assumed to be right (with some margin of error), the 137 mld in Table 8.5 converts to 98 lpcd. Apart from the PWSSB, there is no data source that can provide this information.
5. We attempted to get from the Central Ground Water Board, and from the Punjab State Pollution Control Board in Ludhiana and Patiala (headquarters), some description of the nature of water use by the key industries and the nature of their effluents, to assess their impact on resource use, but were unsuccessful.
6. Note that there is no anomaly in the decline in the number of persons having access to sewerage. In most cities, a sewer connection installed in violation of procedures predetermined by the service provider, is usually treated as unauthorized and is likely to be disconnected without notice. For instance, see the Delhi Jal Board's website, http://www.delhijalboard. nic.in/.
7. Movement towards taxation of residential property involves transaction costs such as the identification of properties, their valuation, setting tax rates, revenue collection, and other compliance costs that are not the focus of this chapter.

CHAPTER 9

Urban Reforms
A Case Study of Rajkot
(*with* Navroz Dubash)

As we have emphasized and discussed in earlier chapters, cities in India are severely stressed on account of inadequate and poor quality infrastructure and services, and are unable to productively absorb new activities and population. This concern is supported by the fact that aggregate investments in urban infrastructure, that is, water and waste water disposal services, solid waste collection and management, city-wide roads, and street lighting, has been stagnating at about 2.5–2.75 per cent of the total developmental expenditure, which is far below the level that is needed to wipe out the infrastructure deficit and to simultaneously provide for the requirements of fast-growing urban populations. Several studies and government documents, notably the various India Infrastructure Reports,[1] the Ninth, Tenth, and Eleventh Five Year Plans have referred to the problems arising out of inadequate urban infrastructure and services, and have underlined the need to accelerate investment in them. These documents have also referred to gross inefficiencies in service delivery and management, and have called for a closer examination and review of the existing systems and procedures that are constraining efficient delivery of urban services.

Seized of these problems, the Government of India (GoI) has, in recent years, taken important initiatives to explore the use of incentives for the state and city governments to undertake long-standing reforms that impinge on infrastructure and service delivery and management, including geographical and functional fragmentation in city management, weak fiscal base and rating, and inefficient service delivery systems. These initiatives which have been brought forward in the form of Urban Reform Incentive Fund (URIF), the now defunct City Challenge Fund (CCF) or its variant, the Jawaharlal Nehru National Urban Renewal Mission (JNNURM), and pool financing are designed to provide incentives in the form of grants to enable states and cities identify a reform agenda for improving the management of cities and their infrastructure. In this context, this chapter on Rajkot looks at the city and its infrastructure, its current level of adequacy and maintenance, and the nature of pressures that city's infrastructure is confronted with. The chapter attempts to assess the role of Rajkot Municipal Corporation (RMC) in service provisioning, financing, and management together with that of other public institutions concerned with services like water, waste water, and developed land of the private sector and the conditions under which it has been brought in. Similar to what we examined in Ludhiana in the previous chapter, this chapter provides a sense of what might be areas of interventions to put Rajkot city's public service delivery on a fast track, orderly growth route.

The chapter uses a somewhat simple framework of analysis: Why supply mechanisms do not respond to the growing demand for infrastructure and services or the lags in infrastructure and services caused by persisting population growth and other factors bearing on infrastructure demand. The framework recognizes that supply responses are a function of complex factors that extend beyond the institutional and financial arrangements, but due to the limitations of space, this chapter limits itself to looking at the institutional and financial factors, similar to what was done in the previous chapter.

The findings in this chapter are based on an examination of budgets provided by the RMC, materials made available by the Rajkot Urban Development Authority (RUDA), and other reports and studies prepared by institutions such as the Centre for Environmental Planning and Technology (CEPT), academic dissertations on Rajkot, and interviews with the Rajkot Chamber of Commerce and other stakeholders.

The chapter is in three parts: The next part provides an overview of the city's profile, comprising the demographic, economic, and infrastructural attributes of the city. Following this, the next section discusses the respective roles of institutions and organizations that are responsible for the growth and development of Rajkot city and the city's infrastructure, as well as their roles in financing and managing infrastructures. The developmental challenges and options are discussed in the final part of the chapter.

THE CITY OF RAJKOT: DEMOGRAPHIC, ECONOMIC, AND INFRASTRUCTURE ATTRIBUTES

The City

Founded in 1608 as a fortified city on the banks of river Aji, Rajkot over the history has served many needs and situations—as a princely state in the early years of the nineteenth century, as a city developed by the British during 1820–70, as the capital of the former Saurashtra state, and now as a centre of considerable importance in the state of Gujarat, with extensive interests in trade, industry, education, entertainment, and communications. It has country-wide rail and road linkages.

Demography

Rajkot has, over the decades, grown at impressive rates, enabling it to rise from a small town of 36,151 persons in 1901 to an urban agglomeration of over 1 million persons in 2001 (1,002,160 according to the 2001 Census). It now forms a part of the club of thirty-five one-million population cities in India. The population growth of Rajkot has, however, been uneven; during 1941–51, it registered an extraordinarily high rate consisting essentially of refugee migrants from Pakistan. A second period of high growth during 1991–2001 was driven principally by the incorporation of new settlements into the Rajkot municipal jurisdiction. Incorporation or merger[2, 3] of such settlements—the Census calls them outgrowths—represent a phenomenon that now characterizes several of India's metropolises and large cities, and present a challenge of how best to organize and manage services in the merged areas. In Rajkot, as this chapter explains in some detail, this process of urban consolidation is behind many of the most significant urban development challenges the city faces today.

Table 9.1 summarizes population change during 1991–2001 in Rajkot Urban Agglomeration (UA) for its various constituents and outgrowths. It shows that a few local governments experienced more than 100 per cent population growth during this period, with an overall growth rate of nearly 53 per cent for the UA, which testifies its rapid growth during the past decade. Figure 9.1 presents the population change for Rajkot city (the municipal corporation [MC]) since 1901, which summarizes the spurts and growth the MC has been subjected to in the twentieth century. After a peak of 99 per cent population growth during 1941–51, population growth has been highest at 73 per cent during 1991–2001. During this period, the outgrowths have also become relatively more important.

TABLE 9.1
Population Change in Rajkot

Constituents of Rajkot Urban Agglomeration (UA)	Population		Per Cent Growth 1991–2001
	1991	2001	
Rajkot UA	651,007	1,002,160	53.1
Rajkot MC	556,137	966,642	72.8
Kotharia OG	–	11,016	–
Anandput OG	4,923	7,272	47.7
Madhapur OG	3,134	3,744	19.5
Bedi OG	–	3,312	–
Mota Mava OG	1,953	3,046	55.9
Manharpur OG	1,136	2,793	145.9
Munjka OG	1,498	2,192	46.3
Vavdi OG	1,382	2,143	55.1
Mavdi OG*	22,243	–	–
Nana Mava OG*	16,610	–	–
Raiya VP*	41,991	–	–

Source: Census of India, Primary Census Abstract, 1991 and 2001.
Notes: * Merged with the RMC.
UA: Urban Agglomeration; MC: Municipal Corporation; OG: Outgrowth; VP: Village Panchayat.

Rajkot's demographic growth is accompanied by a phenomenal growth in slum population and illegal and unauthorized settlements. Nearly 20 per cent of the city's population is estimated to be living in slums, which, like in other cities, are devoid of basic services and

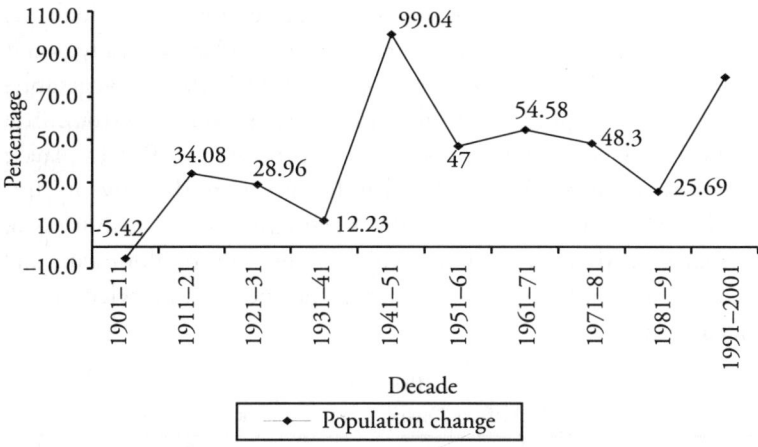

FIGURE 9.1 Population Change in Rajkot City

Source: RMC.

infrastructure such as water, waste water disposal facilities, and road networks. Incorporation of new settlements into the municipal limits in 1999 has affected the social composition of Rajkot city; the percentage of those who live in slum and unauthorized settlements has risen from 20 per cent in the pre-1999 period to about 30 per cent now, suggesting insufficient control over lands therein by the RUDA.

Economic Base

Rajkot has a strong manufacturing economic base, with a market that extends not only beyond the state of Gujarat, but even the national boundaries. In its early history, Rajkot was organized around the establishment of cloth mills. More recently, the emphasis has shifted to small and medium industries, dominated by foundries, oil engine manufacture, machine tools, engineering and automobile works, castor oil processing, gold and silver jewellery, handicrafts, readymade ladies garments, spices, medicines, and wall clocks. Manufacturing activities are concentrated in two main industrial estates, namely, Aji Industrial Estate and Bhaktinagar Industrial Estate; in addition, many small units are scattered through the city.

For its centralized location, Rajkot has a history of being a vibrant trading centre for the Saurashtra region. It boasts of a stock exchange that is linked with the exchanges in Mumbai, Kolkata, and New Delhi. Rajkot also serves as a market town for agricultural produce from the surrounding areas. Although Saurashtra region is a water-scarce region, groundnut, bajra, cotton as well as vegetables are grown by tapping the limited groundwater available. Groundnut and oil seeds are major crops sold and processed in Rajkot. There are currently five large edible oil mills and more than twenty-five small mills in the city. Table 9.2 summarizes the distribution of economic activity in Rajkot, which shows the predominance of manufacturing, trade and commerce, transport, and services in the city's employment.

TABLE 9.2
Activity Distribution in Rajkot

Activity	Per Cent of Workers
Agricultural and allied activities	3.8
Household industries	3.0
Manufacturing (other than HH)	28.2
Construction	5.5
Trade and Commerce	21
Transport	10.2
Services	28.4
Total	*100.0*

Source: RMC, 2001.

Infrastructure

WATER SUPPLY

The availability of water is arguably the greatest long-term problem facing Rajkot. The city lies in a water-deficit region; rains are irregular and there is no perennial source of water. Since the city lies in a hard rock area, the availability of groundwater is limited. Because of this, there is considerable variation in the per capita water availability even though municipal water networks claim to reach 80 per cent of Rajkot's population (and 73 per cent of land area, see Table 9.3), 90 per cent of population in the old city area, and 70 per cent in the newly merged areas. Water is supplied for twenty minutes a day which, the RMC contends, delivers 79.4 lpcd, well below the 135 lpcd recommended by the National Commission on Urbanization. According to the Chamber of Commerce, the municipal network supplies are generally supplemented by water tankers and deep tube wells. During summer months, even slum dwellers are reported to buy water from the private sources.

Table 9.3 summarizes the state of the water supply infrastructure in the city. Given the daily production of 109 mld, the city has an overall water shortage of about 56 mld, when leakages of the order of 27 per cent (29 mld) and the national standard of 135 lpcd are factored in. The total number of house connections are only 122,000 for 189,221 households, and an additional 2,100 stand-posts and 1,700 hand pumps are installed by RMC. Nearly 250 private tankers supplement the water demand of the city. Overall, only 72 per cent of the city's population has access to tap water and nearly 91 per cent of slum population is claimed to be served. Only 78 per cent of the water is being treated which means that the remaining 22 per cent untreated water is a potential health concern. The storage capacity of the city also leaves much to be desired, with its capacity at 54 per cent of what is produced (Table 9.3). The RMC plans to draw 160 mld from the Narmada river at a price of about Rs 6 per kl (excluding any capital expenditure) and Rs 9 per kl if capital expenditure is included. The stability of this source

TABLE 9.3
State of the Infrastructure: Water Supply

Attribute	Component	Indicator
Service delivery	Water demand	135.2 mld @ 135 lpcd
	Water produced	108.8 mld
	Water supply claimed by RMC	112.22 mld @ 112 lpcd
	Water wasted due to leakages	29.4 mld
	Water discharged to the people	79.4 mld
	Water supply per capita per day	79.24 lpcd
Coverage	Total number of house connections	122,000
	Total number of standposts	2100
	Total number of hand pumps by RMC	1700
	Number of tankers (10,000 l)	250
	Percentage population having tap-based water	72
	Percentage of slum population served	91
	Percentage area covered	73
Treatment	Percentage water being treated	78
storage capacity	Percentage of water that can be stored	54

Source: RMC and City Corporate Plan for Rajkot City, 2003, and water demand calculated.

of water is linked with the state-level political compulsions that are beyond the control of RMC. Also, if the source is to be sustained, water pricing will be a major issue. Thus, even in a water-deficient area, the marginal cost pricing of water discussed in the earlier chapters has some relevance, in that water can be sourced from a distance, as long as some part of the additional costs incurred to do this can be charged from the consumers. This also means that water-deficient areas are in need of subsidies to provide the service.

Figure 9.2 shows the trend in coverage of land area and population with water supply networks. While the population coverage has only marginally increased from 75 per cent in 1993 to 80 per cent in 2003, the area covered has actually declined over the decade (especially so in 1998) due to the continually increasing area of the city.

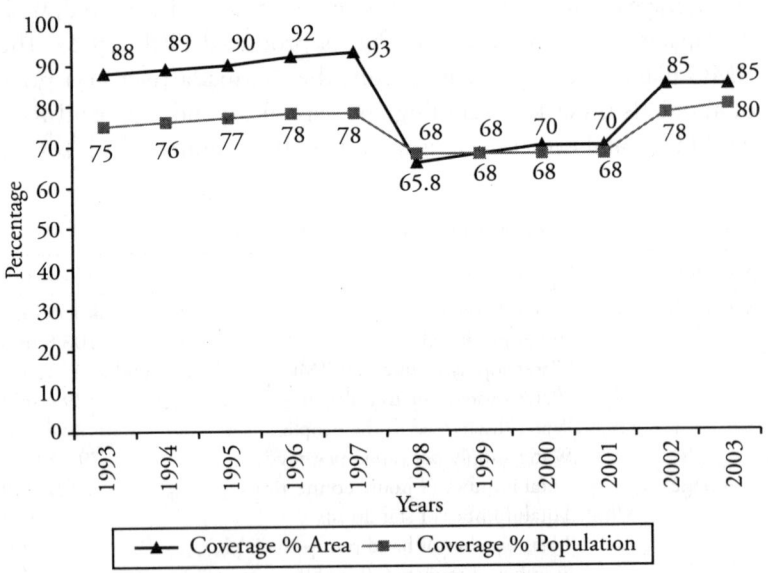

FIGURE 9.2: Water Coverage, RMC, 1993–2003

Source: RMC.

SEWERAGE AND DRAINAGE

Table 9.4 summarizes the state of sewerage and Figure 9.3 summarizes its coverage in the city over time. The sewerage network in Rajkot consisting of a 460 km long collection system, currently serves 55 per cent of city's population and only 44 per cent of households, although in terms of area, it remains at the same level as in 1993 (see Figure 9.3). Also, the sewage treatment plant has a capacity to treat only about 55 per cent of the sewage that is generated in the city. The plant has, however, been non-functional for technical problems and financial constraints. These are highly inadequate taking into account the Ministry of Urban Development's recommended standard of 100 per cent coverage and 100 per cent sewage treatment capacity. A substantial portion of the sewage—approximately 35–40 mld—is discharged into open drains, *nallas*, septic tanks, and soak pits, and is a major source of insanitation in the city.

TABLE 9.4
State of the Infrastructure, RMC: Sewerage

Attributes	Component	Indicator
Treatment	Per cent of wastewater treated	55%
Service coverage	Per cent of population coverage	55%
	Per cent of household coverage	44.43%

Source: Study estimates based on formulae suggested by City Managers' Association Gujarat (CMAG) Urban Indicator Program for Rajkot.

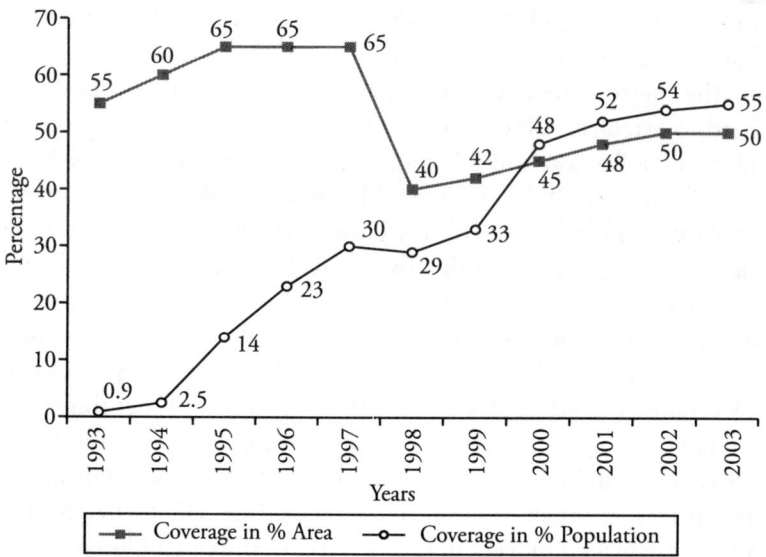

FIGURE 9.3: Sewerage Coverage, RMC, 1993–2003

Source: RMC.

Rajkot relies on a natural drainage system for storm water disposal. The RMC considers the option of having an underground drainage system as too expensive in relation to its potential use. It justifies its choice not to invest in underground drainage for reasons that Rajkot is a low rainfall area and that it has a natural drainage system; however, it has under consideration a study to assess the costs and benefits of such a system.

SOLID WASTE

Rajkot city generates about 470 metric tonnes of solid waste per day of which the RMC and its extended arms are able to collect about 350 metric tonnes, accounting for a waste collection efficiency of 74 per cent (see Table 9.5). The extended arm of RMC includes the private contractors and community based organizations. Primary collection of waste is done by about 3,000 *safai karamcharis* or cleaners of the Corporation and by private sweepers who operate in the three wards of the newly merged area. The RMC has outsourced transportation of the waste to disposal sites to private contractors in thirteen out of twenty-three wards; municipal employees continue to be responsible for the remaining areas. On the basis of the information in Table 9.5, clearly, vehicle capacity is inadequate to handle the waste being generated.

The performance of outsourcing arrangements is, however, hard to establish. One measure of effectiveness is the promptness of waste collection and transport for final disposal. There is a bin only for every 3.38 km (Table 9.5) which is inadequate. Of a total of 75 per cent of waste collected, only 20 per cent is collected on day one, 30 per cent on day two, and the remaining 50 per cent on days three and four, which suggests low level of performance. There is no doubt that RMC falls short of the 100 per cent solid waste collection efficiency recommended by the Ministry of Urban Development (MUD) for cities of this size. It is clear that this is not explained by finances alone. The Rajkot Chamber of Commerce also expressed dissatisfaction with solid waste services and observed that private contractors in the newly merged areas do no better than the municipal employees in the old city. In the case of Surat, as we have learned from Chapter 6, it was better urban management that

TABLE 9.5
State of the Infrastructure, RMC: Solid Waste Management

Attributes	Component	Indicator
Service level & coverage	Per cent of waste collection	74%
	Per cent of vehicle capacity to waste generated	45%
	Average spacing of waste collection bins	3.38 km/bin

Source: Study estimates based on formulae by CMAG Urban Indicator Program for Gujarat.

led Surat to the status of a clean city. Hence, there are lessons of management to be learned from there.

ROAD SYSTEM

With a road length of 2,250 km, half of which being non-bituminous, Rajkot's road network is both inadequate and of poor quality. Only 64 per cent of roads are surfaced (Table 9.6). The coverage is 20 km of road for every square kilometre of land. Table 9.6 suggests that the cost per kilometre of road length is Rs 20,800. For the 2,250 km of road length, the cost (expenditure) is Rs 468 lakhs. Per capita, this works out to Rs 48.42, which is well below even the lower end of financial norm (of Rs 1,260.24 per capita in 2004–5 prices) recommended by the Planning Commission for municipal roads (see Mathur et al., 2007, Table 2).

The traffic is multi-modal, and with no separate traffic grids, the city remains congested with the associated high costs. Two wheeler traffic and auto rickshaws dominate the traffic mix, accounting for about 65 per cent of all traffic. Cars constitute only 1.5–3 per cent of the total traffic. When combined with non-motorized

TABLE 9.6
State of the Urban Infrastructure, RMC: Roads

Attributes	Component	Indicator
Surfaced roads	Per cent of roads surfaced	64%
Physical coverage	Road density	20 km/sq. km
Financial management	Cost per km of road length	Rs 20,800/km

Source: Study estimates based on formulae suggested by CMAG Urban Indicator Program for Gujarat.

traffic, the result is multiple forms of transportation sharing the limited roadways, with resultant loss of speed. The problem is compounded by the prevalence of uncontrolled or manually managed intersections. Rajkot has no public transport system; however, a vibrant privately operated transport network fills in to meet the mobility requirements of the city.

STREET LIGHTING

Street lighting is managed by the RMC in conjunction with the Gujarat Electricity Board (GEB) and private contractors. The institutional arrangement is that poles are owned by the GEB, while the distribution network is provided and managed by the RMC. The RMC, in turn, contracts out maintenance of street lighting to private contractors for sixteen out of twenty-three wards. As with other services, the newly merged areas present to the RMC a formidable task in respect of street light provisioning.

Table 9.7 and Figure 9.4 describe the state of the art infrastructure with respect to street lights. The street lights per capita have declined during 1997–2003, reflecting the problems of the newly merged areas. Table 9.7 shows that the number of street lights per kilometre of road is twenty-five, accounting for a total number of 56,250 street lights for the 2,250 km of roads. This works out to one street light for every 40 m compared with the international norm of one street light for every 30 m. Figure 9.4 further corroborates that the number of street lights per capita has have in fact declined during 1997–2003. Hence more street lights are needed (see Box 9.1). Table 9.7 also reports the cost per street light to be Rs 1,350. We work out the total cost (expenditure) for the 56,250 street lights to be Rs 75,937,500. At RMC's 2001 population, this works out to be

TABLE 9.7
State of the Infrastructure, RMC: Street Lighting

Attributes	Component	Indicator
Street light coverage	Number of street lights per km of road length	25
Cost	Cost per street light	Rs 1350

Source: Study estimates based on formulae suggested by CMAG Urban Indicator Program for Gujarat.

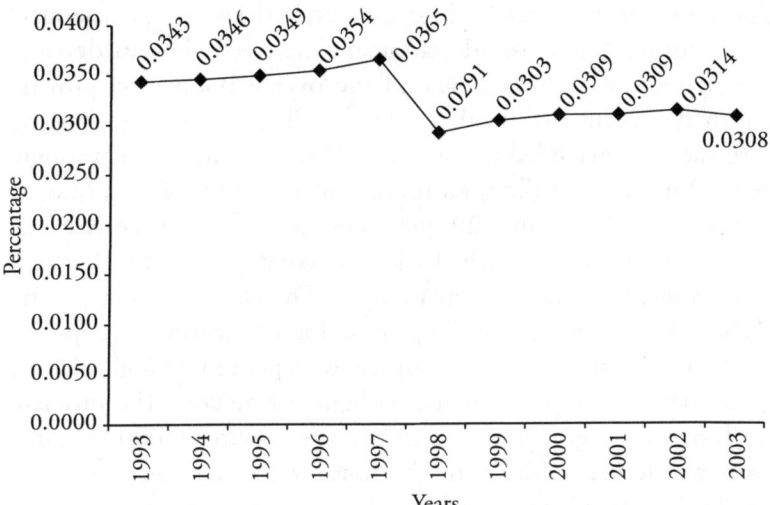

FIGURE 9.4: Street Lights Per Capita, Rajkot City, 1993–2003

Source: RMC.

Rs 78.56 in per capita terms. This is also quite low when compared with the Planning Commission's low end of the financial norm suggested for street lighting which is Rs 377.60 in per capita terms (2004–5 prices) (see Mathur et al., 2007).

PHYSICAL ATTRIBUTES AND LAND USE

Rajkot is characterized by a pattern of multiple land uses. The total area developed for urban activities constitutes 77 per cent of the Rajkot municipal area. Residential use occupies about half of this area, while industries occupy a fifth and commercial zones occupy less than 2 per cent. Although a development plan has been prepared, poor implementation and enforcement result in quite different ground realities. Rajkot is plagued by problems of informal sector including slum development, illegal colonies, commercial encroachments, lack of industrial zoning, and unplanned mixed land use, quite similar to that in Ludhiana.

Informal residential use

Residential use occupies almost 50 per cent of the total land area, and is split into both high-density development, mostly in the older areas, and low-density development, in the newly incorporated areas. Formal residential development has been slow to develop, and it now seriously lags behind the overall population growth. Informal settlements in the form of illegal and unauthorized construction have filled in the gap, and now occupy an alarmingly high 60 per cent of the total residential area. Out of this, 'jhuggi-jhopri' clusters occupy 20 per cent and the rest consists of unauthorized colonies, which do not comply with the General Development Control Regulations (GDCR). According to the RMC, 75 per cent of dwelling units for low-income groups, 55 per cent for middle-income groups, and 25 per cent of high-income group housing are constructed without permission. The problem is, if anything, growing. On an average, around 6,000 dwelling units are added annually to the housing stock as against 1,600 applications that are received by RMC for formal approval.

A substantial portion of unauthorized construction is accounted for by what are known as 'Suchit Societies', which are planned illegal colonies constructed by converting agricultural lands to non-agricultural uses. Development of these colonies is explained by two factors: first, development permission and building applications procedures are extremely lengthy (see Figure 9.5),[4] leading households to bypass the procedures and build illegally. Second, conversion of agricultural into non-agricultural lands is a relatively simple process, and is often used for conversion into farmhouses. The RMC has no role in this process, even when it has to ultimately assume responsibility for extending services to such areas.

Informal commercial use

Commercial use accounts for 1.7 per cent of the total area or 2.1 per cent of the developed area. There are two wholesale markets in the city which are supplemented by a large and vibrant informal trading sector. The informal sector consisting of predominantly large encroachments is spread out over the entire city, with no effective regulation either by the RMC or by the RUDA. Importantly, there has not been any systematic discussion on understanding either the role of this sector or the alternative ways in which it can be integrated into the economy of the city.

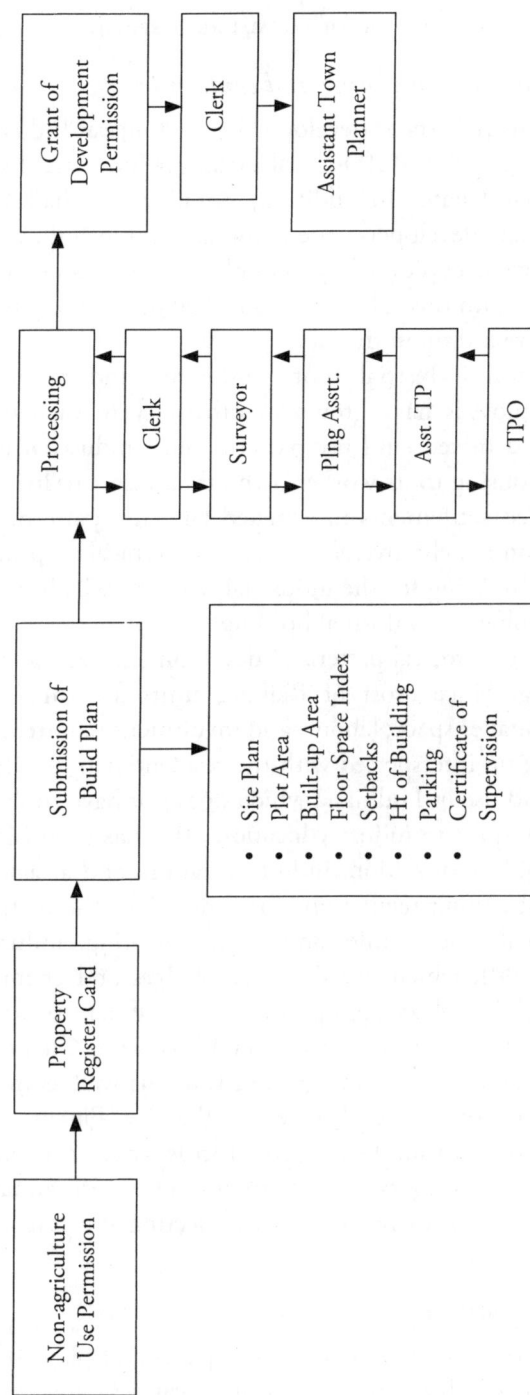

FIGURE 9.5: Path of Approval of Building Plan

Source: RUDA.
Note: TP—Town Planner; TPO—Town Planning Officer.

Industrial use—the lack of zoning and conformity

There are two industrial estates developed by the Gujarat Industrial Development Corporation (GIDC): Bhaktinagar Industrial Estate and Aji Industrial Estate. In addition, Sorathiawadi had been developed by private developers. The National Textile Mill, which is non-operational, occupies a large chunk of prime land in the centre of the city. With this valuable land locked up, it is easy to see why land prices are bid up in the city.

For its historical industrial roots, industries and residences of industrial employees have grown in proximity to each other, showing itself in a mixed land use pattern. Most industrial units do not provide housing to its workers, who then resort to living in slum unauthorized settlements in a mixed land use pattern. The Aji's riverbed is completely covered with slums, a typical by-product of the absence of housing for the industrial workers, which further aggravates the problem of informal housing.

In addition, the historical pattern of development has inhibited efforts at zoning. Since most of Rajkot's units are small-scale industries with smaller space, labour, and investment requirements, they have sprung up interspersed with the residential areas. This is similar to the land use in Ludhiana which does not have zoning or regulation with respect to industry location. This has been further propelled by rapid urbanization, industrialization, and absence of enforcement and zoning regulations for industries. The scattered location of small-scale textile and screen-printing industries (approximately 400), which use a variety of dyes and chemicals, reduces the possibility of setting up of common effluent treatment plants, quite similar to what we observe in Ludhiana (see Chapter 8). These chemicals pollute the underground water as well as the Aji river which is a major source of water for the city. Finally, these small-scale industries within the residential areas are creating undue pressure on the already stressed infrastructure of water, sanitation, and solid waste management, as well as affecting the residential character of such areas.

Public and semi-public use

Public purpose spaces include open space, parks and playgrounds, recreational spaces, education and health facilities, government

Box 9.1
What Then is the City?

In sum, Rajkot city is a growing city with a strong manufacturing and trading base. The city's infrastructural services are not only inadequate in relation to national standards and benchmarks, but as the graphs show, their level when measured in relation to either area or population has not improved over the years. Quite the contrary, all services show a discontinuity corresponding to the additional demands of the merger in the late 1990s. The city has barely managed to hold on, in a wider sense, to the 1993 level of infrastructural services. Spatially, infrastructure pressures have risen in the older areas, and the newer areas remain grossly underserved. A significant portion of the city has grown outside of the building controls and is indicative of either the arduous procedures which households, business and industry find costly to follow,[5] or inadequate coordination between different institutions that hold responsibilities for the growth and development of the city. The city continues to be at high risk on account of its dependence on rainwater; any reduction in such risks is dependent on the new water links and how these are fostered outside the political arena.

offices, and other institutions. The major recreational facility is the race course complex, which houses an international cricket stadium, indoor stadium, hockey ground, football ground, a garden, and an open ground. Other recreational spaces are Shastri Maidan, Zilla Garden, Jubilee Garden, and Aji Dam. The percentages of public purpose space to total area and developed area are 9 per cent and 11 per cent, respectively. A description of land use thus indicates that public purpose spaces are in deficit in the old city area.

Institutional and Financial Frameworks

STATUTORY AND INSTITUTIONAL FRAMEWORK

Land, infrastructure, and services provide the foundation for the development of a city. Their efficient and equitable provisioning is central to economic growth and poverty reduction. Within the general pattern observed over much of the country, the development and provision of land, infrastructure, and services in

Rajkot is regulated by a string of laws, procedures, and government orders, whose administration and enforcement rest with the state government, city government, and specific-purpose authorities. These laws together with the Constitutional (74th) Amendment Act, 1992, provide a framework for service provision and management in terms of the powers that the different levels of government and authorities can exercise, their territorial and functional domain, and the channels of communications between them.

Table 9.8 illustrates the statutes and the institutions (RMC, RUDA, Gujarat Industrial Development Corporation, Gujarat Water Supply and Sewage Board [GWSSB], and most recently the Gujarat Infrastructure Development Board [GIDB] in 1999 created by the Gujarat Infrastructure Development Act) created as a result of the statute, as they apply to Rajkot. It is easy to imagine that there is an overlap of functions between the RUDA and GIDB, and between the RMC and the GWSSB. This is elaborated further below.

TABLE 9.8
Statutory and Institutional Framework for
Land, Infrastructure, and Services

Statute	Institutional Set-up
The Bombay Provincial Municipal Corporation Act, 1949,* as amended for Gujarat, 1989	Rajkot Municipal Corporation (RMC)
The Gujarat Town Planning and Urban Development Act, 1976	Rajkot Urban Development Authority (RUDA)
Gujarat Infrastructure Development Act, 1999	Gujarat Infrastructure Development Board (GIDB)
The Gujarat Industrial Development Corporation Act, 1962	The Gujarat Industrial Development Corporation (GIDC)
Gujarat Water Supply and Sewerage Board Act	Gujarat Water Supply and Sewage Board (GWSSB)

Source: State government of Gujarat.
Note: * Except in case of primary education, most of the provisions in the Bombay Provincial Municipal Corporations Act, 1949 are based on the city of Bombay Municipal Act, 1888, with most lawmakers claiming that this Act has stood the test of time.

Rajkot Municipal Corporation (RMC)

The RMC is the key institution for the provision and management of basic urban infrastructure such as water and waste water disposal services, garbage disposal, city-wide roads, and street lighting. Following the incorporation of the Constitutional (74th) Amendment Act, 1992, the RMC is also entrusted with two additional functions, namely, (*a*) planning for economic and social development and (*b*) urban forestry, protection of the environment, and promotion of ecological aspects.[6] Drawing its power and authority from the Bombay Provincial Municipal Corporation Act, 1949 as applicable to the state of Gujarat, the RMC is also responsible for a host of regulatory functions which give them enough power to regulate any activity, for example, building permits, vending licenses, and industrial permits (see Table 9.9 for a list of functions envisaged by the Bombay Provincial Municipal Corporation Act for the RMC); however, these powers are subordinate to the provisions in some of the state-level laws. Not all the functions listed in the Act are performed by the RMC.

The Corporation consists of a council of sixty-nine members from twenty-three wards with a Mayor as its head. Committees at the ward level are absent. Functionally, the RMC is organized around a powerful standing committee with power to sanction contracts and a number of other sectoral committees. There is a parallel administrative structure organized around twenty-five sectoral departments led by a Commissioner in whom all executive powers of the Corporation vest. The capacity of this executive arm is extremely low.

Of the 5,000 employees of the RMC, 3,000 are unskilled safai karamcharis displaying a large base of workers with lack of any skills. With regard to professional qualifications, the RMC includes only one chartered accountant, four MBAs, and two environmental engineers in its ranks. In addition, while it is an extremely difficult claim to substantiate, there are also indications that political connections and political parties play a role in RMC staffing and promotion decisions, which undermine the scope for development of a merit-based internal structure.

While difficult to ascertain, the political and executive wings of the RMC do not operate in concert at the level of broad direction

TABLE 9.9
Authority and Functions, RMC

Act/Authority	Functions as Envisaged for the Authority
Bombay Provincial Municipal Corporation Act, 1949, amended for Gujarat 1989	• Managing municipal property and liabilities • Formation of public and private streets, building regulations and improvement schemes
Authority Rajkot Municipal Council (RMC)	• Watering, scavenging, and cleansing of all public streets and places in the city and removal of all sweepings therefrom • Water works management comprising construction, management and maintenance of municipal water works, and construction of new works necessary for a sufficient supply of water for public and private purposes • Collection, removal, and treatment of sewage, offensive matter, and rubbish • Lighting of public streets, municipal markets, and public buildings vested in the Corporation • Construction and maintenance of public markets • Entertainment of a fire brigade • Construction and maintenance of public hospitals

Source: RMC.

and strategic vision. Instead, the executive views the Mayor and Corporation members as an obstacle to its functioning which have to be side-stepped wherever possible. As Paul (2008) points out, urban local bodies (ULBs) need democratically elected mayors for a longer term and with powers and capacity to lead and take complex decisions rather than merely play ceremonial roles. The practice of commissioners deputed by state governments who act as de facto power centres need to be abolished. For their part, the elected members are adamant that there are certain political realities, such as the difficulty of full cost pricing of water services, which it is their role to transmit to the executive. More generally, the current lack of, and the difficulty of forging, a shared transformative agenda across the political and executive arms of the RMC is likely to be a substantial obstacle to development and implementation of a reform agenda.

Gujarat Town Planning and Urban Development Act

The Gujarat Town Planning and Urban Development Act (GTPUDA), 1976, applicable to the entire state, regulates the future development of land, infrastructure, and services in cities and towns; the RUDA set up under the provisions of this Act, is responsible for orderly development of Rajkot city and its environs, formulation of a master plan/perspective plan, and development of new areas with proper infrastructure and services. It formulated in 1999 a development plan for Rajkot, 2011 AD, which is under consideration of the state government. Table 9.10 summarizes the functions of RUDA and the institutional set up for its creation.

TABLE 9.10
Institutional Set-up and Functions of RUDA

Act/Authority	Functions as Envisaged for the Authority
Gujarat Town Planning and Urban Development Act, 1976	• Undertake the preparation of a development plan for the urban development area
Authority Rajkot Urban Development Authority (RUDA)	• Undertake the preparation of town planning schemes in urban development areas for matters pertaining to planning, development, and use of urban land • Control the development activities in accordance with the development plan in the urban development area • Execute works in connection with water supply, disposal of sewage, and provision of other services and amenities • Acquire, hold, manage, and dispose the movable or immovable property as necessary • Carry out the development work in urban development areas as assigned to it by the state government • Enter into contract or arrangement with any local authority/person or organization for development purposes

Source: RUDA.

Clearly, as stated, there is an overlap of functions between the RUDA as stated by the Gujarat Town Planning and Urban Development Act and the GWSSB.

Gujarat Infrastructure Development Board

The GIDB set up under the Gujarat Infrastructure Development Act, 1999, is meant to promote public–private partnership in infrastructure development and advise the state government on policies relating to private participation in such projects (see Table 9.11). The Act provides 'a framework for participation by persons other than the state government and government agencies in financing, construction and operation of infrastructure projects'. Thus Rajkot has been much more proactive than Ludhiana in promoting private participation in infrastructure projects.

TABLE 9.11
Functions of GIDB

Act/Authority	Functions as Envisaged for the Authority
Gujarat Infrastructure Development Act, 1999	• Promote private sector participation in financing, construction, maintenance, and operation of infrastructural facilities
Gujarat Infrastructure Development Board (GIDB)	• Advise the state government on matters of policies related to private–public participation • Coordinate and monitor projects

Source: GIDB.

Gujarat Industrial Development Corporation (GIDC)

The GIDC set up under the GIDC Act 1962 has a vital stake in the economic development of the state, including that of cities and towns such as Rajkot. The Corporation establishes and manages industrial estates at places selected by the state government, and provides loans for the establishment of factories in such estates. The GIDC enjoys power under the GIDC Act to provide amenities and common facilities in the estates and is responsible for their maintenance. The Corporation has developed the two industrial areas in Rajkot, and as per the statutory provisions, is responsible for its O&M. Then there is the GWSSB which provides water to the rural areas and undertakes augmentation of water supply in selected urban areas of the state. The set of institutions in Rajkot indicates that it is more conscious of investors than the set of institutions in Ludhiana, Punjab, indicate.

HOW DOES THE INSTITUTIONAL FRAMEWORK WORK IN PRACTICE?

To what extent has this institutional structure helped to build, augment, and maintain the services in Rajkot? To what extent has it constrained efficient and equitable service delivery? The proliferation of Acts and corresponding issues can and does lead to implementation problems, as we have seen in the case of Ludhiana as well. The existing institutional structure rests on two premises, both of which contribute to sub-optimal outcomes: (*a*) local governments and their interests and priorities are subordinate to larger, state-level priorities and (*b*) spatial and functional domains of the different institutions are distinct.

First, local and municipal mandates are often subordinated to state-level priorities. For example, under the Gujarat Industrial Development Act, 1962, the GIDC is empowered to 'establish and manage industrial estates at places selected by the state government', without requiring it to consult with the RMC, presumably on the ground that economic and industrial development is outside the purview of the municipal government. But in reality, economic and social development is within the purview of the RMC (see the section on RMC, section on statutory and institutional framework). However, the GIDC is not accountable to local constituents. Industrial estates in Rajkot are a case in point. The industrial estates were established by the GIDC in accordance with norms that are not in conformity with those of the RMC. The RMC demands that the estates be handed over to them and that the pipes be changed before they will provide water. GIDC insists that they do not have the necessary funds to change pipes and that RMC should nonetheless provide water. As a result, the industrial estates in Rajkot are today faced with problems of water and infrastructure management within the estate areas. Such provisions in the Gujarat Industrial Development Act fail to recognize the role of RMC in planning for economic and social development. As far as local services are concerned, only local authorities should be in a position to decide regarding their delivery since they know and can reflect the local preferences better.

Second, jurisdictional overlaps across institutions leave scope for shedding of responsibility. Both the Bombay Provincial Municipal Corporation Act and the GTPUDA include provisions governing water supply and sanitation, thereby conferring responsibility on both RMC and RUDA for these services. Since the GTPUDA does not specify a timeframe or provide sufficient guidance on requirements for completion of water and sanitation services, these responsibilities tend to be underplayed by RUDA. For example, as discussed further below, RUDA failed to provide these services to the 'new areas' that were merged with the RMC area in 1998, leading to continued contentions by the two authorities that the failure to provide timely water and sanitation rests with the other. Since each institution is constituted under separate acts through separate processes, there has been little effort at rectifying this institutional overlap.

In addition, complex procedures require coordination across multiple institutions. For example, approval for town planning schemes involves the RMC and the RUDA and is sent to the Gujarat state town planner for modification and approval as necessary. This process is overly elaborate. Moreover, the coordination problem can be exacerbated by the state town planner's lack of familiarity with the local context, which could introduce locally inappropriate decisions. Finally, the lengthy approval procedures have the perverse effect of encouraging unauthorized colonies, as the costs of formal approval are too high.

The institutional context for Rajkot's urban development is further illuminated by a focus on two additional themes: the merger of RUDA areas into RMC and the emergent use of public–private partnerships.

THE MERGER OF RUDA AREAS INTO RMC:
A MAJOR INSTITUTIONAL CHALLENGE

In June 1998, three village areas with a population of more than two lakhs were merged with Rajkot city, which then had a population of approximately 6.6 lakhs, representing a 37 per cent increase in the city's (RMC's) population. This merger also increased the city's area by 33.6 per cent (see Figure 9.6 for a visual representation of these changed boundaries). Figures 9.2 and 9.3 tell a story of a steep drop in levels of service provision (of water supply and sewerage) in 1997, as the newly merged areas with highly inadequate levels of service provision were added to Rajkot. Behind this merger lies a story of institutional dissonance.

As per the GTPUDA, 1976, the newly merged areas were declared urban development areas and brought under the control of RUDA, prior to their eventual merger into the RMC. During the period of RUDA control, while population grew and economic activity flourished in anticipation of the merger, the development of the area in terms of service delivery failed to keep pace. As a result, the RMC is now faced with digesting an enormous area and population. The merger poses the largest set of urban development challenges Rajkot would face in the coming years, particularly in the areas of land use, water, and sewerage.

RUDA insists that their responsibilities are, in order of priority, preparation and periodic revision of a development plan, preparation of town planning schemes, and, finally, infrastructure development. Thus, plans are regularly prepared on paper; RUDA fulfils its obligation to revise development plans every decade. RUDA officials argue that since infrastructure is their last priority, provision of infrastructure to the new areas should not be seen as their responsibility. However, the GTPUDA does not provide any support to this contention. The matter is further confused, because the GWSSB is responsible for rural parts of the state, including rural parts of RUDA areas.

As a result of this mismatched perception, the newly merged areas were transferred to RMC with highly inadequate infrastructure. RUDA provided only a basic street network, leaving provision of other services to the RMC. For example, RUDA had provided only 500 standposts for water supply for a population of about 100,000 (or a standpost for every 200 population). Despite this lack of basic facilities, at the time of the merger, high rise buildings and other signs of advanced development already dotted the new areas, relying on water tankers and soak pits.

Rajkot and Its Outgrowth—1991

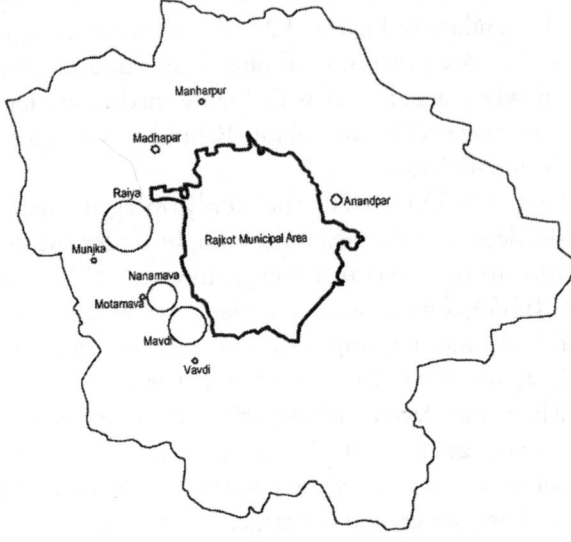

Rajkot and Its Outgrowth—2001

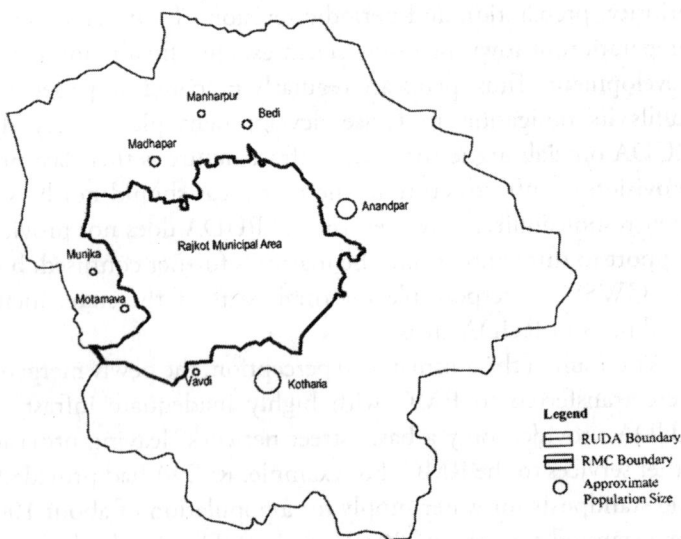

FIGURE 9.6: Change in Area and Population of
Rajkot and Its Outgrowths, 1991–2001

Source: RMC.
Note: Map not to scale.

As a consequence of institutional overlaps, and lack of clarity, the RMC now faces a steep task ahead. It has had to invest a substantial portion of its capital budget for upgrading facilities in the newly merged areas, a pattern that is likely to continue in the future. For example, scheme expenditures increased between 1998–9 and 1999–2000 from Rs 21 crore to Rs 52 crore, largely accounted for by massive increases in water supply, new area development, and town planning. In undertaking this task, the RMC will have to do a back-filling provision of services in an area that is already substantially developed, a far more challenging and expensive task than laying infrastructure early in the development cycle.

EMERGENT PUBLIC–PRIVATE PARTNERSHIPS

The RMC's emphasis on private sector involvement is an important emergent institutional trend in the city's management, quite in contrast with that of Ludhiana's. Specifically, using provisions of the Gujarat Infrastructure Development Act, 1999 as also of the Bombay Provincial Municipal Corporations Act (as applied to Gujarat), the RMC has an aggressive attitude to promote outsourcing of municipal services where possible. To date, they have established a 'zonal contract system' for laying water pipelines, O&M of sewerage and drainage, solid waste management and transport of solid waste to dump sites, and maintenance of street lights. Moreover, they use what they describe as build-operate-transfer (BoT) contracts (described further below) for construction of public facilities such as fire stations and community centres.

The pursuit of greater economic efficiency is the major reason given by the RMC for the emphasis on outsourcing. For example, the RMC finds that private contractors used for transporting solid waste deploy capital-intensive trucks more efficiently than they were used under municipal control. Privately employed drivers work longer hours, getting better use out of the trucks. Contracts are written based on number of trips with a designated load. The performance of these outsourced arrangements is, however, hard to establish. While RMC officials express satisfaction with the outsourcing arrangement, Chamber of Commerce members dispute this assertion, suggesting that private contractors who manage sweeping in the new areas do no better than the municipal employees in the old city. Moreover, as stated earlier, about half the waste remains uncollected after two days.

Outsourcing is also used as a way of side-stepping politically volatile labour management issues. As described earlier, about half the RMC's staff (3,000 workers) consists of safai karamcharis or sweepers and cleaners responsible for collection and consolidation of solid waste. These cleaners are organized into several strong unions, which, according to RMC officials, place obstacles in the way of more effective functioning and certainly oppose any lay-offs. The issue is further compounded by the fact that most of the safai karamcharis belong to the same caste, which is protected as a 'scheduled caste' under the Atrocities Act. RMC officials claim that the employees misuse the protections under this Act in the course of labour negotiations.

Taking advantage of the lack of existing municipal workers, the new areas are entirely serviced by outsourced solid waste contracts. The RMC aims to expand upon this base until 50 per cent of the service is provided through outsourcing. The benefits of outsourcing, from an RMC perspective, are that private contractors are better able to exact labour discipline from workers, since they are 'headstrong' people. In order to obtain results, the RMC must 'turn a blind eye' to the methods of the contractors. There may indeed be legitimate concerns about inefficiencies derived from politically organized municipal workers. However, use of outsourcing as a political instrument also risks undercutting the original purpose of labour protections and protections for scheduled castes. In the absence of a broader set of robust social protections and credible enforcement, outsourcing may have perverse results in Rajkot's context.

The RMC has also made liberal use of so-called 'build-operate-transfer' (BOT) projects as a partnership vehicle with the private sector. In essence these are contracts to private developers for construction of a specific facility—fire station, community centre, or others—as specified in the Rajkot Development Plan. In exchange for construction of the facility, the private contractor receives rights to develop a portion of the land for commercial use or sale. For example, the RMC has contracted with a developer to build a fire station and housing for firemen, at zero cost, on a plot of land specified for the purpose in the Rajkot Development Plan.

On the basis of a plan drawn up and approved by the RMC, the fire station and housing was constructed on about 40 per cent of the plot area, leaving the remaining 60 per cent or so at the disposal of the contractor to be developed as a multi-storey shopping complex and community hall. The contractor rents the community hall for functions and leases the shops, both at market rates.

Since the land, once zoned for a public purpose, cannot legally be sold or used for any purpose other than a fire station, this arrangement appears to benefit both sides. The contractor benefits from access to land in a prime commercial area. Moreover, since the contractor normally will collect rental or sale income in 'black' (or unaccounted for) money as well as 'white' money, they realize the true economic value of the property. RMC officials also candidly admit that the contractor, by taking payment in black (or unaccounted) money, can come close to realizing the market value of the land.

Such arrangements raise a basic question. Does the provision of a public facility at no cost—such as a fire station—represent fair compensation to the RMC in exchange for prime commercial land? The answer rests in part on the details of the contracting and bidding process, which would determine whether the RMC extracted the true value of the property. These empirical questions were beyond the scope of this chapter, but are certainly necessary to explore before this sort of arrangement is widely adopted.

More fundamentally, the RMC's BOT arrangement represents an attempt to side-step the rigidities of the zoning arrangements. In essence, it allows commercial use of a substantial portion of land allotted for public use. The RMC would likely be better served by an arrangement that allowed it to sell off a portion of the land explicitly for commercial use, reap the full market value, and use the proceeds to build a public facility on the remaining land. Doing so would, however, require a change in the zoning rules.

THE FINANCES OF THE RMC

The RMC maintains a single entry/cash-based accounting system; consequently, the receivables and payables do not form a part of its financial accounts as in a double entry system of accrual accounting. Nor are its liabilities adequately accounted for. The

RMC classifies all receipts into four categories, viz., revenue receipts, capital receipts, scheme receipts, and other (miscellaneous) receipts. Revenue receipts are further divided into two main heads: (*a*) own revenue receipts and (*b*) state transfers. Own revenue receipts consist of taxes, user charges, and other fees and fines that are levied and collected by RMC. Own resource receipts, that is, the fiscal base of RMC consists of octroi, consolidated property tax, theatre tax, vehicle tax, and non-tax receipts, mainly from sale of water. Receipts under state transfers consist of education cess, which is returned to the Corporation either in full or part, and grants-in-aid under general purpose and specific purpose categories. Capital receipts represent loans contracted for various projects and from sale of assets. Scheme receipts are amounts that the RMC receives for various project-specific schemes and works. Other receipts consist of deposits, advances, and the like.

Expenditure heads are also divided by the RMC into four categories, namely, revenue expenditure, capital expenditure, scheme expenditure, and other expenditure (miscellaneous). Revenue expenditure has three categories: (*a*) expenditure on establishment, wages, and salaries; (*b*) expenditure on operation and maintenance; and (*c*) debt servicing. Expenditure is classified for each department such as general administration, fire, lighting, public health, water supply, medical care, pre-primary education, primary education, higher secondary education, technical education, public buildings, and on commercial activities. Expenditure on developmental works is shown as capital expenditure, whereas expenditure on various project-specific schemes is shown under schemes.[7]

In 2002–3, the RMC spent Rs 1265 per capita (Table 9.12). Annual revenue expenditure, that is, expenditure on the O&M of services and regulation of activities accounts for 59 per cent of the total expenditure, which was Rs 742 per capita (in current terms) or Rs 553 (in 1997–8 prices) in 2002–3. Of this, Rs 398 was spent on establishment, wages, and salaries, an amount equal to 54 per cent of the revenue head or 31 per cent of total expenditure, with the remaining, that is, 27 per cent spent on O&M expenditures. Expenditure on pensions and other retirement benefits forms 7.4 per cent of the total expenditure. Next in importance to revenue expenditure is expenditure on schemes; in 2002–3, expenditure on schemes constituted 28.9 per cent, and only the balance of 5.1 per cent was incurred on creation of new assets. Table 9.12 describes the composition of RMC(s) expenditures.

TABLE 9.12
Composition of RMC's Expenditure, 2002–3

| Nature of Expenditure | Per Capita (Rs) | | Per Cent of Total |
	Current	1997–8 Prices	Expenditure
Revenue	742.14	553.40	58.67
Establishment and salaries*	397.98	296.77	31.46
O&M and others*	344.16	256.63	27.21
Capital	64.13	47.82	5.07
Schemes	365.20	272.32	28.87
Pensions and other deposits	93.49	69.72	7.39
Total	1264.96	943.26	100.00

Source: RMC and authors' computations.
Note: * Included in own revenue expenditure.

How is this spending level financed? The RMC raises, with the revenue-raising powers that it has access to, Rs 1,424 per capita (including state transfers). Over 57 per cent of RMC's own income is derived from octroi, an indirect tax on goods entering the municipality, perceived to be generally producing distortions but a preferred option with most municipalities where it exists. Notwithstanding the proposition that municipal governments should make better use of charges and direct taxation (property) to finance services, there is resistance to do so as discussed further below.

Earning from property taxes which uses an annual rateable value (ARV) base are 24.5 per cent of revenues of the RMC. The general property tax rate rises with the ARV, with the highest slab of greater than Rs 10,000 attracting a tax rate of 30 per cent to which are added a conservancy tax of 4 per cent on domestic properties; non-domestic properties are taxed at higher rates for conservancy and are required to additionally pay a fire tax. By most reckoning, it is a high tax regime and has persisted on account of the inability of RMC to periodically revise the ARVs or improve collection.

State transfers to supplement the financial resources of RMC are, in relative terms of lesser significance, accounting for about 8 per cent of the total revenue receipts. A greater part of the transfers accrue to RMC in the form of education cess grant. Table 9.13 summarizes the structure of RMC's revenues.

TABLE 9.13
Structure of RMC's Revenues, 2002–3

Revenue Identity	Per Capita (Rs)		Per Cent of Total Revenue Receipts
	Current	1997–8 Prices	
Own revenues receipts	968.68	722.33	68.00
Tax receipts*	909.96	678.54	63.88
Non-tax receipts*	58.73	43.79	4.12
State transfers	113.66	84.75	7.97
Other miscellaneous	78.27	58.36	5.49
Capital receipts	48.34	36.04	3.39
Scheme income	103.96	77.52	7.29
Pension and other deposits	111.53	83.17	7.82
Total receipts	1,424.44	1,062.18	100.00

Source: RMC and authors' computations.
Note: * Included in own revenue receipts.

At the first stage of analysis, the finances of the RMC portray a positive profile in the following ways:

1. The corporation has a revenue account surplus; in 2002–3, the revenue account surplus formed 36 per cent of the total revenue receipts. Few municipalities in India are able to claim such surpluses.
2. It is not a revenue-dependent corporation, and its dependency ratio on state resources is extremely low, similar to that of Ludhiana, consisting primarily of education cess grant.
3. It is able to apply its surpluses for capital improvement works, a distinction that is achieved by, at best, a few municipal corporations in India.

A closer examination of RMCs finances, however, shows several disturbing features. These are as follows:

1. Maintaining a revenue account surplus is of little consequence when there are serious service shortages and deprivations, for example, a 79 lpcd water supply with a coverage that has rarely exceeded 80 per cent of population, 45 per cent of households which remain unconnected to sewerage system, and the inability

of RMC to be able to exercise enough control and regulation on land use. In per capita terms, the RMC spends Rs 2.03 per day on running the city's services which, by any reckoning, in insufficient for purposes of growth, equity, or quality of life.

2. Aggregate per capita expenditure levels have risen marginally over the past five years and have, in fact, registered a decline at 1997–8 prices at a rate of 4 per cent per annum. Combined with the fact that expenditure levels, when compared with nationally recommended norms, are low and the fact that the RMC is unable to hold on to even these levels tends to suggest a deterioration in the levels of infrastructure services in the city of Rajkot.

3. Octroi is yet another issue over which the finances of RMC are vulnerable. The state government of Gujarat has abolished octroi in all municipalities, but has so far retained it in municipal corporations. Given the nation-wide trends where octroi stands abolished in all states excepting municipal corporations of Gujarat and Maharashtra, its abolition in these places would seem likely. There appears to be no preparedness on the part of the RMC to operate its activities in a revenue-regime without octroi levies, a revenue source that currently accounts for 57 per cent of revenues.

4. Property tax is the most likely alternative for municipal corporations to at least partially offset octroi levies (although the state government would come up with a compensation package, as in other states). However, the RMC does not show evidence of thinking ahead to build up the property tax regime and its efficiency ahead of abolition of octroi. There are several possible areas for proactive steps. First, the RMC could consider shifting from the ARV method of assessment to a more manageable and transparent unit area based system. Second, despite provision in the Bombay Provincial Municipal Corporation Act (1949) for revisions in ARV every four years, the RMC has allowed the values to remain unchanged for over a decade, since 1992. Third, and arguably most significant, property tax collection efficiency is poor and needs to be improved. In 2001–2, for example, the property tax bill was Rs 21 crore, arrears were 140 crore, and collections were a

mere 16 crore, not even sufficient to cover current charges, let alone arrears. Indeed, a number of lawsuits are pending on property tax issues. In an attempt to deal with this problem, the RMC waived arrears up to Rs 15,000 per property, which seems to have subsequently had some impact on collection efficiency—collection in 2002–3 went up to Rs 25.5 crore—but at the cost of a one time financial adjustment.

5. The water account is another disconcerting feature of the finances of RMC. Water provisioning is perhaps the most important function of RMC, more so as Rajkot is located in a water-scarce region. The RMC spends approximately 18 per cent of its total budget on water, inclusive of expenditure on establishment, O&M including electricity charges and augmentation of water supplies. While there is no consistency in the pattern of expenditure, expenditure on electricity appears to be on the rise. It is one component which is exogenous to the RMC's operations. Table 9.14 describes over time the trend in the water accounts, and shows both revenues and expenditures.

TABLE 9.14
Water Accounts of RMC
(Rs Lakh)

Year	Total Expenditure	Revenue Expenditure	Receipts	Receipts as a Per Cent of	
				Revenue Expenditure	Total Expenditure
1998–9	1628.66	1422.86	245.36	17.24	15.07
1999–2000	3642.34	1467.42	265.27	18.08	10.03
2000–1	3863.55	1102.38	288.14	26.14	7.46
2001–2	2458.30	1343.11	244.52	18.20	9.95
2002–3	2404.51	1392.39	531.20	38.15	22.09

Source: RMC and authors' computations.

As Table 9.14 demonstrates, the RMC recovers only a fraction of the total expenditure on water, while it is increasing. Of the total expenditure on water, the RMC recovered 22 per cent in 2002–3—an improvement over the previous years on account of an increase in the flat rate that it charges per household, but significantly below what would appear necessary for making water provision a sustainable proposition. Even on the assumption that capital and schematic investments are payable over a longer duration with zero burden on the existing population, recoveries from water are significantly low (see Box 9.2). As stated earlier, the RMC supplies water for 20 minutes a day and water connections in Rajkot are unmetered, with few exceptions such as the high-rise apartment and industry and business.

Box 9.2
What Do We Conclude?

The statutory and institutional structures were created on the principle of separate, distinct functional and spatial jurisdictions, with little recognition that there are important interdependencies, both functional and spatial. Actions taken by RUDA have direct implications for RMC. There is evidently a need to revisit the statutory provisions. The finances of RMC are in an unsatisfactory state, despite a surplus on revenue account and its ability to finance a part of capital expenditure out of its own resources. There is little long-term thinking about the significant prospect of octroi abolition, and the related problem of ineffective property tax collection. Water accounts are the most vulnerable and water pricing does not reflect the scarcity value of water, that is, the economic cost.

As Rajkot begins to increasingly rely on Narmada river water which is expected to cost Rs 6 per kl (excluding capital cost),[8] supplying water at current rates would seriously affect water supply, and consequently its other activities.

AREAS OF INTERVENTION

Rajkot's profile is typical of most Indian cities that, on the one hand, are growing and economically viable, and, on the other hand, continue to face increasing stress on infrastructure and services, confront institutional rigidities, and grapple with a stagnant fiscal base. In this generalized framework, cities move on at a pace that permits them to absorb the incremental population and activities, albeit in informal ways, often with services that are supplied by the private sector. Rajkot appears to be in this mould, growing and continuing to acquire economic diversification, without any significant augmentation of its infrastructural base or fiscal rejuvenation, the Constitutional (74th) Amendment notwithstanding. Rajkot has barely managed to hold on to service levels of a decade ago.

The question is: Can Rajkot break out from this routine growth curve? Where is it possible to intervene? This chapter first explored the larger context for urban reform in Rajkot; it now examines in greater detail a few areas, which seem to hold the key to Rajkot's role in Gujarat's economy. Based on this assessment, there are several obstacles to the emergence of a strategic reform programme in Rajkot.

First, there is no obvious locus of dynamism and change in Rajkot today. The city appears to be run from year to year, without any larger plan, and with little ability to anticipate future situations and develop a strategic vision.[9] Instead existing institutions operate within the narrow confines of their statutory and legal framework, such as RUDA grinding through its decadal plan revisions with little regard to final outcome. The institutional dissonance discussed in this chapter, such as between RMC and RUDA, also contributes to the strategic vacuum. The net result is a complete lack of incentives for broader strategic visioning and planning. Indeed, our interviews with officials and citizens suggest a low-level equilibrium of low expectations and low quality service delivery; poor urban functioning has become an accepted way of life.

Second, there is extremely limited capacity within the body that will likely have to play a leadership role in crafting a reform agenda—the RMC. As described and discussed earlier, few of the RMC staff have professional qualifications, and are exposed to the ideas that would allow them to see beyond the confines established by current institutional limits and conventional practice. Limited capacity beyond the very top layer also suggests that implementation of a reform vision will also be a significant challenge. The combination of limited capacity and cross-institutional conflict is particularly problematic.

Third, the urban political economy in Rajkot does not suggest any ready actors to stimulate change. The relationship between the executive and the political arms of the RMC suggests an oppositional relationship rather than a collaborative one.

While elected councillors do indeed play their role by representing the popular public sentiment on issues such as user charges for water and property tax reform, this representation shows little signs of growing into an enlightened leadership. To do so would require the political leadership to spell out the contours of a reform programme that credibly promises better service delivery in the medium term in exchange for short-term public concessions. Such a political bargain would form the basis for a partnership between political and executive wings.

External actors, such as the Chamber of Commerce, do not appear to be moving toward a productive catalytic role either. The Chamber is heavily critical of the RMC and its limited ability to provide services effectively. However, as is common with higher income groups in urban India, they see little incentive to promote change because they are able to meet their private needs through private provision—water tankers instead of piped water. From this privileged perspective, the costs and risks associated with engaging public organizations to change the public infrastructure are far higher than the likely benefits. The merger of the new areas is a further obstacle to unified urban action. The new areas are likely to demand a disproportionate share of financial and managerial resources, which will leave older parts of the city disinclined to pay additional taxes or user charges.

Fourth, in the absence of a larger strategic framework and adequate accountability mechanisms, efforts at greater private sector involvement risk being sucked into patronage politics and shaped by political rather than economic context. In this assessment, the available evidence on the economic gains from either outsourcing or 'BOT' contracts was inconclusive. A more in-depth study of contractual terms, obligations, bidding processes, and eventual outcomes is needed. However, the BOT arrangements were used as a way around a restrictive planning framework (in the case of a fire station) and outsourcing street cleaning was seen primarily as a way of side-stepping fraught labour relations suggests the primacy of politics in public–private partnership. Mitigating this bleak picture are a few potential triggers for reform.

First, that Rajkot does not suffer from the parlous state of municipal finances that many other Indian cities grapple with provides some room for experimentation.

Second, and related, the merger of new areas provides a relatively blank canvas for experimentation; a problem could be turned into an opportunity. The current experiments—such as private sweepers—are limited and undertaken with narrow aims, in this case undercutting the sweepers union. By being more bold and creative and, most important, focusing on delivery of improved final outcomes, the RMC may be able to use the new areas as the vanguard of a larger project of urban renewal. To do so would require a strategic vision focused on these areas, combined with an intensive communication campaign to the public.

Third, the anticipated shift away from octroi and toward other forms of municipal financing may have at least two positive long-term effects. First, it could force the RMC to grapple with the question of user charges and property tax reform to ensure a viable base. Second, making greater financial demands on citizens would necessarily stimulate a broader public debate about service delivery and lead to scrutiny and demands for accountability. In particular, the peculiar situation of deeply flawed service delivery— such as 20 minutes of water a day—despite a substantial revenue account surplus and scope for financing capital expenditures out of the city's income would come into focus. While painful and politically charged, such public ferment and debate is necessary to create demand for a strategic vision and, equally important, public ownership of and commitment to a reform agenda.

Moving from broad forces and patterns to specific first steps, a few areas are key to Rajkot's future:

1. *Greater autonomy and authority to the RMC consistent with the parameters of the Constitutional (74th) Amendment Act, 1992.* From all the secondary evidence analysed in this chapter, there is little indication or suggestion that the 1992 amendment has made any impact on the functioning or the finances of the RMC. The RMC continues to be negatively impacted by the intersecting web of laws and their attendant institutions. The relationship of RMC with either the GIDC whose mandate

is to spur industrial growth in the state or even the RUDA which is responsible for projecting and planning Rajkot's hinterland, has not undergone any change, as a result of the 1992 Amendment. Thus, the GIDC continues to develop industrial estates and industrial areas in areas that it considers appropriate from the standpoint of the state and RUDA, in accordance with its mandate, formulates a development plan for Rajkot and its environs to the year 2011 AD.

There will, of course, continue to be significant roles for institutions other than RMC. However, to complement local autonomy there need to be clear demarcations between institutions and formal mechanisms for the RMC to participate in the process of decision-making on issues such as where to locate estates or what areas should accommodate the new growth. The absence of such mechanisms has affected service provisioning in Rajkot and its environs. Even on a broader scale where Rajkot's development is to be coordinated with that of other towns and villages, that is, by the District Planning Committee (DPC), progress has been tardy, if not insignificant. For example, the office of the district is concerned with conversion of rural lands into urban or quasi-urban use, but not with the integration of such lands into the overall physical and infrastructure development.

The key to the problems of fragmentation and coordination lie in revisiting the statutory frameworks in the context of the Constitutional (74th) Amendment Act, 1992, and simultaneously the institutional structures that are created under those frameworks. This is a substantial problem and has to be undertaken at the state level.

2. *Positioning of the informal sector in Rajkot's economy.* At 60 per cent of the total residential area and accounting for substantial proportions of commercial activity, the informal sector of Rajkot cannot be ignored. It contributes significantly to the city's economy and invariably places considerable demands on services. Over the years, there has been an extraordinary growth in informal housing, mostly in the form of unauthorized colonies which do not conform to any developmental regulations and informal businesses that are

scattered over the city. This pattern of growth is explained in terms of tardy growth of formal housing, inadequate supply of developed lands, lengthy and arduous procedures for building permits, and inability of the RMC and RUDA to control unauthorized construction (or is it rent seeking)? While it is not possible to quantitatively estimate the benefits that might be derived by regulating the sector and providing it a legitimate place, it is evident that it is inescapable. Moreover, if a strategic reform vision is to address the issues of user charges, property tax, and the like, doing so without factoring in the informal sector is to define away a substantial proportion to the problem. A necessary first step is simply to obtain better information on the dimensions of the problem, and categorize the drivers of the informal sector—regulatory, financial, governance, or a combination of these. This understanding will then have to inform any strategic vision, and in particular each sectoral component of a reform agenda, whether in terms of water, solid waste, or roads.

3.   *Raising the financial profile of the RMC.* Even with a surplus on revenue account, the finances of the RMC are in an unsatisfactory state. It is surprising, as this Corporation has not seized the vast opportunities available to it, in three spheres (*a*) property reform of taxation, (*b*) water price reform, and (*c*) using debt market for strengthening municipal infrastructure.

Property tax reform is long overdue in Rajkot. As stated earlier, the total revenues from property taxation which in Rajkot is a composite tax comprising a tax on property, a conservancy and a fire tax, are a meager Rs 25.52 crore from about 200,000 assesses. There are five slabs of ARVs, with each slab carrying a different tax rate that rises to 30 per cent for properties that have an ARV of Rs 10,000; such high rates have evidently not been revenue-friendly, evidence of which is in large arrears. The state of Gujarat has moved towards a major reform of property tax system, which however, has been slow to be incorporated by the RMC. Property taxation is the most legitimate local tax and needs to be effectively used.

Water pricing is an important sphere for consideration of reform, as discussed in Chapter 5, particularly since water scarcity is likely to be a fact of life for Rajkot well into the future. The currently extremely high levels of subsidy are unsustainable, especially in the face of dependence on future high cost supply from the Narmada (implying the importance of the marginal cost, as argued at the beginning of this book). The city is faced with a stark choice, of either biting the political bullet and raising user fees or strengthening the long-term state of public finances in order to provide a transparent and sustainable subsidy for water consumption. In this context, attention to more efficiency of water use, on the supply and demand sides, would appear to be a no-lose strategy in Rajkot's water-scarce environment.

Debt financing of urban infrastructure is an accepted strategy in many parts of the developing world, including India, and particularly Gujarat. The example of Ahmedabad seeking capital market funds for financing infrastructure is still fresh to induce other municipal corporations to instil fiscal discipline and use it for augmenting service levels. In Rajkot, debt servicing (loans from the state government) is relatively insignificant and the RMC perceives it to be a positive feature of its finances. It has made use of its surpluses for capital improvements and schemes, without using the market funds. This is one area where fiscal rating may be a possible route for improving own finances and financing the city's infrastructure.

The state government has a vital stake in the city's growth and development. Apart from reconciling the statutory provisions under different Acts with the aim of giving primacy to RMC, there are two other spheres where state government interventions are necessary. These are: (*a*) accounting systems which is the case of Rajkot are single entry/cash-based and which do not permit a realistic appraisal of its finances, and (*b*) implementing the recommendations of the State Finance Commission.

In conclusion, Rajkot faces many problems typical of urban India—a fractured institutional structure, low capacity, chronically poor service delivery, and a sense of apathy and resignation to crumbling urban spaces, not very different from what we find in Chapter 8, in the case of Ludhiana. At the same time, it has a reasonably healthy financial base, albeit one that is threatened and inadequately used. To envision a serious reform of Rajkot, three factors appear to be paramount. First, much will hinge on the future of octroi in Gujarat. If octroi is to be abolished, the state must allow cities time to plan, and Rajkot and other cities will have to rise to the challenge. Second, many hurdles to Rajkot's reform, as with Ludhiana's, lie outside its control, at the level of state institutions and frameworks. Any urban reform effort will have to be undertaken in concert with a larger state-level effort. Third, the current political disconnect between citizen and elected officials, and elected officials and administrative bureaucracy, bode ill for the full life cycle of reform—from conceptualization through design and implementation. To be credible and politically sustainable, urban reforms in Rajkot, as elsewhere, will need the support and understanding of the citizenry. Forging the local political conditions means for public debate and effective governance mechanisms to sustain reform are a pre-condition to urban renewal in Rajkot.

Having analysed urban reforms in Rajkot, the next and final chapter summarizes all the findings regarding the costs and challenges of providing local public services, and contains concluding remarks.

NOTES

1. The India Infrastructure Reports (IIRS) are published every year as a collaborative partnership of the Infrastructure Development Finance Corporation (IDFC), Indian Institute of Technology Kanpur, and the Indian Institute of Management Ahmedabad, which has been named as the 3iNetwork.

2. An urban agglomeration is a typical Indian concept, similar to what other countries would call a metropolis. An urban agglomeration in India would comprise at least one central city—normally with a population in excess of 100,000, and several smaller cities and villages.

3. City-county merger or consolidation is a major issue in many developed and developing countries, and is linked with questions of scale, efficiency, and management. It is not a routine business of expanding or changing boundaries.

4. First, non-agricultural use permission has to be obtained for the land following which a property register card is issued. Next, a building plan is submitted which includes details such as the site plan, plot and built-up areas, floor area ratio, setbacks, height of building, parking, and certificate of supervision for processing. The 'processing' of the plan has to pass through the clerk, surveyor, planning assistant, assistant town

planner, and finally the town planning officer. The processing leads to the grant of development permission.

5. This is a typical de soto syndrome: doing anything legally is more cost.

6. The Bombay Provincial Municipal Corporation Act, 1949 also provides for four other functions of Schedule 12 but in the category of discretionary functions.

7. The Rajkot Municipal Corporation (RMC) undertakes and implements schemes in the spheres of water supply, drainage, town planning, Aji Industrial Settlement Yojana, slum development, and the like.

8. Note the consistency of this unit (operating) cost with the marginal cost estimates in Chapter 4.

9. This has, however, changed now with the city preparing a strategic City Development Plan (CDP), according to the requirements of the JNNURM, indicating its current status and where it would like to go in the future.

CHAPTER 10

Towards Sustainable Urbanization
Summary and Conclusions

We started this book by answering questions regarding the marginal costs of water supply and expenditures on other services. We studied the mechanisms of pricing and charging mechanisms not only with respect to water, but also with respect to other services, more importantly solid waste. Further, we also made an attempt to broadly understanding reform of public service delivery in a couple of representative cities, dwelling on institutional factors, rising above the issue of costs, pricing, and finances.

Making an attempt to separate expenditures from costs, we found that a few cities in the country (specifically those in Bihar, Madhya Pradesh, Rajasthan, and Uttar Pradesh [BIMARU] states) spend abysmally low on all services including water supply. When these low-spending cities are excluded, we find that the supply of every additional kilolitre of water imposes extra burden on the cities ranging from Rs 2.77 to Rs 5.08, as marginal operating costs. This, while being lower than the evidence from the literature, excludes the capacity costs of creating assets such as civil works and plant/equipment needed to supply water. Judged against these short-run marginal cost estimates, based only on O&M expenditures, we have found some Indian cities such as Jaipur and Pune under-pricing their water. So it is possible that closing the doors of cities to in-migration is not required, it is really the pricing that needs correction, as Williamson (1988) points out. The provision of such services to low-income residents of cities can be cross-subsidized through differential pricing. National urban reform initiatives such as the

Jawaharlal Nehru National Urban Renewal Mission (JNNURM) and Urban Infrastructure Development Schemes for Small and Medium Towns (UIDSSMT) do specify phased cost recovery through user charges, while they do not mention marginal costs.

Since this book has been about the costs as well as challenges of locally provided urban services, we take here the opportunity to visit the JNNURM and UIDSSMT, the flagship programmes of the Ministry of Urban Development (MUD) covering urban India, whose objectives are to promote better infrastructure in the large, small, and medium towns in the country, respectively. We examine below the JNNURM's reform agenda requirements for cities, for them to be eligible to access funds and document its success in encouraging cities to reform.[1]

The JNNURM specifies several mandatory and optional reform agenda items required to be fulfilled by state governments and urban local bodies (ULBs). At the ULB level, the following mandatory reforms are required by JNNURM and UIDSSMT:

1. Movement to accrual-based double entry system of accounting
2. Improvement in property tax coverage to 85 per cent (of all properties)
3. Improvement in property tax collection efficiency to 90 per cent
4. Full cost recovery as far as water supply and solid waste are concerned
5. Internal earmarking of funds for services to the urban poor
6. Provision of basic services to the urban poor
7. Setting up of e-governance

State-level reforms that are required for access to JNNURM funds are as follows:

1. Transfer of functions outlined in the Twelfth Schedule, as specified by the 74th Constitutional Amendment Act (CAA)
2. Constitution of District Planning Committees, per the 74th CAA
3. Transfer/integration with city planning functions
4. Transfer/integration with water supply and sanitation
5. Reform in rent control

6. Stamp duty rationalization to 5 per cent
7. Repeal of Urban Land Ceiling and Regulation Act (ULCRA)
8. Enactment of community participation law
9. Enactment of public disclosure law

Finally, there are certain optional reforms required both at the ULB and state levels. These relate to the introduction of property title certification system, streamlining the approval process, and more generally, revision of building bye-laws, earmarking 25 per cent developed land in all housing projects for economically weaker sections (EWS) and low-income groups (all at the ULB-level), along with several other administrative and structural reforms.

With regard to building bye-laws, there is in fact evidence that building bye-laws in India as they relate to floor area ratio (FAR) restrictions are highly conservative when compared with cities internationally (see Bertaud, 2004). For example, in Indian cities, the maximum permissible FAR in the central city is very low (ranging from about 0.5 to 2 or so), compared with an FAR ranging from 5 to 15 (in Manhattan) in other major cities of the world. In most large cities of the world, as technology and infrastructure improve, the FAR (floor space index [FSI]) in the city centre tends to increase. The progressive increase in FSI has two purposes, as the urban economics and planning literature point out: first, it allows households and firms to consume more floor space as their incomes increase without having to move to new areas in the suburbs; and second, an increase in FSI contributes to a decrease in the city spatial expansion (or suburbanization), decreasing population dispersion, transport costs, and pollution due to transport. Without higher FAR, real estate projects are also usually not financially feasible. Sridhar (2007a) examines the impact of land use regulations such as restrictive FAR on suburbanization in the context of Indian cities and finds that population density is higher in suburbs where a higher FAR is allowed.

While the JNNURM has a clause relating to building bye-laws, it ensures revision of bye-laws to make rain harvesting mandatory in all buildings and adoption of water conservation measures. It also optionally mandates bye-laws for reuse of recycled water. However the JNNURM is surprisingly silent regarding the conservative floor area ratio restrictions prevalent in the Indian cities. This is a potential area of reform for the JNNURM as it is currently being implemented and if extended to other cities of the country.

Tables 10.1–10.3 respectively summarize commitments made by the cities and states with regard to mandatory ULB-level, mandatory state-level, and optional (state or ULB-level) reforms. As presented in Table 10.1, with regard to mandatory reforms required at the ULB-level, the time-line commitment made by cities is the shortest for movement to a double entry based system of accrual accounting, the time frame being about 3.33 years on average which is the commitment made by cities to attain this target. This is followed by commitment to setting up of e-governance which has, on average, a commitment of 3.5 years made by cities. There are, however, cities that have committed to taking twice as long, that is, seven years to set up e-governance as with all the other mandatory reform agenda items required of them. With respect to the reform

TABLE 10.1
Mandatory Reforms at ULB Level: Commitment to JNNURM Reforms

Reform Agenda	Average Time (in Years) Committed for the Reform	Maximum (in Years)	Minimum (in Years)	Number of Observations (Cities)
E-governance set-up	3.49	7	0	61
Shift to accrual based double entry accounting	3.33	5	0	61
Property tax (85% coverage)	4.80	7	0	61
Property tax collection (90% collection efficiency)	5.03	7	0	58
Full cost recovery (water supply)	5.50	7	0	58
Full cost recovery (solid waste)	5.70	7	1	46
Earmarking of funds for urban poor	2.33	7	0	57
Provision of basic services to urban poor	6.31	7	3	59

Source: Compiled from Memoranda of Understanding submitted under JNNURM and authors' computations.

which is the most directly related to one of the objectives of this book, full cost recovery of the charges of water supply, the cities on average make a commitment of 5.5 years, reflecting the political will or inability to attempt full cost recovery immediately. There are a few cities, however, which have committed to full cost recovery of the provision of water supply and solid waste immediately.[2]

As far as state-level mandatory reforms are concerned, Table 10.2 shows that repeal of ULCRA is the most successful as most of the states have repealed the Act, since on average, less than a year is required to complete that commitment. The other more successful reform mandated at the state level is the constitution of the District Planning Committees, as specified by the 74th CAA, for which an average commitment of less than two years has been made by the states of cities included in the JNNURM. Other relatively more successful attempts at reform at the state level are the transfer/integration with city planning functions, transfer/integration with water supply and sanitation, and transfer of 12th schedule functions to ULBs, for which about three years are committed on average by the states.

However, the reforms taking the longest time for commitment by the states are the reform of rent control and rationalization of stamp duty to 5 per cent, given this could have fiscal implications for some ULBs (such as the Municipal Corporation of Delhi), which stand to lose substantially in their share from the state, should stamp duty were to be rationalized. The reform of rent control could have favourable fiscal implications in many states given that variants of the archaic rental value system still continue to be followed in a number of states.

Finally, with respect to optional reforms required at the ULB or state-level (Table 10.3), we find the introduction of the property title certification system in ULBs is the slowest, with an average time commitment by cities of nearly six years.

A computerized information system has to be in place for fool-proof property title certification, which is the reason why a commitment to the property title certification system is a relatively longer period. The reform taking a relatively short period for commitment, as far as optional reforms at the ULB or state level is concerned, is the revision of building bye-laws by ULBs, for which

TABLE 10.2
Mandatory Reforms at State Level: Commitment to JNNURM Reforms

Reform Agenda	Average Time (in Years) Committed for the Reform	Maximum	Minimum	Number of Observations (Cities)
Transfer of 12th Schedule functions	3.10	7	0	61
Constitution of District Planning Committee (DPC)	1.78	4	0	60
Constitution of MPC	3.73	7	0	30
Transfer/integration with city planning	2.85	7	0	60
Transfer/integration with water supply and sanitation	2.38	6	0	52
Reform in rent control	4.08	7	0	49
Stamp duty rationalization (to 5%)	4.90	7	0	58
Repeal of ULCRA	0.72	6	0	46
Enactment of Community Participation Law	3.41	6	0	59
Enactment of Public Disclosure Law	3.20	5	2	59

Source: Compiled from Memoranda of Understanding submitted under JNNURM and authors' computations.

the average period is two years. As discussed earlier, these bye-laws pertain to rain water harvesting.

However, despite the importance of efficiency and the need for marginal cost pricing in the case of water supply, the results and focus in Chapters 2–5 of this book do not imply that marginal cost pricing is the only solution for provision of safe and adequate water supply. There could be some grounds on which disadvantaged areas such as hilly and mountainous regions cannot recover their costs which can be very high. We have examined only Bangalore (which is 930 m above mean sea level) in this study. Cities such as Ooty (which is at an altitude of 2,240 m above sea level), Nainital (which is located 1,939 m above sea level), and Shimla (being 2,213 m above sea level) suffer from even more accentuated topography. There are several such regions in the country. While quantitative

TABLE 10.3
Optional Reforms at ULB or State Level: Commitment to JNNURM Reforms

Reform Agenda	Average Time (in Years) Committed for the Reform	Maximum	Minimum	Number of Observations (Cities)
Property title certification system in ULBs	5.79	7	0	53
Revision of building bye-laws (streamlining the approval process)	3.50	7	0	58
Revision of building bye-laws (mandatory RWH in all buildings)	2.07	6	0	57
Earmarking 25% developed land in housing projects for EWS/LIG	4.44	7	0	48
Simplification of framework for conversion of agricultural land	3.79	6	1	33
Computerized process for registration of land and property	3.78	7	0	50
Bye-laws on reuse of recycled water	4.32	7	1	53
Administrative reforms	4.76	7	3	51
Structural reforms	4.13	7	2	46
Encouraging public–private partnership	3.17	7	0	42

Source: Compiled from Memoranda of Understanding submitted under JNNURM and authors' computations.

estimates regarding the cost of providing water supply or other services in such cities are not available, it is easy to imagine that such cities would have to spend a lot to provide a reasonable level of services to their residents.

If we were to apply the marginal cost principle, or even the average or for that matter, the total cost principle, to such disadvantaged regions/cities, then the reform initiative of raising user charges to cover costs (either unit or marginal costs) would imply that residents living in such areas would have to pay higher user charges for services, just because they happen to live in some of those disadvantaged locations. This is unfair, and an important reason why urban reform programs cannot be applied across the board to all cities. In fact, the JNNURM and UIDSSMT recognize this and specify that cities in the north east and special category states may recover at least 50 per cent of O&M charges initially, but they also should graduate to full recovery in a phased manner. The central finance commissions, in their transfer mechanisms, do take into account criteria that are applicable to special category states, but not *special category cities* (located in *general category states*), which have to provide local public services such as water and municipal roads. Further, the list of criteria and weights suggested by the states in their memoranda submitted to the Twelfth Finance Commission (TFC) also, while among other things, includes an index of infrastructure, forest cover, and irrigation effort, but does not explicitly include cost disabilities a state/region faces in providing public infrastructure services. However it is desirable that this criterion is taken into account by the states and future finance commissions in the interests of equity. Prohibitively high costs of providing local public services can be met partly through inter-governmental transfers, but not entirely through marginal cost recovery or pricing.

Even in the case of services other than water supply, for instance, for building roads and tunnels in mountainous regions, more time and effort are required, necessitating more manpower, and more expensive equipment (for snow shoveling where it is required), increasing costs. However, even here, we have found that cities' per capita expenditures on basic services such as sanitation and sewerage (forget about roads or street lights) appear to be abysmally low, let alone adequate in any sense to meet the demands of an increasing population. Further, while spending alone is not sufficient, since O&M expenditures might just mean increased salaries without improving service levels, we find weak municipal finances might still be the core of the issue.

When it comes to practical pricing aspects, we find that while it is possible for us to discern distinct cost structures in city's expenditures, especially so as it relates to water supply, cities do not make any attempt to separate out costs from their actual expenditures. Further, cities to the extent possible, keep a check on the unit cost of providing water supply. Estimates of marginal costs as it relates to water supply are very rare. A *quid pro quo* relationship between service delivered and a charge is even rarer to find in the case of other services such as solid waste, municipal roads, and street lighting which are usually financed from general property taxation. However, it is important for the cities to keep a check on costs and expenditures as it relates to water supply and other services, as it has implications for marginal cost pricing of water supply and some cost-based pricing of other services. Such distinction also has implications for determining the extent of inter-governmental transfers, since it is not fair for a city to charge residents extra just because they live in a place where several factors outside of the city's control contribute to the costs of providing several public services. Finally, such pricing can regulate the quantity of the service (e.g., solid waste generated) that is required by sending signals to consumers that it is potentially costly to litter on the roads. Thus a system of pricing has to be combined with penalties and fines for better enforcement and better service delivery.

Our findings in the study of reforming public service delivery in Ludhiana (Punjab) and Rajkot (Gujarat) strongly suggest that over and above the issue of finances, institutional and statutory overlap of functions explain poor service delivery in the case of many Indian cities. The response here is that cities should ideally have one local-level institution for all locally provided services, to avoid a statutory overlap of several institutions dealing with the same service, and a 'passing the buck' attitude. It is desirable for local-level institutions to be adequately equipped with resources, skills, powers, and more or less similar expenditure responsibilities with respect to provision of local services. The case of Rajkot demonstrates that even when privatization is practiced with respect to some services, public monitoring is necessary for better outcomes.

This book has been one small step in studying what ails public service delivery in this country. It has made some attempts at examining both costs and the challenges of improving service delivery. While pricing methods and financial instruments for cities in the form of municipal bond markets are continually evolving, future research should build upon this work to study what more could be done to minimize statutory overlaps in the creation of institutions, and more generally, to reform public service delivery.

All said and done, while the three tiers of government (central, state, and local) are indeed too much with us, private and corporate sector are becoming more important as drivers of growth. Despite this, much can be said about the growing importance of cities and the role played by urban local governments in making attempts to improve their finances and public service delivery (see Sridhar, 2007b). It is useful to reiterate that municipal bodies are the primary providers of key urban services like water supply, sewerage, sanitation/solid waste management, and city-wide roads. It is instructive to note that currently, 50 per cent of India's gross domestic product (GDP) is generated in its cities, which is expected to reach 65 per cent by 2011. There are currently seventy-three municipal corporations, 1,770 municipal councils, 229 town area committees, and 717 notified area committees in the country, with state governments having the discretion in deciding the status of urban settlements. In some cities, municipal bodies account for a significant share of total public spending in the metropolitan areas. For instance, local expenditure accounted for a significant 43 per cent share of the estimated total (central, state, and local) government spending in the Mumbai metropolitan area, while in Ahmedabad, the share of local expenditure in total government expenditure was 31 per cent. However, despite this and increasing urbanization with the consequent pressure on urban services, the financial powers of municipal bodies have undergone negligible changes.

With the control of fiscal deficit becoming a critical area of management for the central and state governments, budgetary allocations to municipal bodies cannot be expected to increase substantially and may even decrease. Concessional funding from financial institutions is unlikely. Access to multilateral and bilateral funding is likely to be conditional, as donor countries have always insisted on bringing about greater accountability and commercial orientation in the projects financed by them. Municipal bodies therefore need to identify new sources of funds, such as municipal bonds, for financing their infrastructure.

Under these circumstances, several urban local governments in the country have been very innovative in their urban management practices. Ahmedabad Municipal Corporation became the first local body in the country in 1996 to tap the capital market to obtain funds through issue of a bond. Such initiatives by a number of cities have led to a market for credit rating of cities, based on their financial management. A number of other cities have also shown the way in other innovative methods of financing of urban services. Indore has come up with a model—a 50:50 programme in which citizens of a jurisdiction get their roads revamped from a private contractor and the municipal corporation foots the remaining 50 per cent of the bill. Surat, once afflicted by the plague, has now been transformed into a beautiful city, post-1994, because of innovative urban management practices discussed in this book. Many cities have privatized their mass transport systems.

Last, but not the least, the Right to Information Act was passed in India's Parliament in 2005, which is indeed a very powerful weapon in the hands of the common man. This law can be used to seek information on various aspects of government functioning and service delivery, which has implications for the public. While this law cannot be used to seek solution to public problems, it certainly can be used to seek more information about the problem and to know more about its cause(s). This itself in many cases would have been obfuscated without the Act, hence is a major check on public corruption, making the government much more accountable as a service provider.

It is true that these initiatives are drops in the ocean, and a lot more needs to be done to reinvent and reengineer the government. But we have to start somewhere and the journey has begun.

NOTES

1. UIDSSMT's reform agenda requirements are identical to those of the JNNURM.
2. Chennai has committed to full cost recovery of water supply immediately and Vishakhapatnam has committed to full cost recovery of solid waste within a year.

References

3iNetwork (eds) (2006). *India Infrastructure Report 2006: Urban Infrastructure.* New Delhi: Oxford University Press.

Agarwal, O.P. (2006). 'Urban Transport', in 3iNetwork (ed.), *India Infrastructure Report 2006: Urban Infrastructure.* New Delhi: Oxford University Press.

All India Institute of Local Self-Government (2004). *Action Plan for Implementation of MSW Rules 2000 in Maharashtra.* New Delhi: All India Institute of Local Self-Government.

American Water Works Association (1991). *Water Rates Manual.* Denver, Colorado: American Water Works Association.

Asnani, P.U. (2006). 'Solid Waste Management', in 3iNetwork (ed.), *India Infrastructure Report 2006: Urban Infrastructure.* New Delhi: Oxford University Press.

Auzins, A. (2004). 'Institutional Arrangements: A Gate towards Sustainable Land Use', *Nordic Journal of Surveying and Real Estate Research,* 1(1), 57–71.

Bagchi, S. (2001). 'Financing Capital Investments in Urban Infrastructure', *Economic and Political Weekly,* 27 January, pp. 385–98.

Bertaud, A. (2004). *Mumbai FAR Conundrum: The Perfect Storm: The Four Factors Restricting the Construction of New Floor Space in Mumbai.* Retrieved from http://alain-bertaud.com.

Census of India (2001a). *Town Directory.* New Delhi: Registrar General of India.

————— (2001b). *Data Highlights: Migration Tables.* New Delhi: Registrar General of India.

————— (1991a). *Town Directory.* New Delhi: Registrar General of India.

————— (1991b). *Series 28—Ludhiana (Part VA and VB-D Series) Migration Tables.* Chandigarh, Punjab: Directorate of Census Operations.

————— (1991c). *Series 20—Part IVA-C Series, Socio-cultural Tables.* Chandigarh, Punjab: Directorate of Census Operations.

Chernick, H. and A. Reschovsky (2004). 'Improving the Fiscal Health of Large Cities: Lessons from Other Countries', A Research Proposal, September, University of Wisconsin, Madison, WI.

Cole, M.A. (2004). 'Economic Growth and Water Use', *Applied Economics Letters,* January, 11 (1/15): 1–4.

Davis, J. (2004). 'Corruption in Public Service Delivery: Experience from South Asia's Water and Sanitation Sector', *World Development,* 32(1): 53–71.

de Bartolome, C.A.M. and S.L. Ross (2003). 'Equilibrium with Local Governments and Commuting: Income Sorting versus Income Mixing', *Journal of Urban Economics,* 54, pp. 1–20.

Dinar, A. (2000). 'Political Economy of Water Pricing Reforms', in *The Political Economy of Water Pricing Reforms.* New York: Oxford University Press and the World Bank.

Economic Times (2005). '*Maha* Strategy to Clean up States', 24 July.

Foster, D. (2006). 'Hidden Cost of Intermittent Water Supply', in 3iNetwork (ed.), *India Infrastructure Report 2006: Urban Infrastructure.* New Delhi: Oxford University Press.

Foster, V. (2001). 'The Design of Pro-Poor Subsides in Urban Water and Sanitation Services in India'. Mimeo.

Fox, W. (1994). 'Strategic Options for Urban Infrastructure Management', Urban Management Programme Policy Paper, The World Bank.

Fox, W. and K. Edmiston (2000). 'User Charge Financing of Urban Public Services in Africa', Working Paper 00-4, International Studies Program, Georgia State University.

Government of Delhi (2004). *Economic Survey 2003–4.* New Delhi: Government of Delhi.

Hanke, S. and R. Wentworth (1981). 'On the Marginal Cost of Wastewater Services', *Land Economics,* November, 57(4): 558–67.

Lahiri-Dutt, K. and G. Samanta (2001). 'Million Cities of India: A Review of 2001 Census Data', *Urban India,* 21(2): 97–110.

Llorente, M. and M. Zerah (2002). 'The Urban Water Sector: Formal versus Informal Suppliers in India', *Urban India,* 22(1): 35–49.

Link, H. (2003). 'Estimates of Marginal Infrastructure Costs for Different Modes of Transport', Paper submitted to the 43rd Congress of the European Regional Science Association, 27–31 August, Jyvaskyla, Finland.

Mathur, M.P., R. Chandra, S. Singh, and B. Chattopadhyay (2007). 'Norms and Standards of Municipal Basic Services in India', National Institute of Urban Affairs (NIUA) Working Paper 07-02, January.

McNeill, R. and D. Tate (1991). *Guidelines for Municipal Water Pricing*. Social Science Series Number 25, Inland Waters Directorate, Water Planning and Management Branch, Ottawa, Canada.

Ministry of Urban Development (2008). *Handbook of Service Level Benchmarks*. New Delhi. Retrieved from http://urbanindia.nic.in/moud/what'snew/main.htm, last accessed 17 October 2008.

Ministry of Urban Affairs and Employment (1996). *Report of the Working Group on Urban Water Supply and Sanitation Sector for the Ninth Five Year Plan (1997–2002)*. New Delhi.

Mohan, R. (1996). *Report of the Expert Committee on Commercialization of Infrastructure (or the India Infrastructure Report 1996)*. New Delhi: Government of India.

Monitor (2004). *Rapid City Assessments of Hyderabad, Bangalore, and Alandur*. Submitted to Water and Sanitation Program, April.

National Commission on Urbanization (1988). *Report of the National Commission on Urbanization*. New Delhi.

National Institute of Public Finance and Policy (2007). *Improving the Fiscal Health of Large Cities: A Pilot Study from Kolkata*. Draft Report submitted to the World Bank, June.

————— (2005). 'Improving the Fiscal Health of Large Cities: Evidence from India', A Research Proposal, March 2005.

National Institute of Urban Affairs (1998). *Financing Urban Infrastructure in India*. Research Study Series Number 59. Prepared for the Urban Sector Profile Project of the Asian Development Bank, Manila, Philippines.

Noll, R., M. Shirley, and S. Cowan (2000). 'Reforming Urban Water Systems in Developing Countries', in Anne O' Krueger (ed.), *Economic Policy Reform: The Second Stage*. London: University of Chicago Press.

Operations Research Group (ORG) (1989). *Delivery and Financing of Urban Services*. New Delhi: Operations Research Group.

Paul, S. (2008). 'Urban Governance in India: The Way Forward, Key Note Address', Third International Conference on Public Policy and Management, Indian Institute of Management, Bangalore, India, August.

Paul, S., S. Balakrishnan, K. Gopakumar, S. Sekhar, and M. Vivekananda (2004). 'State of India's Public Services', *Economic and Political Weekly*, 28 February, pp. 920–34.

Planning Commission (2005). *Mid-term Appraisal of 10th Five Year Plan, 2002–2007*. New Delhi.

————— (2002). *The Tenth Five Year Plan*. New Delhi.

————— (1997). *Ninth Five Year Plan*. New Delhi.

PricewaterhouseCoopers (2001). *Infrastructure Development Action Plan for Chhattisgarh*. New Delhi.

Raghupathi, U.P. and V. Foster (2002). 'Water Tariffs and Subsidies in South Asia'. Mimeo.

Raju, K.V., N. Praveen, H.L. Shashidhar, and B.K. Anand (2004). *Groundwater in Urban Market: Can it Sustain? A Case Study of Kolar City in South India*. Draft Version, Research Report, Cerna, New Delhi.

Rana, P.S. (2003). 'Pricing of Water for Sustainability'. Mimeo.

Rao, G.M. and V. Aggarwal (1991). 'Central Transfers to Offset Fiscal Disadvantages of the States: Measurement of Cost Disabilities and Expenditure Needs', *Indian Economic Review*, 26(1): 13–34.

Reedy, D.E. (1986). 'Domestic Water Use and Sanitation in Lagos, Nigeria', Background Paper, Washington, D.C.: World Bank, West Africa Projects Department.

Report of the Third Working Group on Norms and Standards for Provision of Basic Infrastructure and Services, prepared for State Finance Commissions (1995).

Reschovsky, A. (2006). 'Expenditure Needs Compensation in a Horizontal Fiscal Equalization Program', in Robin Boadway and Anwar Shah (eds), *The Theory and Practice of Intergovernmental Fiscal Transfers*. Washington, D.C.: World Bank.

The Royal Town Planning Institute in Ireland (2001). *Institutional Arrangements for Land Use And Transport in The Greater Dublin Area*. Response to the Department of Environment and Local Government and the Department of Public Enterprise on their consultation paper, June. Retrieved from http://www.rtpi.org.uk/resources/policy-statements/2001/jun/pol20010628.pdf.

Roy, J., Subhorup Chattopadhyay, Sabyasachi Mukherjee, Manikarnika Kanjilal, Sreejata Samajpati, and Sanghamitra Roy (2004). 'An Economic Analysis of Demand for Water Quality: Case of Kolkata', *Economic and Political Weekly*, 10 January, pp. 186–92.

Saleth, R.M. and A. Dinar (1997). *Satisfying Urban Thirst. Water Supply Augmentation and Pricing Policy in Hyderabad City, India*. Papers 395, World Bank—Technical Papers.

Savage, D. and S. Dasgupta (2006). 'Governance Framework for Delivery of Urban Services', in 3iNetwork (ed.), *India Infrastructure Report 2006: Urban Infrastructure*. New Delhi: Oxford University Press.

Shah, S. and S. Buechler (2004). 'Water Sector Reforms in Mexico: Lessons for India's New Water Policy', *Economic and Political Weekly*, 14 January, pp. 361–70.

Singh, K. and B. Ta'i (2000). 'Introduction', in Kulwant Singh and Behnam Ta'i (eds), *Financing and Pricing of Urban Infrastructure*. New Delhi: New Age International (P) Limited, Publishers.

Sridhar, K.S. (2007b). 'Re-engineering Government', *The Economic Times*. 10 December.

————— (2007a). 'Impact of Land Use Regulations on Suburbanization: Evidence from India's Cities', Institute for Social and Economic Change (ISEC) Working Paper No.185/2007.

————— (2003). 'Firm Location Decisions and Impact on Local Economies', *Economic and Political Weekly*, 27 September, 38(39): 4121–30.

Sridhar, K.S., O.P. Mathur, and A. Nandy (2006). *Costs of Urban Infrastructure: Evidence from India's Cities*. South Asia Network of Economic Research Institutes and Global Development Network, May.

Sridhar, K.S. and S. Bandyopadhyay (2007). *Improving the Fiscal Health of Indian Cities: A Pilot Study of Pune*. Draft, World Bank, June.

Suresh, V. (1998). 'Indian Experience in Urban Water Supply and Sanitation', Country Presentation/Case Study' Presented in the ESCAP Sub-regional Workshop on Private Sector Involvement in Water Supply and Sanitation, New Delhi.

Swamy, S., A. Vyas, and S. Narang (2000). *Transformation of Surat: From Plague to Second Cleanest City in India*. New Delhi: Urban Management Program for Asia and the Pacific and the All India Institute of Local Self-Government.

Tata Energy Research Institute (1999). *Urban Services Environmental Rating System*. TERI Project Report No. 1999EE41 prepared for the Ministry of Environment and Forests and United Nations Development Programme, New Delhi.

Tiebout, C. (1956). 'A Pure Theory of Local Expenditures', *Journal of Political Economy*, 94, pp. 416–24.

Times Research Foundation (1997). *Municipalities in India: The Devolution Paradox* (Volume 3). New Delhi: Times Research Foundation.

Tiina Idström, J.T. (2004). *Marginal Rail Infrastructure Costs in Finland 1997–2002*. Helsinki: Finnish Rail Administration, Traffic System Department. Retrieved from http://www.rhk.fi/english/research/a604e. html, last accessed on 29 May 2006.

Turvey, R. (1976). 'Analyzing the Marginal Cost of Water Supply', *Land Economics*, May, 52(2): 158–68.

The University of Birmingham (1999). 'The Role of Government in Adjusting Economies', Paper 35, India: Urban Water Supply, International Development Department, School of Public Policy.

Urban Water Council (UWC), the United States Conference of Mayors (2000). Retrieved from http://www.usmayors.org/USCM/urbanwater/case_studies/, last accessed on 23 September 2005.

Warford, J. (1997) 'Marginal Opportunity Cost Pricing for Municipal Water Supply', Special Paper, International Development Research Centre, Ottawa, Canada.

Water and Sanitation Program: South Asia (2005). 'City Assessments and Urban Services: Reform Trajectory', Workshop organized by the WSP: South Asia on 'Policies and Strategies for Improving Urban Services in India', Administrative Staff College of India, Hyderabad, 23–4 June.

_____ (2000). *The Cancellation of the Pune Water Supply and Sewerage Project*. Case Study 23723, December.

_____ (1994). *Peru: Lima Water Rehabilitation and Management Project*. Staff Appraisal Report Number 13206-PE, LA3 Department, Environment and Urban Development Division, Latin America and the Caribbean Regional Office, November.

Whittington, D. (2002). *Municipal Water Pricing: Getting Started on Tariff Reforms and Subsidies in South Asia*. New Delhi: National Institute of Public Finance and Policy.

Williamson, J.G. (1988). 'Migration and Urbanization', in Hollis Chenery and T.N. Srinivasan (eds), *Handbook of Development Economics* (Volume I). Amsterdam: Elsevier Science B.V.

World Bank (2004). *World Development Report 2004*. Washington, D.C.: The World Bank.

_____ (1999). *Urban Water Supply and Sanitation*. New Delhi: Allied Publishers.

_____ (1997). 'Water Pricing Experiences: An International Perspective', World Bank Technical Paper No. 386.

_____ (1995). *Urban Water Supply and Sanitation*. Quoted in UNDP-Water and Sanitation Program's, Water for India's Poor: Who Pays the Price for Broken Promises, October 1999.

_____ (1994). *Lima Water Rehabilitation and Management Project*. Report No. 13206-PE, Environment and Urban Development Division, Latin America and the Caribbean Regional Office.

Zakaria Committee (1963). *Augmentation of Financial Resources of Urban Local Bodies*. Report of the Committee of Ministers, Constituted by the Central Council of Local Self Government, Government of India.

Zérah. M.H. (2006). 'Urban Water and Waste Water', 3iNetwork (ed.), *India Infrastructure Report 2006: Urban Infrastructure*. New Delhi: Oxford University Press.

_____ (2002). *Water Supply and Sanitation in Vijayawada: Analysis of Households' Situation towards Modes and Cost of Access, Consumption and Level of Satisfaction.* Research Report, Cerna, New Delhi.

_____ (2000). *Water: Unreliable Supply in Delhi.* New Delhi: Centre De Sciences Humains.

Index